COBRA

COPENHAGEN BRUSSELS AMSTERDAM

Peter Shield
with an essay by Graham Birtwistle

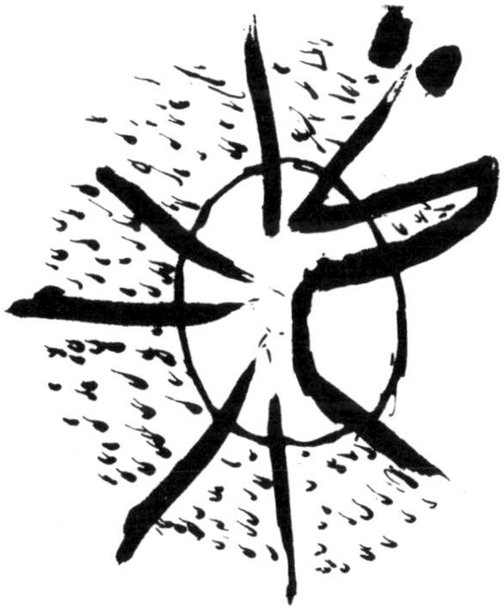

National Touring Exhibitions/Hayward Gallery

Published on the occasion of *Cobra: Copenhagen, Brussels, Amsterdam*, a National Touring Exhibition organized by the Hayward Gallery, London for the Arts Council of England in collaboration with BALTIC

Exhibition tour:

BALTIC, Gateshead	1 March – 21 April 2003
Manchester Art Gallery	2 May – 15 June
Irish Museum of Modern Art, Dublin	3 July – 21 September

Exhibition curated by Peter Shield with Roger Malbert and Sune Nordgren
Exhibition organized by Roger Malbert, assisted by Sandra Dodson, Julia Risness and Miranda Stacey, earlier stages organized by Suzanne Cotter, assisted by Jessica Fisher
Contextual material and educational resources produced by Helen Luckett

Catalogue designed by Herman Lelie
Typeset by Stefania Bonelli
Printed in England by PJ Print

Front cover: Constant, *Animaux* / Animals (detail) (cat. 52)
Inside front and back covers: Karel Appel, from Karel Appel and Hugo Claus, *De Blijde en Onvoorziene Week* / The happy and unforeseen week (cat. 134)
Title page and pages 20, 23, 28 and 35: untitled drawings by Pierre Alechinsky (cat. 12)
Page 7: Title from *Cobra* 4 (cat. 129)
Back cover: Karel Appel, *Vrijheidsschreeuw* / Cry of freedom (cat. 25)

Published by Hayward Gallery Publishing, London SE1 8XX, UK

ISBN 1 85332 231 8

Hayward Gallery Publishing titles are distributed outside North and South America by Cornerhouse Publications, 70 Oxford Street, Manchester M1 5NH, UK (tel. +44 (0)161 200 1503; fax. +44 (0)161 200 1504; email: publications@cornerhouse.org; www.cornerhouse.org/publications).

Contents

Lenders to the Exhibition

Belgium

Ellen and Jan Nieuwenhuizen Segaar

Denmark

Carl-Henning Pedersen & Else Alfelt Museum, Herning
Jyske Bank A/S, Silkeborg
Louisiana Museum of Modern Art, Humlebæk
Nordjyllands Kunstmuseum, Aalborg
Silkeborg Kunstmuseum
Vejle Kunstmuseum

France

Pierre Alechinsky

Netherlands

ABN AMRO Art Foundation, Amsterdam
Cobra Museum voor Moderne Kunst, Amstelveen
Frans Hals Museum, Haarlem
Gemeentemuseum, The Hague
Karel and Rosemarie van Stuijvenberg
Museum Boijmans Van Beuningen, Rotterdam
Stedelijk Museum, Amsterdam

U.K.

The Arts Council Collection, Hayward Gallery, London
The British Museum, London
Peter Shield
Redfern Gallery, London
Tate, London

and those lenders who wish to remain anonymous

Preface

This is the first major exhibition in Britain on Cobra, a surprising fact considering the importance of the movement and Britain's geographical proximity to the three countries, Denmark, Belgium and the Netherlands, where most of its manifestations occurred. There have been numerous exhibitions elsewhere in Europe during the past three and a half decades, many accompanied by excellent catalogues, but relatively little has been published in English.

Of the large historical exhibitions on Cobra, some have taken a broad view and included works produced by Cobra artists later in their careers, after the group's formal dissolution in 1951. This exhibition focuses on works shown in one or other of the Cobra exhibitions held in Amsterdam, Brussels, Copenhagen and Paris between 1948 and 1951. It does not attempt to be fully comprehensive – more than sixty artists and poets were associated with Cobra. Twenty artists are represented in this show with a major group of paintings and drawings by each of the key figures: Pierre Alechinsky, Karel Appel, Constant, Asger Jorn and Carl-Henning Pedersen.

There are a few exceptions to the rule limiting the selection of works here to those made between 1948 and 1951. Included are paintings from the early 1940s by the Danish artists who decisively influenced their Dutch colleagues and were exhibited in Cobra exhibitions, and drawings from 1952 and 1953 by the Dutch poet Lucebert, who participated in Cobra mainly as a poet but went on to become a prominent artist in the Cobra manner.

Cobra was anti-specialist and collaborative: poets painted and organized exhibitions; artists wrote manifestos and illustrated and published books of poetry. The literary and polemical aspects of Cobra are not easily conveyed in an exhibition in English. The collaborative atmosphere can be sensed in the books, hand-written and drawn with characteristic Cobra vitality, and the Cobra journals which have the distinctive typographical style and atmosphere of their period. A few paintings and prints on which two or more artists and writers have worked give further evidence. The Belgian Christian Dotremont and the Dutch poets involved with Cobra were among the major poets of their generation within their respective countries. Translated extracts from their writings form an essential element of this exhibition. In a movement dedicated to experiment and improvisation, drawing played a particularly crucial role, and it is appropriate that this is reflected in the emphasis given to drawing here.

Cobra: Copenhagen Brussels Amsterdam is organized by the Hayward Gallery in collaboration with BALTIC. The exhibition's chief curator is the art historian and translator Peter Shield, working with Sune Nordgren, Director of BALTIC, and Roger Malbert, Senior Curator of the Hayward Gallery's National Touring Exhibitions. Peter Shield has contributed in several important ways to this publication, with a brief history and chronology of Cobra, an essay on the Cobra exhibitions in Amsterdam in 1949 and Liège in 1951, and artists' biographies. We thank him for this and for his patient and authoritative guidance on every aspect of the exhibition throughout its development. We are also grateful to the art historian Graham Birtwistle, of the Free University of Amsterdam, for his fascinating and timely analysis of Cobra and 'primitivism'.

When my colleagues Martin Caiger-Smith, the Hayward Gallery's Head of Exhibitions, and Roger Malbert first considered organizing a touring exhibition on Cobra, they quickly learnt of Sune Nordgren's longstanding enthusiasm for the movement. We are delighted to have been able to collaborate with BALTIC on this exhibition. The gallery's beautiful spaces and explicit dedication to the experimental in contemporary art make it an ideal opening venue. Manchester Art Gallery's new exhibition space also provides a superb setting, as does the Irish Museum of Modern Art in Dublin, where a selection of works from the Musgrave Kinley Outsider Collection will be presented alongside the exhibition, suggesting significant affinities. We thank our colleagues at each of these galleries for their wholehearted commitment to the project, in particular: Anne Howes, Vicki Lewis, Chris Osborne and Emma Thomas at BALTIC; Catherine Dickinson and Tim Wilcox at Manchester Art Gallery; and Enrique Juncosa, Sean Kissane, Brenda McPharland, Catherine Marshall and Rachel Thomas at the Irish Museum of Modern Art.

Many institutions and individuals have generously given us encouragement and access to their collections and knowledge. In Denmark, the Silkeborg Kunstmuseum houses the most important single collection of works by Asger Jorn – more than fifty paintings and five hundred drawings – as well as the works he collected by friends and contemporaries, including his Cobra colleagues. The Nordjyllands Kunstmuseum, Aalborg, has a substantial holding of works by Danish and Dutch Cobra artists, which was consolidated after the Museum acquired two major Cobra collections. The Stedelijk Museum in Amsterdam has one of the most significant collections of Cobra works, formed at the outset from the original exhibition held there in 1949 and added to consistently ever since. The Gemeentemuseum in The Hague, in addition to its holdings of Cobra paintings, has an outstanding collection of drawings by Karel Appel on long-term loan from the Karel Appel Foundation. The Museum Boijmans Van Beuningen, in Rotterdam, which organized the first comprehensive survey exhibition of Cobra in 1966, has many fine Cobra works. And most of the other museums from which we have borrowed have important collections.

We would like to express our warmest appreciation to the many individuals who contributed to the realization of the exhibition through their generous advice and assistance. Those to whom we would like to extend our particular thanks are: Deborah Wolf, ABN AMRO Art Foundation, Amsterdam; Irene Olsen and Stine Høholt, Arken Museum for Moderne Kunst; Hugo Bongers, Chris Dercon, Yvette Hollander, Guido Jansen, Saskia de Jong and Jaqueline Rapmund, Museum Boijmans Van Beuningen, Rotterdam; Frances Carey, Antony Griffiths and Janice Reading, The British Museum, London; Aase Dreyer, Anne Kristensen and Sidsel Ramson, Carl-Henning Pedersen and Else Alfelt Museum, Herning; Andrea van Munster, Ruvert Ophorst and Margot Wellen, Cobra Museum voor Moderne Kunst, Amstelveen; Søren Dietz, Flemming Friborg and Sidsel Maria Søndergaard, Ny Carlsberg Glyptotek, Copenhagen; Mai Melgard, The Royal Danish Embassy, London; Mabel Hoogendonk and Karel Schampers, Frans Hals Museum, Haarlem; Jonieke van Es, Ap Gewald, Wim van Krimpen, Peter Loorij, Maria Manuel, Kristina Odenhamn and Dr. Frans Peterse, Gemeentemuseum, The Hague; Natacha Derycke, Fonds Henri Storck, Brussels; Jytte Brinch and Viste Nielsen, Den Jyske Bank, Silkeborg; Hannah Schwarzbach and Harriet de Visser, Karel Appel Foundation, Amsterdam; Kirsten Degel, Hilde Østergaard and Poul Erik Tøjner, Louisiana Museum for Moderne Kunst, Humlebaek; Kirsten Andersen, Anne Lie Stokbro and Nina Hoboldt,

Nordjyllands Kunstmuseum, Aalborg; Richard Gault, Richard Selby and Maggie Thornton, Redfern Gallery, London; Dorte Kirkeby Andersen, Troels Andersen and Elisabeth Hvid, Silkeborg Kunstmuseum; Oliver Shuttleworth and Lucy Tagg, Sotheby's, London; Dorthe Aagesen and Hanne Møller, Statens Museum for Kunst, Copenhagen; Beppie Feuth, Rudi Fuchs, W. S. van Heusden and Gert Imanse, Stedelijk Museum, Amsterdam; Ludo van Halem, Stedelijk Museum, Schiedam; Catherine Clement, Jim France, Alison Miles and Sir Nicholas Serota, Tate, London; and Grethe Byrgiel, Nina Damsgaard and Marianne Sørensen, Vejle Kunstmuseum. We are also indebted to the following: Pierre and Micky Alechinsky, Len van den Berg, Cornelie Frech, Ed Frech, Alan Guest, Ellen and Jan Nieuwenhuizen Segaar, Graham Birtwistle, Louis Kaner, Karel van Stuijvenberg, Daphne Thissen, Professor Mike Tucker, Freddy de Vree and Nancy Whyte.

As always, I am grateful to my Hayward colleagues for their contributions to the realization of this project. Suzanne Cotter was responsible for organizing and co-curating the exhibition in its initial stages. Helen Luckett, Education Programmer, has been closely involved in many aspects of its development, researching and providing contextual material and producing a short film. Caroline Wetherilt, Art Publisher, and Jonathan Jones, Publishing Co-ordinator, have edited and produced this publication, which has been designed by Herman Lelie and typeset by Stefania Bonelli. To each of them, and to others too numerous to mention, thank you.

Susan Ferleger Brades
Director, Hayward Gallery

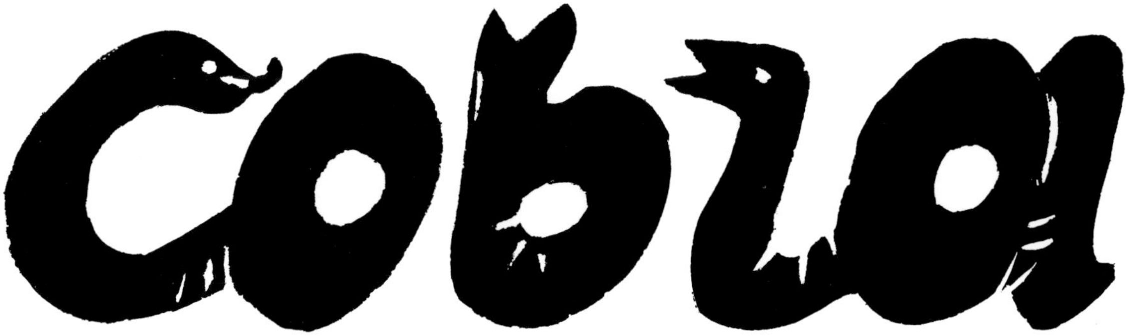

Introduction

Roger Malbert

'Cobra? It's like going on a train journey. You fall asleep, you wake up, you don't know whether you've just passed Copenhagen, Brussels or Amsterdam.'[1] This is how the poet Christian Dotremont, inventor of the acronym 'Cobra' and the group's principal spokesman and co-ordinator, characterizes the informal association of young artists and poets who met, worked, published and exhibited together in several countries between 1948 and 1951. Transience and disorientation: Cobra's brief manifestation in retrospect seems adequate to its historical moment, one of drastic change as Europe recovered from the hell of Nazism, German Occupation and the Second World War. 'Our art is the art of a revolutionary period, simultaneously the reaction of a world going under and the herald of a new world'[2], the Dutch painter Constant wrote in 1948: 'A painting is not a composition of colour and line, but an animal, a night, a scream, a human being, or all of these at once.'[3]

A cry does not last forever, and it is perhaps appropriate that Cobra did not live to consolidate its vision aesthetically, found a school and establish a doctrine. What remains is the romantic ideal, traces of an explosion of youthful revolt, of great significance artistically because of the extraordinary quality of many of the works produced under its banner, but ultimately doomed to extinction. The maturity of the group's decision to dissolve itself in Liège in 1951 saves us the trouble of adjudicating on Cobra's closing date. There is post-Cobra and neo-Cobra, but nothing like the rough and ready expressionism of the collaborative years when Karel Appel, Constant, Asger Jorn, Carl-Henning Pedersen and others were fired up to produce amazing, fearless work that still challenges because it so outrageous, irresponsible, funny and beautiful. That is the artistic legacy. Ideologically, the Cobra spirit spills over into the rebellion of a subsequent generation in 1968 – via Constant and Asger Jorn's involvement in the Situationist International group – and this gives it an edge over other more innocuous artistic movements that have been thoroughly absorbed into the history of painterly style.

The resolute internationalism of the Cobra movement, epitomized in its multilingual publications, is all the more impressive considering the circumstances of the immediate post-war years. Artists of more than a dozen nationalities took part (including two Scots, William Gear and Stephen Gilbert, both based at that time in Paris). Most were in their twenties or early thirties and utterly impoverished: Dotremont, on one train journey, resorted to selling his jacket to help finance the next issue of *Cobra* magazine. Poverty explains the poor quality of the artists' materials (some of their works are not in the best condition today) and it also helps account for the small scale of most Cobra paintings. While New York artists at this time were expanding their field, Cobra's liberating gestures are usually confined to the proportions of a modest easel painting – except when occasionally artists were offered a larger canvas or a wall to work on. The evocative photographs of the murals executed collectively in Amsterdam, Bregnerød and Silkeborg and since destroyed, suggest how overpowering their work could be on a bigger scale.

Another difference between the Cobra artists and the Abstract Expressionists in New York (with whom they were more or less contemporary but had no contact) is immediately striking. Although both, to some extent, grew out of the fertile soil of Surrealism, the Americans mostly chose to suppress or, in Jackson Pollock's phrase, 'veil' their imagery, whereas Cobra artists enthusiastically and joyfully embraced the grimacing, grinning or anguished faces that erupted with spontaneous force from their experiments in improvisation. And this is a clue to a further distinction: the Cobra artists were strongly engaged, both socially and politically – many were socialists or communists – and they were seeking forms of expression that could, in principle, be universally understood. Hence their identification with the imaginative world of children, whose vitality and conviction must have seemed especially poignant, following the recent violent deaths of millions. A return to the original creative impulse was Cobra's aim; those childish, crudely executed images belie the sophistication of their makers, several of whom were widely-read thinkers who argued eloquently for their theoretical position in critiques and manifestos. Cobra's declaration of freedom from artistic convention has a Dadaistic ring of defiance about it – Dada's deliberate childishness was similarly founded in disgust at the ways of 'civilized' men at war.

Like all good *avant-garde* movements, Cobra was aggressively polemical, defining itself in opposition to its many enemies. These included Classicism (harmonies founded on authoritarian principles, falsely reassuring); Formalism (of Mondrian, Dotremont wrote, 'We are sick of him', and Constant, 'Let us fill Mondrian's virgin canvas, even if it is only with our misfortunes!'), Surrealism (of the smoothly finished 'pictorial' variety); and Social Realism (with its spurious claims to popular appeal through hackneyed formulae). Graham Birtwistle, in his essay 'Behind the Primitivism of Cobra', shows the ambiguities and contradictions that were inherent in the movement ideologically. And a glance at the pages of Cobra publications reveals an eclecticism far beyond the range of most journals of 'visual culture' today, with essays on the Great Wall of China, the psychoanalysis of the comic strip, the Carnival at Binche, grafitti and Bessie Smith.

There seems nothing subversive today in Cobra's primitivist aesthetic or belief in the life-affirming energy of the unconscious. The imaginative power of children's art is universally acknowledged and naive expressionism long ago exhausted its potential for innovation. What does an art committed to spontaneity and authenticity have to say to our ironically knowing, self-conscious, post-modern age? It requires an effort to appreciate how challenging Cobra works must have seemed at the time of their creation, when they were widely ridiculed and bought by no one. Now, they are among the most popular and accessible of twentieth-century works in the museums that house them and reproductions serve to brighten up the corridors of hotels and office buildings. Perhaps this is as it should be for a movement whose aim was a 'people's art', a way of seeing that would be within everybody's reach.

In fact, many Cobra works are far from ingratiating and even now the most intense of them would be difficult to live with. The sense of cathartic outburst after terrible catastrophe is still palpable – although few images make explicit reference to war, or to the immediate social situation. Their metaphors are more personal – wild beasts, children, phantoms – and represent an antidote to melancholy, however dark and brooding the spectral presences that sometimes haunt them. The Cobra impulse to create is affirmative, rather than critical, it seems; its strength is in its waywardness and unpredictability. Speed, as with other varieties of automatism – Surrealist,

Abstract Expressionist – is one essential factor: most good Cobra paintings have evidently been produced quickly, short-circuiting the conscious will to reflect, intervene and rationalize. There are no dainty finishing touches – no tidying-up of rough edges, accidents or marks of clumsiness – or modifications of the sheer monstrous ugliness, sometimes, of the image. It is left raw, and that refusal of 'finish' is possibly one of Cobra's enduring challenges, especially in today's product-oriented, technocratic culture.

The experimental attitude implies disinterested curiosity, a willingness to fail and an openness to the unforeseen. This attitude was epitomized by the then Director of Amsterdam's Stedelijk Museum, Willem Sandberg's decision to invite a largely unknown group of young artists to make an exhibition there in 1949. That provocative show, the first Cobra exhibition, scandalized the city and prompted calls for his resignation (Peter Shield recounts the story in these pages). Willem Sandberg, typographer – and during the Occupation a consummate forger of identity papers – graphic designer, poet and exemplary curator, later recalled the events of Cobra's manifestation:

after the war
i asked myself
what art's reply would be
to all this violence
to all these huge changes
in human relationships
the famous artists hardly responded
i was about to turn away
when i noticed a group of young people
who had something to say
and who said it on a new note
violently
in a primitive way perhaps
they were seeking a new language
with much warmth
and resolution[4]

In assessing Cobra today, it must be asked whether the contingencies of geography have contributed to its marginalization. Art history's predominant narrative transports modern art, during and immediately after the War, directly from Paris to New York, leaving artists working in smaller European cities in the shade. The English-speaking world is especially in thrall to this version of events. It is time to shift the balance.

1 Jean-Clarence Lambert, *Cobra*, New York, Abbeville Press, 1983, p. 7.

2 Constant Niewenhuys, 'Manifesto', *Reflex 1*, Amsterdam, Sept – Oct 1948, translated from the Dutch by Leonard Bright. Reprinted in Willemijn Stokvis, *Cobra: an international movement in art after the Second World War*, New York, Rizzoli, 1988, pp. 29–31.

3 Ibid.

4 Willem Sandberg, *The Dutch Contribution to the International Development in Art Since 1945*, The Detroit Institute of Arts, 1963.

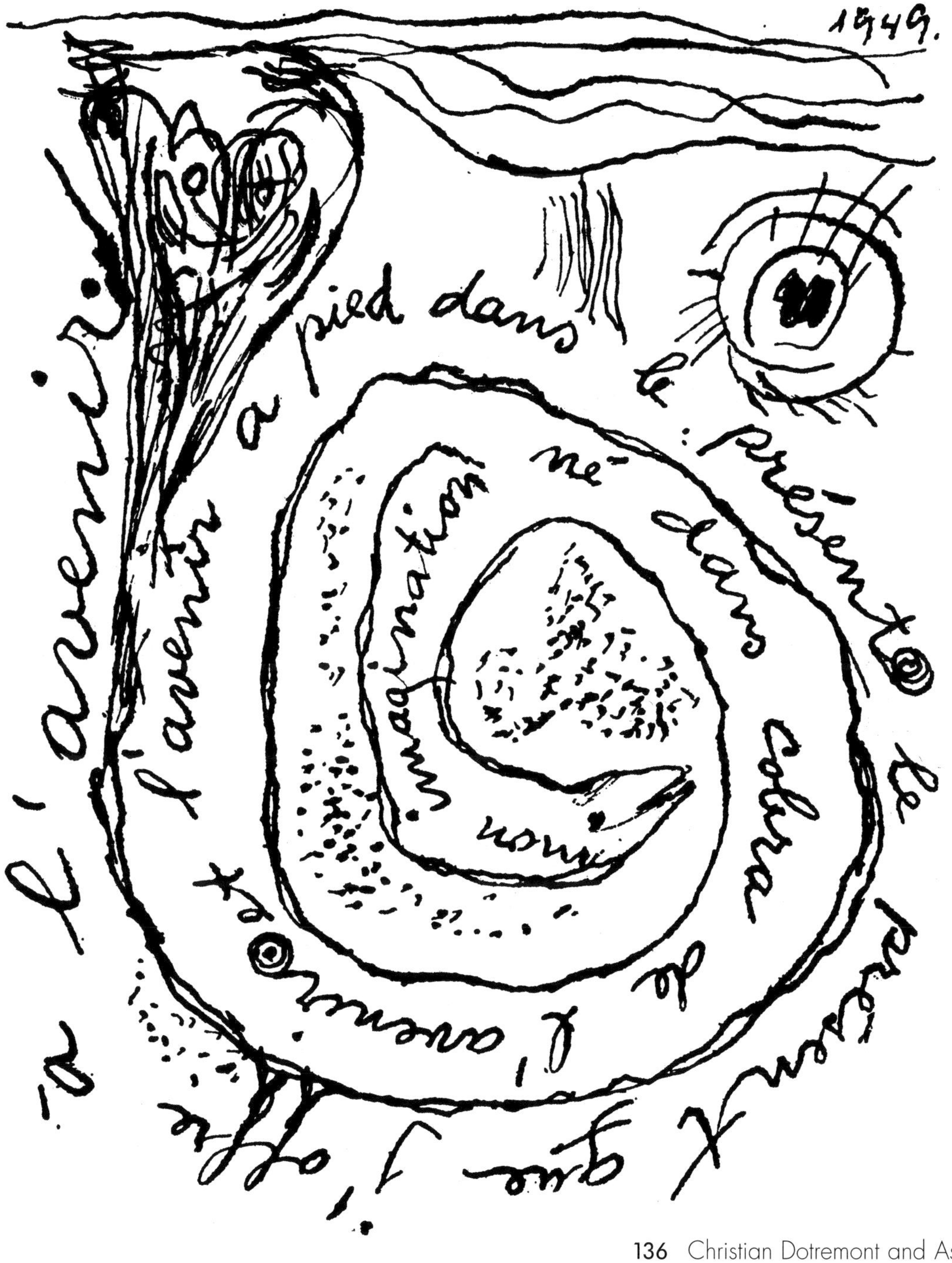

136 Christian Dotremont and Asger Jorn
Untitled drawing, 1949
page from *La chevelure des choses*, 1961
The hair-do of things

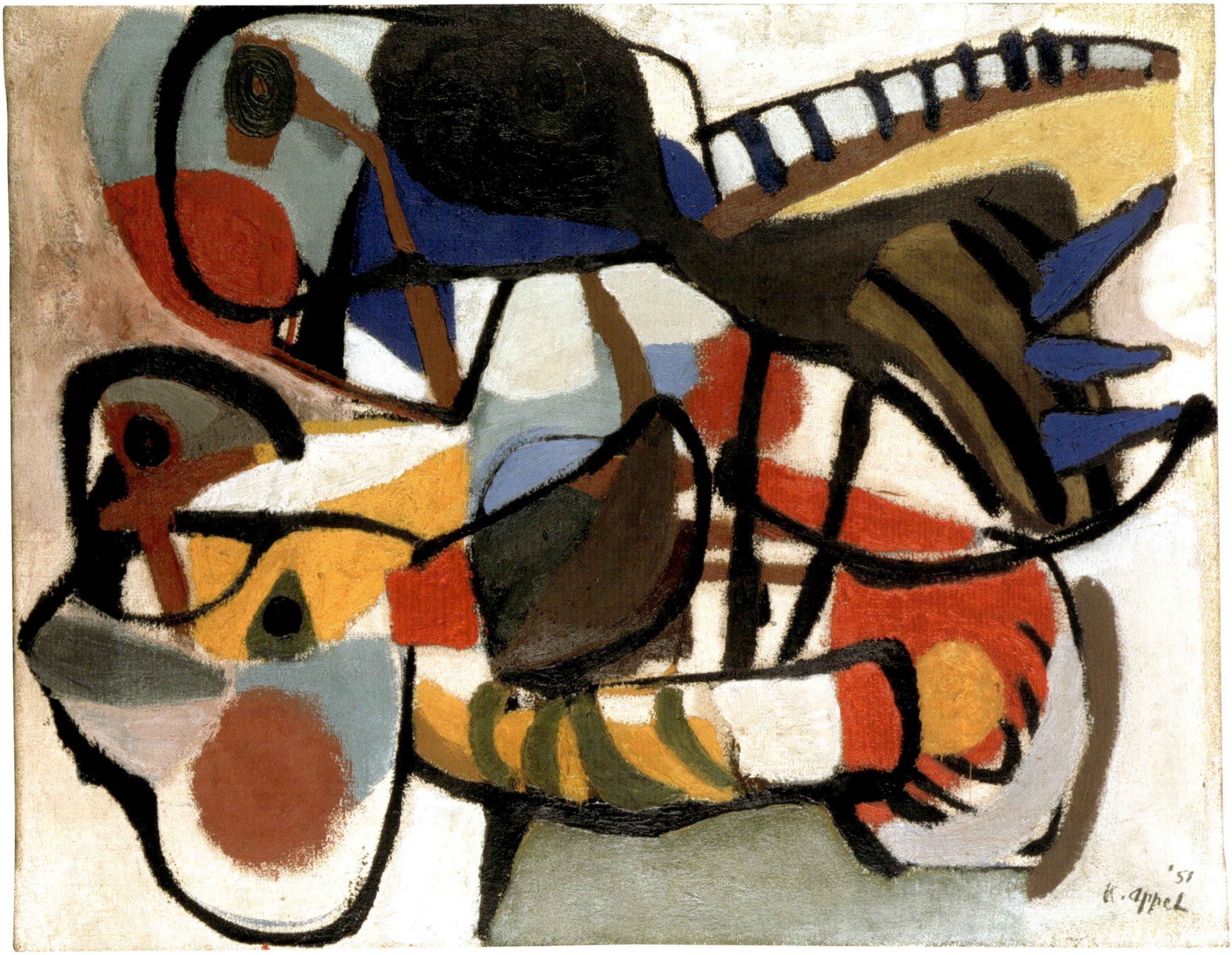

41 Karel Appel
African Mosquito, 1951

A Short History of Cobra

Peter Shield

Cobra was founded at the Café Notre-Dame on the Left Bank in Paris on 8 November 1948. The signatories of the first simple manifesto that spoke of 'an organic experimental collaboration which avoids all sterile and dogmatic theory' were Christian Dotremont and Joseph Noiret for the Surrealist-Revolutionary Centre in Belgium, Asger Jorn for the Danish Harvest Group, and Karel Appel, Constant and Corneille for the Dutch Experimental Group. The Cobra group prioritized spontaneity of expression and to this end found inspiration in child and primitive art. For the sixty or so artists and writers who eventually took part in its manifestations, Cobra was a crossroads, 'not a movement but a moment,' according to Dotremont, where they met others of like mind, exchanged ideas (not always harmoniously) and worked and exhibited together.

The Pre-Cobra period

The Danish Harvest Group

In 1938, a number of Danish 'abstract surrealist' artists from the Line group began to infiltrate a miscellaneous group of landscape artists known as the Harvest Group (*Høst*) and, by 1945, they formed a majority. Their idiom was based on an amalgam of influences drawn from Wassily Kandinsky, Paul Klee, Joan Miró, Yves Tanguy, the masks of Oceanic art and Pablo Picasso's work of the 1930s. During the Second World War, when occupied Denmark was initially under a relatively lax Nazi rule, they founded the magazine *Helhesten* (*The Horse of Hell* – a three-legged harbinger of death) as a cultural resistance to the occupying power. The Harvest Group gradually became known as 'spontaneous abstract' painters and attracted a small but enthusiastic band of national collectors. The principal members were Else Alfelt, Ejler Bille, Sonja Ferlov, Svavar Guðnason, Henry Heerup, Asger Jorn, Erik Ortvad, Carl-Henning Pedersen and Erik Thommesen. Closely associated with them, although belonging to *Grønningen*, another exhibiting group, was the artist Egill Jacobsen. As soon as the War was over, many of these artists travelled to other European countries and discovered that they had developed a unique spontaneous idiom based on the motif of the mask. Jorn, in particular, created a network of contacts from Lapland to the south of France.

The Dutch Experimental Group

The Dutch signatories to the Cobra Manifesto, Karel Appel, Constant and Corneille, who were half a generation younger than the Danes, had followed the fitful and unsatisfactory courses at the Amsterdam State Academy of Art during the Second World War. However, the German Occupation of the Netherlands meant that neither contact with the outside world nor any significant artistic activity was possible until the War ended in 1945. The Dutch Experimental Group rejected the formal models of Piet Mondrian and the de Stijl movement as inadequate to express their wish for immediacy of expression, preferring the recent work of Georges Braque, Picasso, and Henri Matisse that they saw exhibited at the Stedelijk Museum, Amsterdam, in 1945–46.

The somewhat solitary Constant had an interest in exotic animals, which found expression in his painting. In 1946, he travelled to Paris, where he met Asger

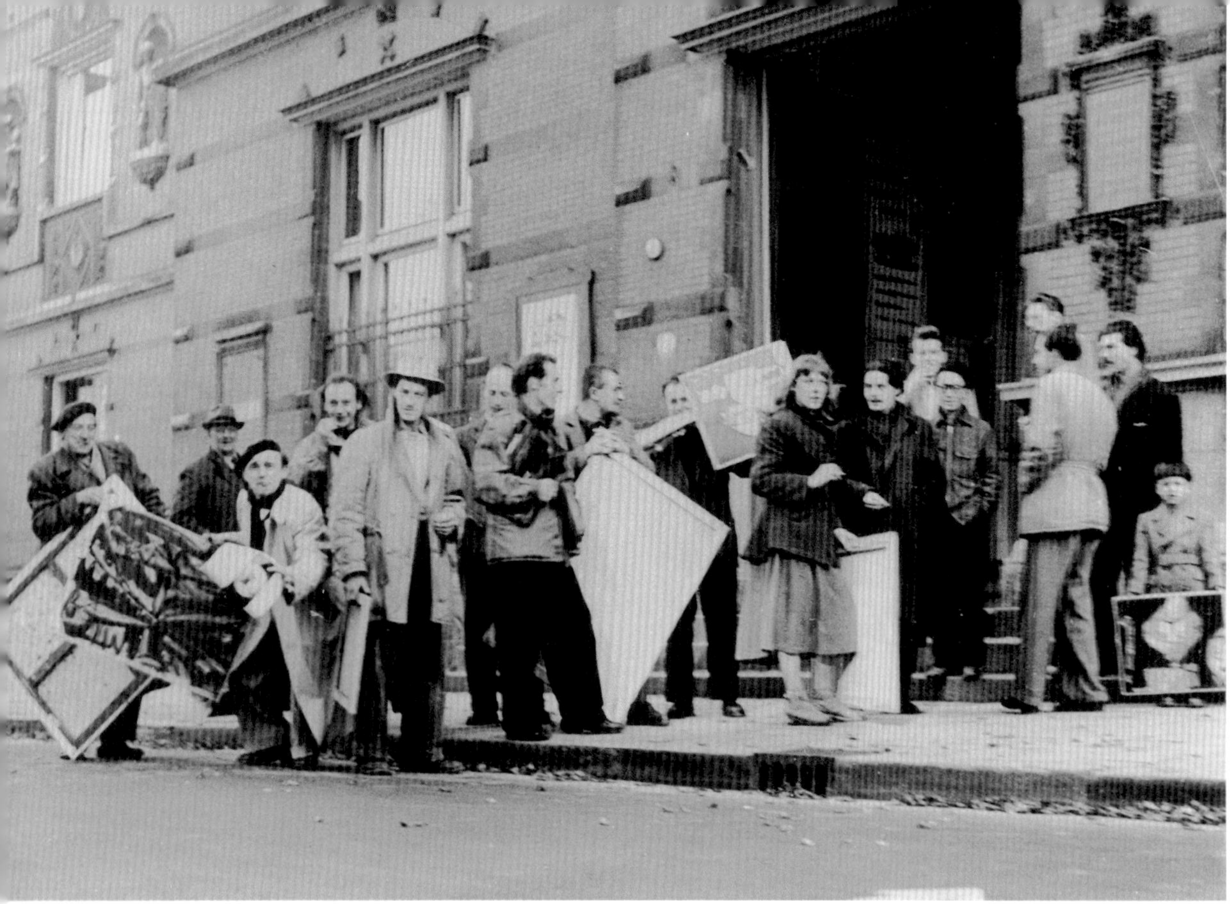

Figure 1
The first *International Exhibition of Experimental Art*, Stedelijk Museum, Amsterdam, November 1949.
Hanging-day. Members of the Cobra movement bringing their work to the exhibition.
Left to right: Anton Rooskens, a passer-by, Bert Schierbeek (carrying a work by Stephen Gilbert), Theo Wolvecamp, Eugène Brands, C.O. Götz, Corneille, Jacques Doucet, Pierre Alechinsky, Tony Sluyter, Lucebert, Jan Elburg, Shinkichi Tajiri, Gerrit Kouwenaar, Constant, Karel Appel, Victor Nieuwenhuys (Constant's son carrying a work by his father). Photograph by Mrs. E. Kokkorris-Syriër. Courtesy W. Stokvis Archive, Amsterdam.

Jorn at a Miró exhibition. Jorn's theories about the primitive impulses of art added much to Constant's theoretical education. A journey to Budapest in 1947 enabled Corneille to see works by Miró and Klee and, while in a bookshop there, he discovered the publications of French Surrealism. Dissatisfied with the stagnation of the Dutch art world on his return to Amsterdam, he joined his friend Appel on a trip to Brussels and Paris to study current trends in painting including both the primitive impulses in the work of Jean Dubuffet and other developments such as Social Realism, which were less appealing to them. When Appel, Constant and Corneille met again in Amsterdam in late 1947, they found that they had a common distaste for bourgeois Dutch society and that they had all developed an interest in the art of children and the insane, and in primitive art. They exhibited together and, in July 1948, founded the Dutch Experimental Group. The group was joined by Jan Nieuwenhuis (1921–86), Theo Wolvecamp, who painted in a free abstract manner influenced by Miró and Kandinsky, and the much older autodidacts Anton Rooskens, whose work had been transformed by his encounter with the art of New Guinea, and Eugène Brands (1913–2002), who specialized in free Dadaist collages and assemblages, but had also begun to explore the possibilities of children's art. Constant, who was the group's theorist, emphasized a liberation towards primitive impulses as an aid to their political aims of a common artistic language. During 1949, the group was joined by the Dutch poets Jan Elburg, Gerrit Kouwenaar, Lucebert and Bert Schierbeek. A couple of issues of a group magazine, *Reflex*, with vigorous polemics, poems and original lithographs, was published in October 1948 and February 1949.

The Surrealist Revolutionary Group

Christian Dotremont modelled himself poetically on the nineteenth-century French poet Arthur Rimbaud, and was soon accepted into the schismatic world of Belgian Surrealism, a movement dominated, with the exception of the painter René Magritte, by poets. In the early years of the Second World War, he took clandestine trips to Paris, where he made contact with the group of Surrealists around the magazine *La Main à Plume*, led by the writer Noël Arnaud. He also met the philosopher Gaston Bachelard and was taken with his ideas. Back in Brussels in 1946–47, he participated in the publication of several small Surrealist magazines, writing in one of them a provocative pro-Stalinist article that paved the way for his break with mainstream Surrealism.

In July 1947, the French Surrealist poet André Breton published the manifesto *Rupture inaugurale*, which rejected all forms of collaboration by the Surrealists with the Communist Party. Dotremont, however, believed in an accommodation between Marxist thought and experimental art and, in October 1947, he founded the Surrealist Revolutionary Group (*Le Surréalisme Révolutionnaire*), and organized an 'international conference' in Brussels with artists and writers from Belgium, Czechoslovakia, Denmark and France. In his editorial for the only copy of the associated magazine *Le Surréalisme Révolutionnaire*, published in Brussels, Dotremont declared, 'For us a communist does not necessarily have to have the experimental spirit as we understand it, but whoever has an experimental spirit must necessarily be communist.' The French section of the Surrealist Revolutionary Group, led by Noël Arnaud, soon came under fire from the French Communist Party and collapsed. Some of the ex-members of the Group called a conference in Paris in November entitled *The International Centre for the Documentation of Avant-Garde Art, (Centre International de Documentation sur l'Art d'Avant-Garde*). Among those attending were Appel, Constant, Corneille, Dotremont, Jorn and the young Belgian poet Joseph Noiret (b. 1927). However, they were so repelled by the sterile discussions at the conference that they were moved to found their own group, Cobra.

A Cobra Chronology

Peter Shield

1948

September: First issue of the magazine *Reflex*, organ of the Dutch Experimental Group, with four inserted lithographs by Karel Appel, Constant, Corneille and Jan Nieuwenhuis.

8 November: Cobra founded in Paris.

Late November: Appel, Constant, Corneille and Christian Dotremont travel to Copenhagen to participate in the annual Harvest Group exhibition, which also includes works by all the Dutch Experimental Group artists. Dotremont later travels to Malmö in Sweden and makes C.O. Hultén and Anders Österlin, of the Surrealist group Imaginist (*Imaginisterna*), aware of Cobra.

1949

January: In Copenhagen, Asger Jorn and Henry Heerup resign from the Harvest Group over the forcing out of the two remaining landscape painters (Aage Vogel-Jørgensen and Sixten Wiklund). Jorn joins The Spiral, a loose association of mainly younger artists.

February: The second issue of the magazine *Reflex* is published with four inserted lithographs by Eugène Brands, Corneille, Jan Nieuwenhuis and Anton Rooskens and a cover designed by the Frenchman Jacques Doucet.

20 February: First issue of *Le petit Cobra*, a stencilled bulletin intended to keep the participants in Cobra in touch, published in Brussels with four issues at roughly annual intervals.

March: Two small exhibitions involving various combinations of artists held in Amsterdam and Brussels. At the latter, the young Belgian painter Pierre Alechinsky meets Dotremont and involves himself in Cobra activities. He has just established *Les Ateliers du Marais*, a studio complex in Brussels where artists could live and work communally, and this now becomes the International Cobra Research Centre.

The first issue of the magazine *Cobra* is published with a collaborative lithographed cover by Egill Jacobsen, Jorn and Carl-Henning Pedersen and original lithographs by Ejler Bille, Jorn and Pedersen, closely followed by the second issue. The two most important articles are by Jorn: 'Discourse to the Penguins', which makes a clear distinction between Cobra spontaneity and automatism as defined by André Breton, and 'Forms conceived as language', which defines a materialist art.

May–July: Appel, Constant and Corneille have a small exhibition in Paris. The two latter artists deliver the works to Paris before joining Constant in Denmark. Constant travels to Denmark with his family, going first to Copenhagen to deliver works by the three Dutchmen for yet another exhibition. He travels to the Baltic island of Bornholm with the Jorn family, intending to meet Appel and Corneille to attend the first international Cobra congress in Bregnerød. However, Constant learns that his wife has left him for Jorn. Appel, Constant and Corneille, therefore, return home without attending the Congress, with Constant threatening to leave Cobra.

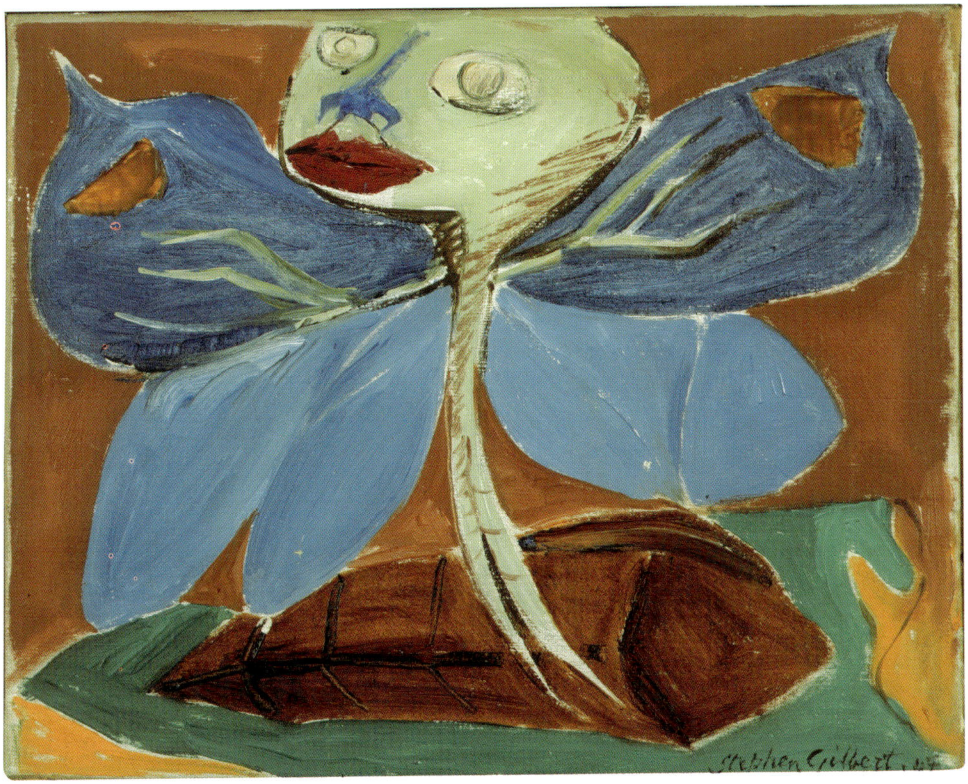

69 Stephen Gilbert
Untitled (Butterfly), 1947

June: The third issue of *Cobra*, published in Brussels, is devoted mainly to articles on experimental cinema.

August–September: The first international Cobra congress, *The Bregnerød Meetings (Les Rencontres de Bregnerød)*, takes place in a students' summer hostel in the woods north of Copenhagen. Else Alfelt, Dotremont, Jorn, Stephen Gilbert, Pedersen and the French writer Édouard Jaguer paint the walls with great swirling murals and visit various Danish artists. Hultén and Österlin and several of Jorn's Spiral Group comrades paint the panels of the hostel's ceiling. In an article, Dotremont reports energetic discussions in a pidgin Franco-Danish.

November: The first *International Exhibition of Experimental Art (Exposition Internationale d'Art Éxperimental)*, and second Cobra congress take place at the Stedelijk Museum, Amsterdam. The fourth issue of *Cobra* serves as the exhibition catalogue.

Jorn exhibits ten canvases at the Paris Salon des Surindépendants.

Appel, Constant, Corneille and the British artists William Gear and Gilbert exhibit with the Harvest Group in Copenhagen. Immediately afterwards, the Group breaks up, leaving only Alfelt and Pedersen as members. Appel, Constant and Corneille travel to Denmark, where they cover the interior of a house with murals, and then to Sweden, where they make a collaborative lithograph with the Imaginist Group.

1950

April: Dotremont suppresses an article by Constant on Social Realism intended for the fifth issue of *Cobra*, published in Hanover by Karl-Otto Götz (b. 1914). The sixth issue of *Cobra*, which concentrates on popular art, is published in Brussels.

May–June: Belgium becomes the active centre of Cobra and host to a couple of what Dotremont calls, 'unifying and decentralizing manifestations', which are attempts to widen the scope of Cobra. One, an exhibition in the small town of La Louvière, including works by Alechinsky, Constant, Corneille, Dotremont, Jorn and Pedersen, is banned because an official finds Dotremont's pamphlet subversive, whilst another, an exhibition by the opportunist *Cobra Réalité* group in Liège, has little to do with Cobra concerns. The Flemish writer-painter Hugo Claus begins a long period of involvement in Cobra activities, especially with the Dutch artists.

Autumn: Several Cobra artists exhibit in various exhibitions in Paris and Brussels.

The seventh issue of *Cobra* is published in Brussels with Dotremont's important essay, 'Signification and sinification', dealing with the problem of signs as language and vice versa.

Appel, Constant and Corneille move to Paris in September and Jorn follows in October.

In November, the final Harvest Group exhibition in Copenhagen is effectively a Carl-Henning Pedersen retrospective. This makes a great impact on Alechinsky on his first visit to Scandinavia. A double Danish issue (8–9) of *Cobra*, is prepared by the Danish poet Uffe Harder (1930 –2002) during the winter, but only reaches proof stage.

1951

April: The exhibition *Five painters of Cobra* – Appel, Balle (whose works did not arrive), Corneille, Jacobsen and Jorn – in a small private gallery in Paris.

May: Jorn returns to Denmark suffering from tuberculosis and malnutrition, and is admitted to the sanatorium in his 'detested' home town of Silkeborg.

Summer: Dotremont travels to Denmark. He too is diagnosed with tuberculosis and Jorn pulls strings to have him admitted to the same sanatorium.

November: The second *International Exhibition of Experimental Art* in Liège. The tenth issue of *Cobra* serves as a catalogue. Alechinsky then moves to Paris to study engraving under S.W. Hayter.

Post-1951

After 1951, some Cobra artists, including Constant and Gilbert, chose a radically different direction, others consolidated and deepened their Cobra language. A few played down their involvement, others exaggerated it. Yet others, Jorn for example, developed complex individual artistic paths. Christian Dotremont continued to promote the idea of a Cobra spirit until his death, bringing other artists into its orbit and encouraging former 'members' of Cobra to continue their collaborations.

Behind the Primitivism of Cobra

Graham Birtwistle

Writers on Cobra have often turned to the word 'primitivism' to characterize the art of the movement. There is certainly good art-historical precedent for this, since primitivism was first established as a term in accounts of those modern movements and artists that are usually reckoned among the antecedents and kindred spirits of Cobra: Expressionism and Surrealism, for example, or Picasso, Paul Klee and Joan Miró, and, of course, that great advocate of l'*Art Brut*, Jean Dubuffet. With its preponderance of mask-like faces and apparently childlike and spontaneous renderings of flora and fauna and fantasy beings, Cobra art can indeed be seen to have extended that earlier primitivist lineage and even to have given it new vitality. It is not surprising, therefore, to find one of the more recent surveys of primitivism in modern art featuring work by a Cobra artist, Karel Appel, on its cover.[1] Since primitivism is a term that is now well and truly attached to Cobra, I will not try to justify its relevance anew. The task I have set myself is to look behind that primitivist art and examine the attitudes and motivations of the artists who made it.

The mention of primitivism can mean that awkward questions are raised. Primitivism has had a bad press in recent years and the term is often used nowadays to refer to the exploitation of 'primitive art' by Western artists and collectors for their own ends. Primitivist taste, it has been argued, preferred to idealize the tribal artists of Europe's colonies and North America as anonymous figures in some timeless, natural state rather than acknowledge them as real people in the real world and as the equals of Westerners. Such, at least, is the tenor of a good many articles and books about primitivism written since the mid-1980s, when a tide of criticism turned against the 'eurocentric' bias of the exhibition *"Primitivism" in 20th Century Art* that William Rubin organized at New York's Museum of Modern Art in 1984. Rubin defined his theme as 'Affinity of the Tribal and the Modern', but in the eyes of his critics he elevated the concerns of primitivist Western artists above those of tribal artists in ways that were deemed inadmissible in a post-colonial era.[2] Opprobrium that started with the reception of Rubin's exhibition then became attached to the concept of primitivism itself, and within a few years a new generation of academics and critics had loaded the term with colonialist and racist implications from a guilty past.[3]

Are we, then, to burden the artists of Cobra with this colonialist guilt? Not in any simplistic way, hopefully, for, like a number of other writers, I have a mixed reaction to those debates of the 1980s.[4] Rubin's theme of 'the tribal and the modern' attracted so much critical attention that other aspects of primitivism – notably ones that had no direct relevance for West/non-West relations and did not present such an obvious target for political critique – were largely ignored. The conception of primitivism popularized by Rubin and his critics was in fact too narrow to take in the complexity of twentieth-century artists' primitivist concerns. The primitivism of Cobra is a case in point. Cobra artists certainly admired tribal and non-Western arts but also, and perhaps more typically, they looked to other models of the primitive that existed within their own Western context: child art, folk art, naive art and the art of psychiatric patients, for instance, as well as examples drawn from medieval art history and Scandinavian archaeology. Because of these and other ramifications, Cobra primitivism is not a subject that can be reduced to any one single issue, let alone that of European attitudes to non-Western cultures.

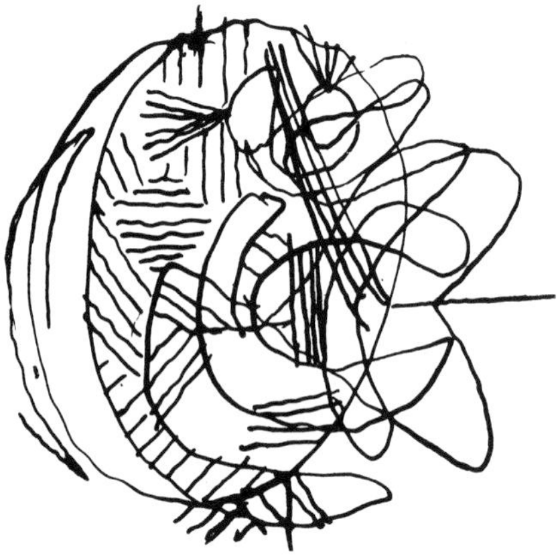

In search of nourishment

If the political critique of primitivism in the 1980s had its faults, it also had its strong points. It alerted attention to eurocentric attitudes in primitivism that had largely gone unexamined in earlier decades, and some of these can inevitably be detected in Cobra circles. For example, Constant wrote in his 'Manifesto' in *Reflex* 1 (published by the Dutch Experimental Group in 1948): 'The child knows no other law than its spontaneous feeling for life and has no other desire than to express this. The same goes for primitive cultures, and it is also this characteristic that lends these cultures such a great appeal for the people of today who have to live in a morbid atmosphere of inauthenticity, lies and unproductiveness.'[5] In equating childlike spontaneity with primitive culture Constant certainly meant to praise both, and his fellow artists undoubtedly took his words in that sense. It is all too evident, however, that his polemical argument rested on an old and obstinate European valuation of primitive culture as representing a continuing 'childhood' of mankind, an assumption that even in the 1940s could still claim a measure of academic credibility as well as serve the primitivist ideals of Constant and his colleagues.[6]

When Cobra artists ventured into Africa, they continued in many respects a pattern laid down by nineteenth- and twentieth-century European artists who had travelled in search of an idealized primitive or oriental art. The Dane Asger Jorn – an admirer of Paul Klee who made his famed *Tunisreise* in 1914 – spent the winter of 1947–48 on the Tunisian island of Djerba studying folk-art motifs (such as 'the hand of Fatima'), which he found significant for his theory of natural and 'living' ornament.[7] The Dutchman Corneille twice visited North Africa in 1948 and 1949, and then in 1951 – accompanied among others by the architect Aldo van Eyck – he made a memorable journey in an old army vehicle across the desert region of the Hoggar in Southern Algeria. Corneille, who has since maintained his love for Africa and its art, later told of that journey: 'We were in search of nourishment. We were looking for special places in the world which could mean something for us. The most important thing about the desert is that not only people but animals, palm trees, camels, buildings – in short, everything you come across – take on an enormously strong presence. [...] Everything there is reduced to its archetypal form. And I believe that because of their continual contact with archetypal forms the lives of the people there take on a kind of *noblesse*.'[8] His account is eloquent and full of personal conviction, yet it can also be seen to typify a certain kind of mid-century primitivism, with its

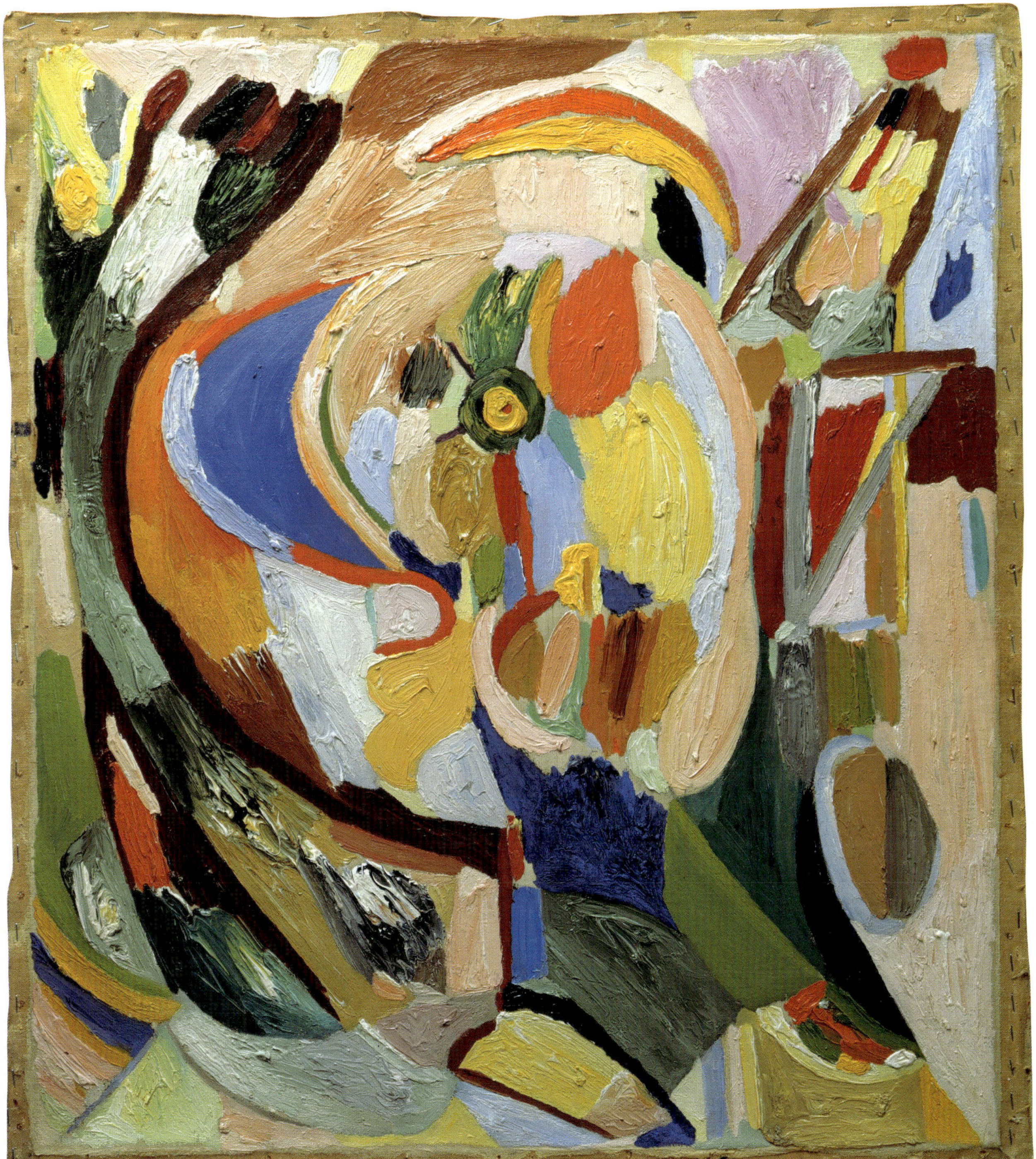

47 Ejler Bille
Untitled, 1942

underlying assumptions still redolent of a colonialist era. It was Corneille the European who searched for nourishment elsewhere in the world. It was Corneille the European who projected an archetypal significance on to the places and people of the Hoggar and whose admiration resonated with a centuries-old notion of The Noble Savage.

Taking account of such factors, then, a certain ambivalence emerges. Cobra primitivism, as I have already suggested, cannot be defined only as a matter of cultural relations between the Westerner and the Other. But since it was a product of its time and could not deny its characteristically European well-springs, Cobra primitivism certainly included its share of attitudes and assumptions that would not pass muster in our present-day cultural politics.

The enemy has always been the classical

The primitivism of Cobra did, however, have much to do with the cultural politics of its own day. The leading Cobra theorists espoused the socialist cause of internationalism and conceived of their movement as unlimited by any national, racial or cultural boundaries (Christian Dotremont, chief editor of *Cobra*, even fantasized in 1949 about a possible Hindu issue of the periodical[9]). Their internationalism contained, on the one hand, a reaction against the destructive nationalism and racism of the Hitler years, and, on the other hand, a counter to the perceived narrowness of bourgeois taste and opinion. Both causes were pioneered earlier by the Danish participants. In the pages of their wartime periodical *Helhesten* the Danes had printed articles on primitive and oriental arts, thereby making their protest against the racist policies of the Nazi occupying powers. And the same artists had written polemics against a bourgeois belief in the Western classical tradition as superior to all other cultures. When in 1940, for instance, Asger Jorn and Egill Jacobsen attacked those who would not acknowledge that 'a good Negro sculpture is just as worthy as a good Greek statue', it was the politics of culture that concerned them.[10] Absence of racial prejudice, openness to the cultural riches of other peoples, and freedom from 'bourgeois "Culture"' they saw as mutually supportive and necessary conditions for a truly socialist society.

The Liberation of 1945 brought an end to the Nazi occupation of Denmark, Belgium and Holland. In the perception of the artists who formed Cobra in 1948, however, liberation from bourgeois society and its culture was something still to be achieved. For Marxian theorists such as Jorn and Constant, it was an alliance of class-society and classical culture that stood in the way of political and artistic freedom. 'The enemy has always been the classical', ran the opening line of a short text in English in the first issue of *Cobra*, 1949 that was about, but not by, Jorn. Written by Michael Ventris for a London architectural journal, the text summarized in a few punchy lines some lengthy polemical articles that Jorn had published in the Swedish architectural press: '[Jorn] analyses the difference between the rational, inhuman *Apollonic* approach of classical art, and the vital *Dionysiac* spontaneity of the "barbarian" East. A shaky Marxist, he identifies Apollo with the old ruling classes, Dionysus with the oppressed and liberated people.'[11] Jorn must have been glad to print this piece in *Cobra* to show his colleagues that someone outside their circle had grasped his point.

Jorn's theories at the time of Cobra portrayed the classical as a current force to be reckoned with (for example, in Le Corbusier's functionalist architecture as well as in the carefully regulated taste of the bourgeoisie), and he held it responsible for enforcing a dualism of form and content in art. In contrast to classical art, Jorn advocated an artistic principle which he identified variously with the Dionysian, the primitive, the oriental, and the arabesque, and which he illustrated from his growing documentary collection of images from world art as well as from the work of modern artists whom he admired. The diversity of his illustrations can seem at first sight bewildering: they include Islamic ornament from a mosque at Isfahan and a mausoleum at Marrakesh, Scandinavian ornaments and rock-engravings from the Bronze Age, medieval wall-painting, model houses from Sumatra, Australian aboriginal sand-ornament, 'yang-yin' symbols, details of plants from the photographic books of Karl Blossfeldt, and paintings by Joan Miró and Paul Klee. Behind their diversity, however, these images all served to exemplify art and design that was not classical and dualistic but a natural and spontaneous expression of the content and form of life itself. In his caption to one such illustration (juxtaposed photographs of a totem pole and a chestnut branch), Jorn wrote: 'The nature of art is not to imitate the external forms of nature (naturalism) but to create natural art. Natural sculpture which is true to its material will be identical to nature's forms without seeking to imitate.'[12] Such claims for a natural morphology in art point to the core of Jorn's particular brand of primitivism: he was looking to nature to establish norms both for art and for society.[13] His main indictment against class-society and classical culture was, in fact, that they were unnatural.

Culture and counter-culture

Much the same indictment was also made by Constant in his 'Manifesto' of 1948 as well as in a text he published in *Reflex* 2 in February 1949, this time under the title 'Culture and counter-culture'. 'Culture' was, for Constant, the legacy of ancient Greece and marked by class division in society and schism in art. Art was schismatic because a natural

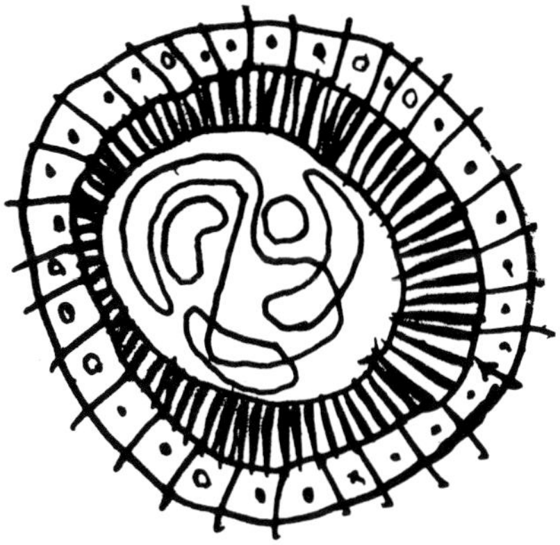

human urge for direct expression remained at odds with the dominant formalism of classical aesthetics ('formalism' was a term much used by Cobra artists to denote the kind of art they rejected). This urge for expression, Constant wrote, had manifested itself from time to time in the art of those 'geniuses' in art history who were initially rejected by the dominant culture and then later assimilated into it. But by assimilating truly expressive artists, formalist culture had increasingly allowed itself to be subverted by a spirit of liberation that it really meant to bridle: 'This impulse towards direct expression, towards the release of bottled-up vitality, which art historians regard as the stimulus for development in culture, is in reality the agent that is demolishing culture.'[14] Natural and spontaneous expressiveness, then, was the driving force behind a 'counter-culture' that, in Constant's view, was getting ever closer to breaking down classical and formalist 'culture'. He concluded his article: 'The exhibition of children's art at the Stedelijk Museum of Amsterdam has demonstrated once again what enormous creative powers slumber in human nature. We shall open the way for an activation of those powers by destroying the last vestiges of formalism that hinder their unfolding.'[15]

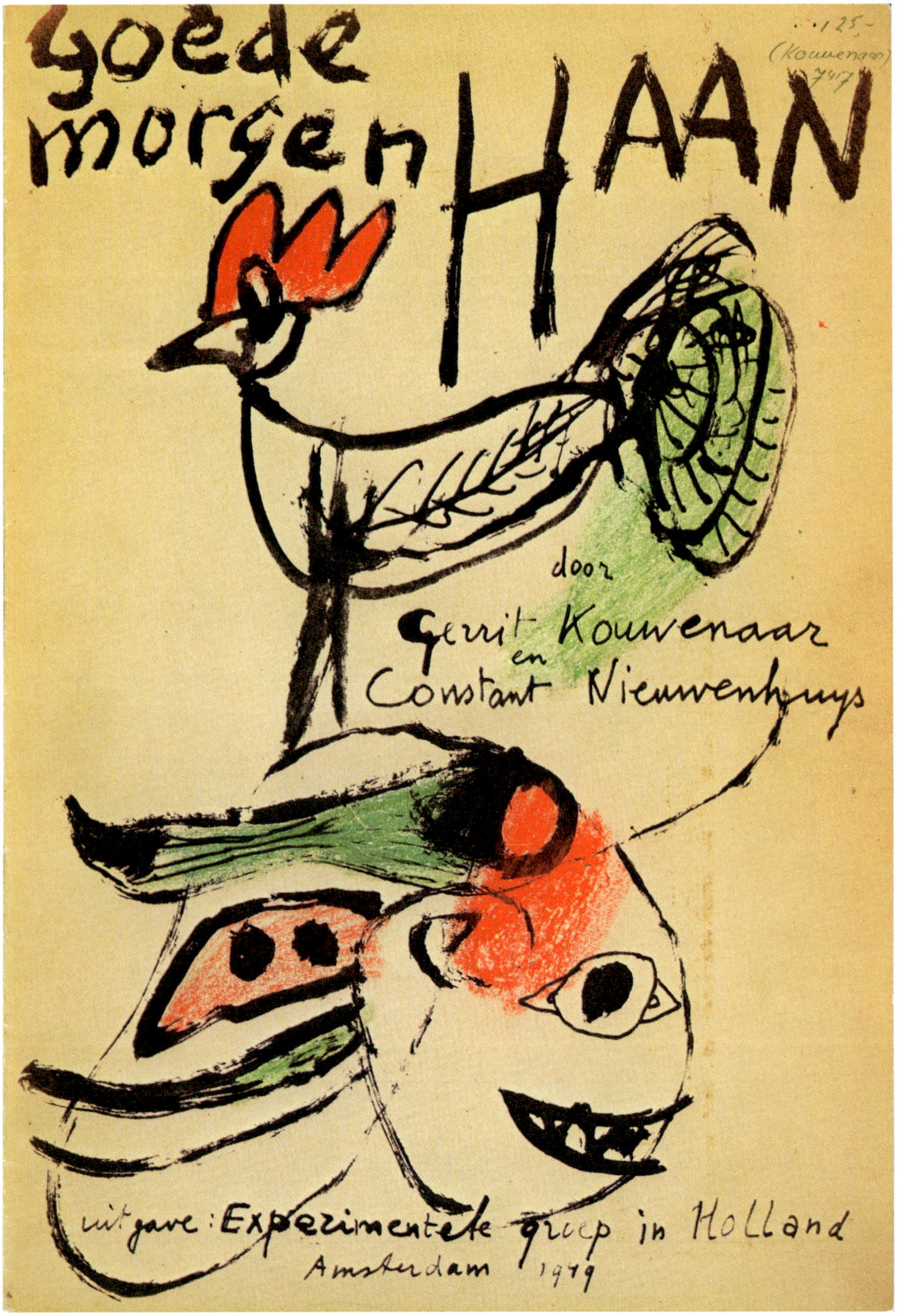

135 Constant and Gerrit Kouwenaar
cover for *Goede Morgen Haan*, 1949
Good morning cockerel

Some twenty years were to elapse between Constant's arguments for a 'counter-culture' in *Reflex* and the widespread use of the same concept to describe the youthful, primitivist opposition that rose up against technocratic and bourgeois society in the later 1960s.[16] The later usage cannot, of course, be attributed to Constant's influence, but it is not too far-fetched to suggest that Constant and Cobra prefigured in some important respects the primitivism that was to mark the counter-culture of the 1960s. Much as Cobra had done in 1949, the counter-culture of 1969 combined a Marxian theme of liberation with an appeal to nature for norms and a subversion of establishment culture by means of spontaneous expression. Constant himself even helped to bridge the historical gap between Cobra and counter-culture. In the mid-1960s, the Dutch youth movement Provo embraced Constant's ideas on the 'homo ludens' from his current project for *New Babylon* and went on to create 'happenings' on the streets of Amsterdam in protest against the establishment.[17] Constant had by then turned his back on the primitivist painting of the Cobra years, but underlying primitivist implications of spontaneity were still in evidence when he proclaimed: 'The world of plenty is New Babylon, the world in which man no longer toils, but plays; poetry as a way of life for the masses, *'la poésie faite par tous et non par un'* [poetry made by all and not by one].'[18] Of course, compared to the mass movement that counter-cultural primitivism became in the 1960s, Cobra primitivism represented only the limited project of a handful of artists and writers. Yet, in theory at least, Constant and his colleagues in Cobra were already concerned with mobilizing the expressive potential of the people and not just of an artistic elite. They wanted, as Jorn put it in *Cobra* 5, 'to make a people of co-workers out of a people of spectators'.[19]

Ye literary ladies and ye literary gentlemen

The poets associated with Cobra generally took the same anti-establishment stance as the artists. For example, in *Reflex* 2 Constant's 'Culture and counter-culture' was followed by the poet Gerrit Kouwenaar's 'Poetry is reality', an article similar in length to Constant's, and, with its Marxian polemics against the dualistic and formalistic culture of class-society, similar in content. Kouwenaar pointed poetry back to its primitive origins in a human need for creative expression and argued for a resurgence of that original vitality in a new poetry of the people: 'a true folk-poetry, [which] does not serve the interests of the ruling class.'[20] And the same issue of *Reflex* contained Lucebert's anti-colonialist poem 'Love-letter to our tortured bride Indonesia', dated Sunday 19 December 1948 and clearly a response to a wave of military repression during the last phase of Dutch colonial rule in the East.[21]

When the poets Lucebert, Kouwenaar and Jan Elburg participated in the major Cobra exhibition of November 1949 under the motto 'There is a poetry that we abolish', it was the literary establishment that they were targeting. In the accompanying *Cobra* 4, Lucebert's poem 'Defence of the 50-ers' harangued 'ye literary ladies and ye literary gentlemen, ye who sit in genteel residences deeply sifting deeds'.[22] In the name of his own generation – the term 50-ers (*Vijftigers*) has subsequently become canonical in Dutch literary history – Lucebert accused the 'literary ladies and gentlemen' of immorality, hypocrisy and petty nationalism. Their sexual experiences were laundered out of their poetry, and though they claimed to read William Blake, Arthur Rimbaud and Charles Baudelaire there was no truly international orientation in their writings. A deep primitivist vein runs through the poem: Lucebert confronts the so-called civilization of these bourgeois writers with a morality that, unlike theirs, is uncompromisingly frank and true to nature. In language that mixes archaic usage and prophetic-sounding incantation with neologism and crude vernacular, Lucebert tears away the façade of civilization to expose the sexualized and animalized life that he and his comrades embrace as reality. His closing line proclaims: 'your heaven will be over-burdened with our festering experience'.

The primitivism of the 50-ers is manifest in their polemics and in the strong emphasis on bodily, sensual experience and the use of street-language in their verses. But it cannot be claimed that their poetry showed the spontaneity of method that we associate with Cobra painting. The 50-ers in general, and Lucebert in particular, turn out to have been careful constructors of their poetry.[23] Lucebert's 'Defence of the 50-ers' is no spontaneous outpouring; it has a complex rhyme scheme, structural features from classical rhetoric, and a layer of intertextual reference to Cabalistic (Jewish) mysticism. There were other activities in Cobra, however, in which poets did seem to approach the spontaneity of painters. When Dotremont and Jorn first made their *'peinture-mot'* collaborations in 1948, poetry and painting joined forces in one rapidly-made word-image work, in which the handwritten text of Dotremont seemed no less spontaneous than the painterly contribution of Jorn. In his article 'Signification et sinification' in *Cobra* 7 (1950), Dotremont developed his thoughts on the pictorial value of handwriting. He shared with Jorn the notion that painting and writing both derived from one common, primitive origin, the characteristics of which were still preserved in calligraphy. After Cobra ended, Dotremont went on to make his own calligraphic *'logogrammes'*: poetic texts that were at the same time spontaneous paintings.

Among the collaborative poet/painter works of Cobra, Constant and Kouwenaar's *Good morning cockerel*, 1949 (cat. 135) must rank as one of the most overtly primitivist examples. Once again, it is the handwriting of the poet that seems to match the painter's spontaneity. Kouwenaar's scrawl wanders in apparently childlike freedom around Constant's similarly childlike images. Moreover, as the critic C. van de Watering has noted, a sentence such as, 'HOORAY is a word that is always having a birthday', seems deliberately designed to call up the primitive thought-world of the child.[24]

...my daughter of three...

The exhibition *Art and the Child* (*Kunst en Kind*), that Constant lauded in his 'Culture and counter-culture', was shown in Amsterdam from 27 December 1948 to 24 January 1949, closing just a matter of weeks before *Reflex* 2 and the first two issues of *Cobra* went to press. Later that year, Constant and his colleagues went on to 'borrow' examples of child art from that very exhibition to illustrate alongside their own art in *Cobra* 4 – the Dutch issue that accompanied the first major exhibition of experimental art at the Stedelijk Museum in November 1949. The exhibition of child art provides one instance – Jorn and Corneille's visits to North Africa were others – of Cobra artists reacting at first hand to works that they valued as primitive models. It was not, however, a reaction that sparked radical changes in the Dutch artists' work, since they were already using childlike modes of representation absorbed from Danish art of the early 1940s and from modern masters who had valued child art, such as Picasso, Paul Klee and Joan Miró. By illustrating children's drawings in *Cobra* 4, the experimental artists were in fact 'coming out' in public for an orientation they had already established in their work.

For example, the striking full-page illustration, in which a child's painting (lent by the Stedelijk Museum, the caption told) with spotted animals was juxtaposed with Karel Appel's similarly spotted sculpture *Wooden Cat*, must have read as a provocative visual manifesto. The affinities between the two images say more about Appel's position than about that of the child, since it was Appel who had chosen to work like a child and not vice versa. The effect was not unlike that of Jorn's comparison of a totem pole with a chestnut branch, where careful selection of comparative images created the suggestion of an alignment between art and nature. The 'nature' with which Appel's art was seen to align itself was, then, the child's immature pictorial method. That this really was a threat to establishment taste in 1949 is evident from the reviews of their exhibition in the Dutch press. The artists' affinity with child art was picked up and treated with scorn by virtually all reviewers, one of whom wrote a tongue-in-cheek eulogy on Appel's *Wooden Cat*: 'Ah, and that puss of Karel's. That Appelpuss! A chubby section of pole with seven little pieces of wood stuck on its backside. And with spots in yellow and azure and vermillion. How I would love to have known that cat in real life!' The reviewer went on: 'And when I came home that evening my daughter of three had made this drawing. A little man under the sun, she said. [...] And we certainly won't offer it to the director of the Stedelijk Museum. It might even be accepted!' His review illustrated some eight works by Cobra artists and one *Little man under the sun*. The comparisons of child art with experimental art printed in *Cobra* 4 were certainly not lost on that reviewer.[25]

Appel's *Wooden Cat* dated from 1947, the year in which he saw work by Dubuffet as well as by patients at the psychiatric hospital of Sainte-Anne in Paris, and the year in which he had written (in December) to his friend Corneille: 'I am now making a powerful primitive work, more primitive than Negro art and Picasso. Why, because I am taking the twentieth century further and overtaking Picasso. Fierce in colour. I have pushed through the wall of Abstract, Surrealism etc. My work includes everything. You shouldn't belong in one compartment'.[26] Though in 1947 Appel's images were closely resembling children's art, this was not something he felt the need to dwell upon in his letter to Corneille. Appel's primitivist concerns were eclectic, so much so that it has proved difficult for art historians to pinpoint when and where child art had a formative effect on his style. What is perhaps most revealing in his letter to Corneille is Appel's self-consciousness concerning his position in the history of primitivist art. He named pioneers of primitivism, such as Picasso, whom he was determined to surpass in primitiveness. Appel conceived his primitivism in a spirit of competition with those who had gone before him, and, paradoxically enough, in typically modernist terms of progress.

Another of the juxtapositions illustrated in *Cobra* 4 – this time a child's drawing on a facing page to Constant's painting *After us liberty*, 1949 (cat. 53) – has been analysed by Jonathan Fineberg in terms of compositional differences and similarities: 'The fantastic character of the animals, the scattered composition, and the lack of depth are remarkably similar. Constant has also eliminated a ground plane, which the child includes, and in the child's drawing the creatures interact in a seemingly narrative way, whereas the images in the painting by Constant hang like masks and idols (which they also resemble).' Fineberg comes down firmly on the side of similarities when he concludes: 'Constant's work of 1948 and 1949 derives more explicitly from child art than the work of any other Cobra artist. They are his greatest works and they number among the greatest paintings of the movement.'[27] Behind the hyperbole, Fineberg may have a point about Constant's painting technique in those years. But it is significant to note that Constant's own words on the matter were not pitched at the level of artistic practice and compositional method. As we have already seen, his 'Manifesto' proclaimed the spontaneity of the child and of primitive culture as an antidote to morbid bourgeois culture, while in *Reflex* 2 his response to seeing the exhibition of children's art was similarly couched in ideological terms. For Constant the artist, child art was certainly an important resource for iconography and compositional method. But for Constant the polemical theorist, child art was to be admired because it exemplified the revolutionary potential of 'counter-culture'.

Cobra primitivism: art or ideology?

Where does this leave us? Looking behind the primitivism of Cobra, do we find a certain kind of artistic practice taking priority? Or, was Cobra primitivism first and foremost a question of ideology and cultural politics? The answer has to be both, though perhaps the movement as a whole did not combine the two concerns so easily as Constant himself apparently did. The artistic production of Cobra was emphasized in the major exhibitions held in Amsterdam in 1949 and Liège in 1951, which can lay claim to being the high points of Cobra achievement, and it is clear that artists such as Appel were more interested in making and showing their primitivist art than in theorizing about it. But as a movement that published polemics against the cultural establishment of the day, Cobra was shaped largely by artists such as Jorn and Constant, who switched repeatedly from the brush to the typewriter, and by Christian Dotremont, who edited Cobra publications from a Belgian office that could be seen to resemble a revolutionary secretariat. Since the movement stood for free expression and claimed to enforce no one stylistic identity, its unity was fragile. The differing concerns within Cobra seem to have co-existed in a state of tension which, in conformity with the dialectical-materialist views of the leading theorists of Cobra, might best be characterized as dialectical. Dialectics do not deal with harmonious relationships, rather with fruitful conflicts.

Conflict was certainly in evidence after the movement ended. When, in 1958, Appel supplied a painting for the UNESCO building in Paris, Constant and Jorn, who were by then engaged in a new movement (the Situationist International), criticized him for turning Cobra primitivism into fashionable art.[28] Dotremont and Constant prolonged in the 1960s their disagreements that had begun in 1948–51 about the aims of Cobra, but they did stand together in refuting art-historical judgements of the 1960s and 1970s that identified the most significant achievement of Cobra as its primitivist iconography and style of painting: the 'language of Cobra'.[29] For Dotremont, the key to Cobra was the way its artists and writers had mixed and swapped disciplines, while, for Constant, the real achievement of Cobra lay in its spirit of liberation. Constant has continued to insist that the primitivist painting of the movement was never a goal but merely a transitional phase *en route* to a yet fuller liberated culture. Perhaps we come closest to finding what lay behind the primitivism of Cobra when we allow the conflicting interpretations to stand.

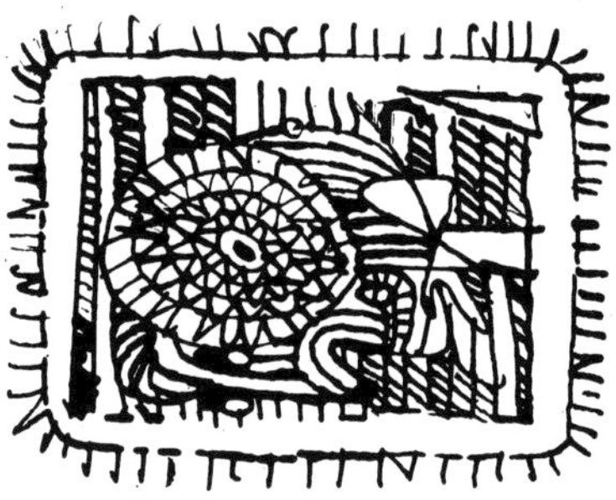

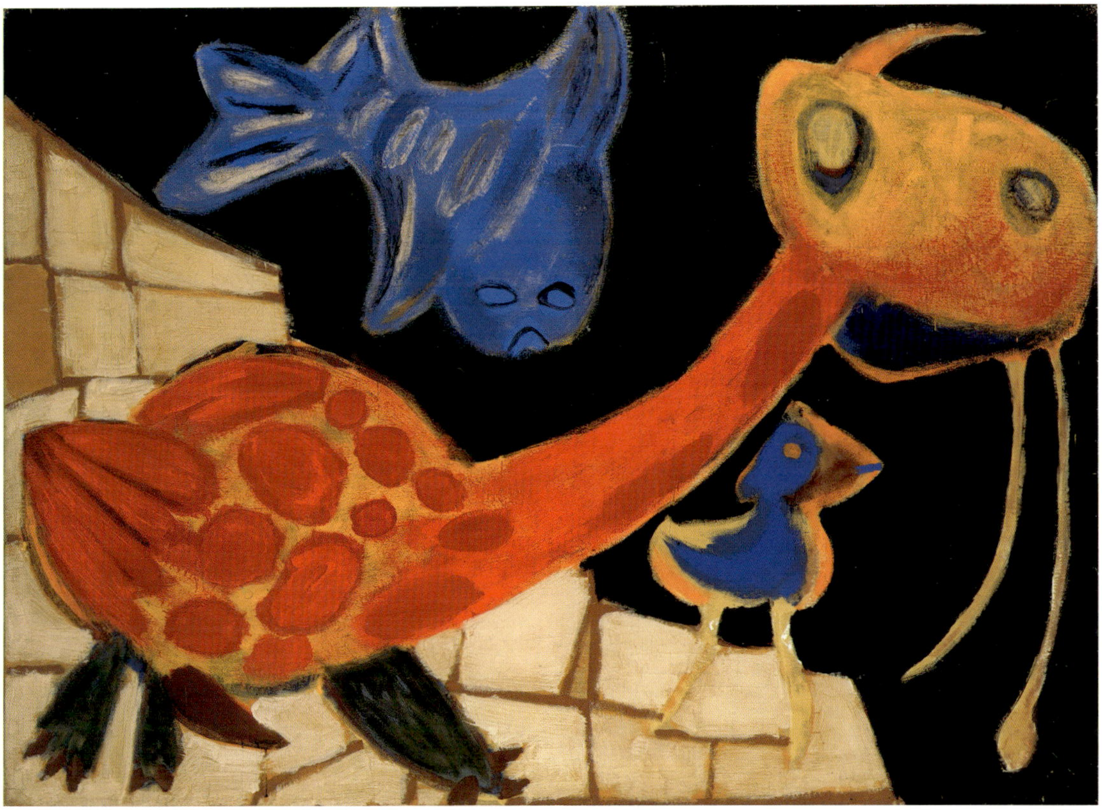

26 Karel Appel
Dieren, 1949
Animals

1 Colin Rhodes, *Primitivism and Modern Art*, London, Thames and Hudson, 1994. The cover features a detail from Karel Appel, *Questioning children* (1949), collection Tate Gallery, London.

2 See, for example, Thomas McEvilley, 'Doctor, lawyer, Indian Chief: "Primitivism in Twentieth-Century Art" at the Museum of Modern Art in 1984', in *Artforum* 23, 1984, pp. 54–60.

3 See, for example, Susan Hiller (ed.), *The Myth of Primitivism. Perspectives on art*, London and New York, Routledge, 1991.

4 Cf. Frances S. Connelly, *The Sleep of Reason. Primitivism in Modern European Art and Aesthetics, 1725–1907*, University Park Pennsylvania, The Pennsylvania State University Press, 1995; James Clifford, *Routes. Travel and Translation in the Late Twentieth Century*, Cambridge Massachusetts and London England, Harvard University Press, 1997. I have outlined my own standpoint in: Graham Birtwistle, 'When skills become obtrusive: on E.H. Gombrich's contribution to the study of primitivism in art', in Richard Woodfield (ed.), *Gombrich on art and psychology*, Manchester and New York, Manchester University Press, 1996, pp. 196–215.

5 Constant Nieuwenhuys, 'Manifest', in *Reflex. Orgaan van de Experimentele Groep in Holland*, 1 (Amsterdam), 1948, p. (6). My own translation from the Dutch.

6 Irena Piotrowska and Michal Sobeski, 'The Primitive', in *Journal of Aesthetics and Art Criticism* 1, 4, 1941, pp. 12–22, assumed that child art provided a key to primitive art.

7 See Graham Birtwistle, *Living Art. Asger Jorn's comprehensive theory of art between Helhesten and Cobra (1946–1949)*, Utrecht, Reflex, 1986.

8 Corneille, interview in: Aldo van Eyck (and others), *Niet om het even wel evenwaardig*, Amsterdam, Van Gennep, undated, p. 42. My own translation from the Dutch.

9 Christian Dotremont, 'Cobra grandit parce qu'il continue', in *Cobra* 4 (Amsterdam), 1949, p. 2.

10 Egill Jacobsen and Asger Jørgensen, 'Kunsten contra Reaktionen', in *Arbejderbladet*, Copenhagen, 15 December 1940, p. 8.

11 Michael Ventris, 'Function and Arabesque', in *Cobra* 1 (Copenhagen), 1949, p. 18; the credited source is *PLAN the Journal of the Architectural Students Association*, 1 (London), 1948.

12 Asger Jorn, 'Hvad er et ornament?', in *Dansk Kunsthaandværk*, 21, 8 (Copenhagen), 1948, p. 124. My own translation from the Danish.

13 The appeal to nature for norms is given a central role by A.O. Lovejoy and George Boas in their 'Prolegomena to the history of primitivism', in *Primitivism and Related Ideas in Antiquity*, Baltimore, The Johns Hopkins Press, 1935.

14 Constant Nieuwenhuys, 'Cultuur en contra-cultuur', in *Reflex. Orgaan van de Experimentele Groep in Holland*, 2, (Amsterdam), 1949, p. (5). My own translation from the Dutch.

15 Ibid., p. (6).

16 Cf. Theodore Roszak, *The Making of a Counter Culture. Reflections on the Technocratic Society and its Youthful Opposition*, London, Faber and Faber, 1970. In 1949, Constant used the Dutch term *'contra-cultuur'*; in the 1960s, the usual Dutch term was *'tegen-cultuur'*.

17 For a contemporary account of relations between Constant and Provo, see *Delta. A Review of Arts Life and Thought in the Netherlands*, 10, 3 (Amsterdam), Autumn 1967.

18 Ibid., p. 53. For a recent study, see Mark Wigley, *Constant's New Babylon. The Hyper-Architecture of Desire*, Rotterdam, Witte de With/010 Publishers, 1998.

19 Asger Jorn, 'Sozialistische Heringe, realistische Ölfarben und Volkskunst', in *Cobra* 5 (Hannover), 1950, p. (11). My own translation from the German.

20 Gerrit Kouwenaar, 'Poëzie is realiteit', in *Reflex. Orgaan van de Experimentele Groep in Holland*, 2, (Amsterdam), 1949, p. (8). My own translation from the Dutch.

21 Lucebert, 'Minnebrief aan onze gemartelde bruid *Indonesia*', in *Reflex. Orgaan van de Experimentele Groep in Holland*, 2 (Amsterdam), 1949, p. (3). Long thought to represent Lucebert's debut as a poet, this is now believed to be his second published poem.

22 Lucebert, 'Verdediging van de 50-ers', in *Cobra* 4, (Amsterdam), 1949, p. 10. My own translation from the Dutch.

23 Cf. C. van de Watering, 'Cobra and literature', various authors, in *Cobra 40 jaar later / 40 years after*, Amsterdam, Sdu uitgeverij, 1988, pp. 58–71.

24 Ibid., p. 60.

25 E. Messer, 'Experimentele tentoonstelling: geklad, geklets, geklodder in Stedelijk Museum', in *Het Vrije Volk*, Amsterdam, 12 November 1949, p. 3. My own translation from the Dutch.

26 Appel's handwritten letter is illustrated in Willemijn Stokvis, *Cobra. Geschiedenis, voorspel en betekenis van een beweging in de kunst van na de tweede wereldoorlog*, Amsterdam, De Bezige Bij, 1974, p. 56. My own translation from the Dutch, with punctuation added.

27 Jonathan Fineberg, *The Innocent Eye. Children's Art and the Modern Artist*, Princeton, Princeton University Press, 1997, p. 192.

28 Constant (and co-editors), 'Ce que sont les amis de "Cobra" et ce qu'ils représentent', in *Internationale Situationniste* 1, 1958, pp. 4–6.

29. The concept of the 'language of Cobra' was introduced by the art historian Willemijn Stokvis in her dissertation of 1974 (see note 26). I have given an account (in German) of the disagreements between Constant, Dotremont and Stokvis in: Graham Birtwistle, 'Cobra: Polemik, Rezeption, Nachleben', in H. van den Berg and R. Grüttemeier, *Manifeste: Intentionalität*, Amsterdam and Atlanta GA, Rodopi, 1998, pp. 289–317.

Figure 2
The first *International Exhibition of Experimental Art*, Stedelijk Museum, Amsterdam, November 1949.
Aldo van Eyck and Tony Sluyter hanging the exhibition (Rooms 6).
Photograph by Mrs. E. Kokkorris-Syriër. Courtesy W. Stokvis Archive, Amsterdam.

The Cobra Exhibitions in Amsterdam and Liège

Peter Shield

The Cobra group had only the most rudimentary structure and most of the organizational work was done in informal meetings. The founding members – Karel Appel, Constant, Corneille, Christian Dotremont and Asger Jorn – travelled to each others' countries for eager discussions, and more and more artists were drawn into the group (and left again). Financial support was sparse and ephemeral and most participants lived from hand to mouth. Nevertheless, the Cobra artists succeeded in publishing magazines, organizing a couple of congresses and setting up *Les Ateliers du Marais* in a tumbledown Brussels building as a centre for collaboration. These insolvent and almost unknown artists also managed to get the financial support for and to organize two of the most remarkable exhibitions of the years immediately after the Second World War in Europe.

The Cobra artists had a model for these exhibitions. In November 1948, the annual exhibition of the Harvest Group in Copenhagen was augmented by a

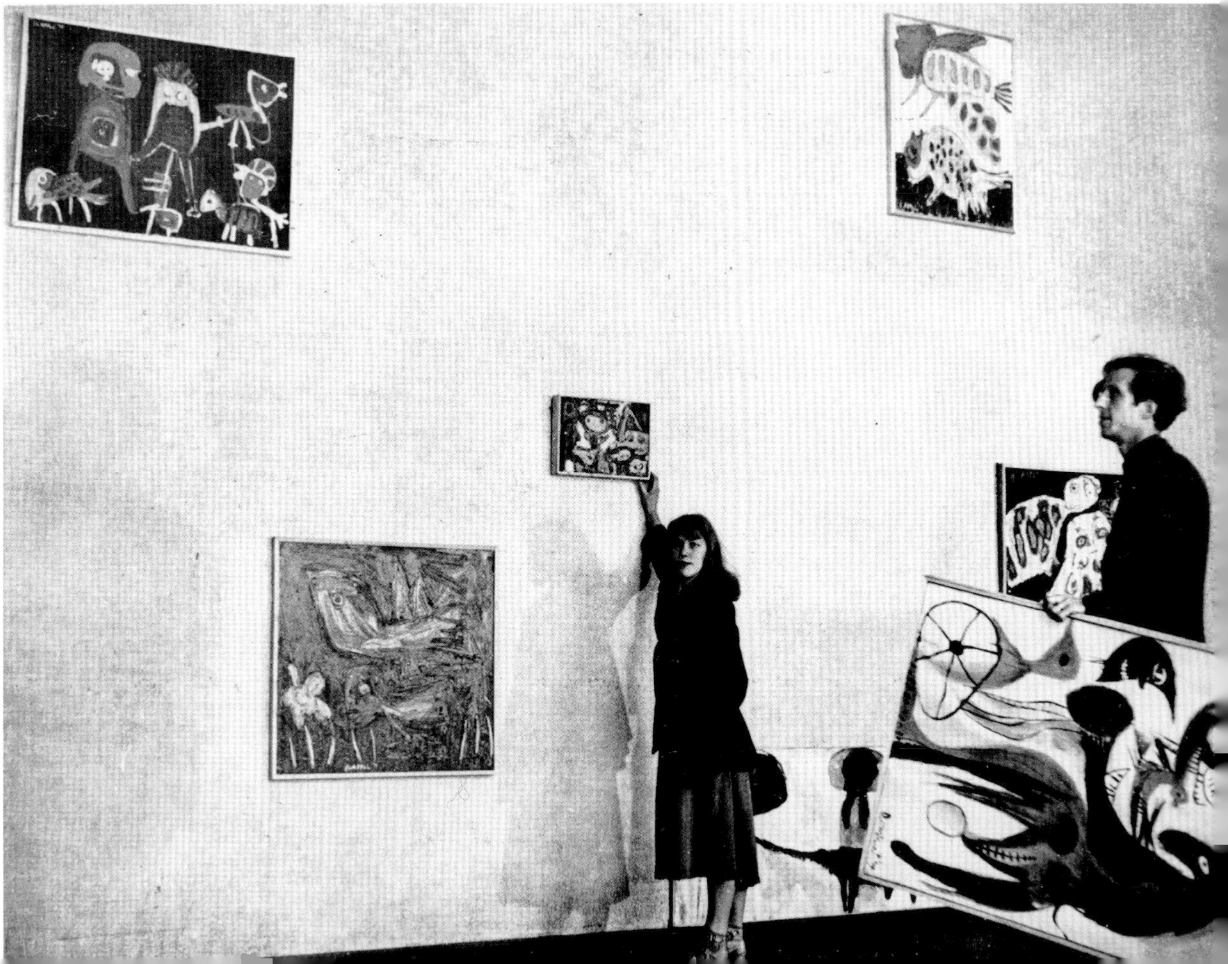

guest showing of works by all seven of the Dutch Experimental Group artists. As the members of both groups had been enrolled in Cobra in Paris only a few days previously, this was the first manifestation of this union. Appel, Constant and Corneille travelled to Denmark for the opening, as did the Belgian poet Christian Dotremont. In a newspaper interview, they declared that they had been invited to demonstrate that others outside Denmark were working 'to create a more common human language within art'[1]. They were obviously overwhelmed by their impressions and both Constant and Corneille wrote enthusiastic articles about the Danish works and the co-operative atmosphere in which they were exhibited.

At this time in Denmark, the art-dealer's role was insignificant, and most artists banded together for economic, theoretical or ideological reasons in legally constituted artists' associations that organized annual selling exhibitions in venues other than museums. Like-minded guest artists were also invited to exhibit. To the visiting artists, who had hitherto few opportunities for exhibiting, this artist-led model with its collaborative implications seemed very attractive, giving them personal control over the exhibition of their works.

Amsterdam, 1949

When the Dutch Experimental Group was promised an exhibition at the Stedelijk Museum in Amsterdam by its director Willem Sandberg – himself a talented typographic designer, occasional poet, and 'the most amazing museum director of the post-war years'[2] – it seemed natural to them that they should curate it themselves, and include a wider spectrum of the 'experimental artists' associated with Cobra. Constant and Corneille set about preparing lists of names to invite. The exhibition took place in November 1949 and over one hundred works by twenty-nine artists of ten nationalities were received (although not all were hung).

When it became apparent that most of the works would be of small format, Sandberg offered some of the Dutch artists very large canvases to be painted specially for the exhibition. This factor also influenced the revolutionary exhibition design by an early supporter of the Dutch Experimental Group, the influential architect Aldo van Eyck (1918–98), in which 'he incorporated the vitalistic expressions of the Experimentals into Mondrian's geometry of the universal.'[3] By hanging some works very high, others very low, resting on the ground even, and juxtaposing the few large canvases strategically, he avoided a regular line of many small works. The sculptures and works on paper were displayed on low plinths, which were alternately black and white to a rectangular de Stijl-like rhythm not to be found in any of the works exhibited. The smallest gallery was furnished with an interior cage and the walls painted black for the Dutch experimental poets. The bars of the cage were hung with the poets' self-illustrated poems, and on the end wall were pinned works by contemporary Dutch and French writers with the provocative slogan 'There is a poetry that we abolish.' Despite a carefree atmosphere on the day of installation (fig. 1, p. 14), there were the usual anxieties of group exhibitions. The Dutch painter Anton Rooskens recorded that van Eyck's design was reluctantly accepted by some of the artists, and that there were attempts both to change and to defend the hanging policy.[4]

The first *International Exhibition of Experimental Art (Exposition Internationale d'Art Experimental)* was opened on 3 November to the loud boom of recorded drumming from Central Africa. Visitors to the exhibition were met by the huge intimidating canvas *La Barricade* by Constant, painted for the exhibition, and this confrontational spirit permeated

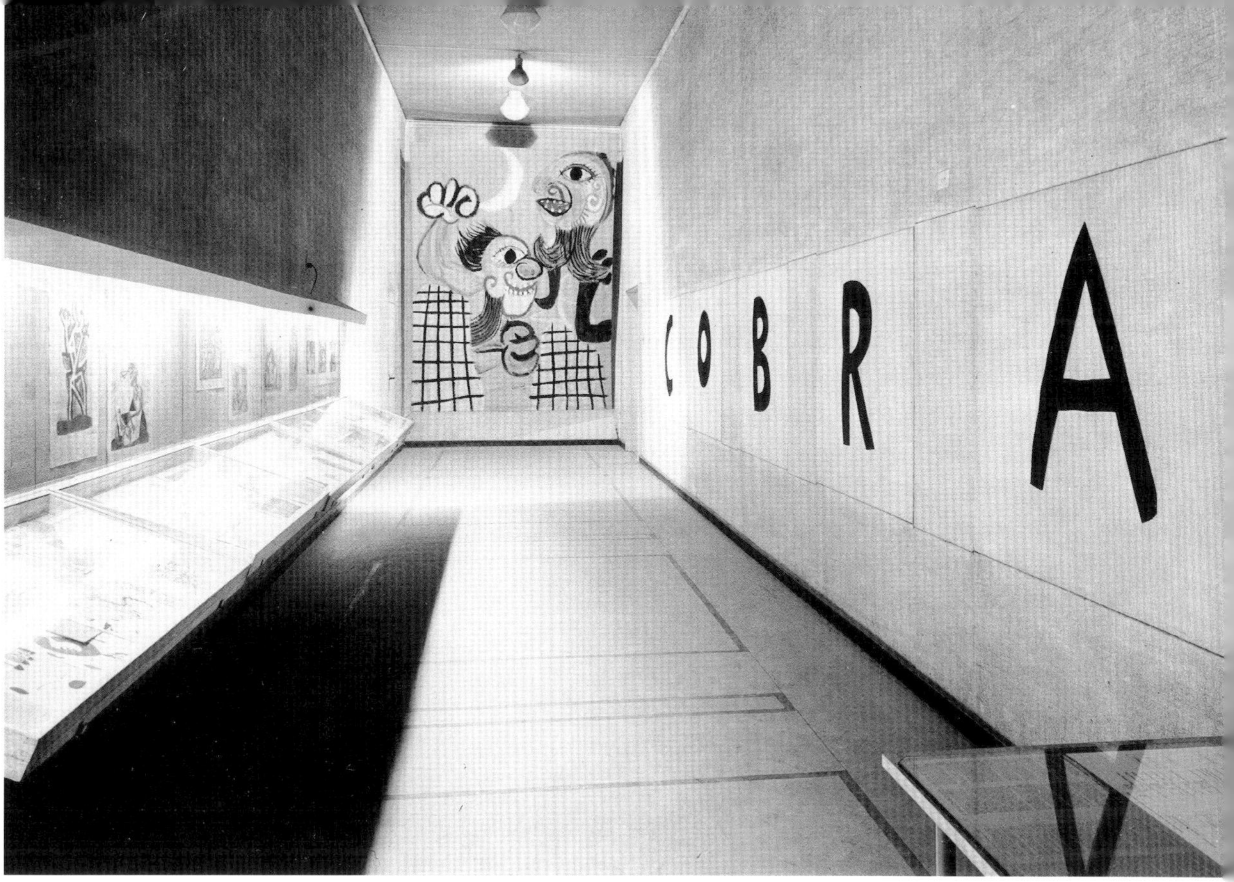

Figure 3
The first *International Exhibition of Experimental Art*, Stedelijk Museum, Amsterdam, November 1949.
The entrance room with Constant's *La Barricade*.
Photograph courtesy Stedelijk Museum, Amsterdam.
Constant: © DACS 2003

the whole exhibition (fig. 3). As the prevailing 'modern' tendency in Holland at the time was either a mannered figuration or a dark and austere Expressionism, the combination of raw, bright colours, primitive techniques and fantastic beasts on the walls of the Stedelijk was an intense provocation. Being mostly middle-class themselves, these artists knew their targeted bourgeois values and constraints at first hand. Moreover, Jorn's parents were adherents of a narrow Protestant sect, whilst Dotremont's were fervent Catholics. There were some exceptions: Appel, Henry Heerup and Carl-Henning Pedersen, for example, had suffered the hardships and prejudices of working-class childhoods.

The nations of Cobra were not equally represented in the show. The only Belgian representative was the 22-year-old Pierre Alechinsky, who was to become a major figure in the Cobra group, and who showed a series of Tarot-like engravings (cat. 2) and some paintings in a naive style. However, the entire Dutch Experimental Group exhibited, together with the associated Frenchman Jacques Doucet, but not all the Danish Harvest Group was represented. This contributed much to the discord already taking place within that group. Corneille had written to Jorn in July asking only for paintings by Else Alfelt, Ejler Bille, Jorn, Erik Ortvad and Pedersen and sculptures by Heerup and Erik Thommesen.

Most of the exhibited works by the Dutch Experimental Group dated from 1949, but all of the Danish contributions dated from previous years, one by Bille being as early as 1938. This was probably due to the artists' wish to reserve their current works for the annual Harvest Exhibition that was to begin on the 19 November in Copenhagen. A year later, Dotremont was to chide the Danes bitterly for their tendency to prioritize exhibitions in Denmark over those in other countries. However, the Danes knew they could sell at home, and abroad was an unknown situation. Whatever the reason, the group of earlier Danish works presented an overview of the tendencies that had struck the Dutch artists so forcibly the previous year.

The Danish and Dutch works were, in the main, in what has become known as 'the Cobra language': a spontaneous welter of expressive masks and fantastic human or zoomorphic beings, the Danes tending towards the mythic, the Dutch to childlike surrealistic figures. The main intent, particularly on the part of the Dutch, seemed to be to demonstrate an animal lust for life. None of the titles betrayed a political or social concern except for Constant's *Barricade* and *After us liberty* (cat. 53) both from 1949. In this regard, a striking omission was anything from Appel's major series *Questioning children* (cats. 24 and 32) from the previous year, which had been prompted by the sight of starving children on railway platforms as he travelled across a war-devastated Germany to Denmark.

The rest of the exhibitors in the show were *déplacés*, artists at odds with the prevailing artistic climates of their respective nations, and they had mostly been picked out by Constant and Corneille at various Parisian exhibitions – an ironic situation given that the group, initially at least, was opposed to the Parisian hegemony. Two Scots, who were resident in Paris at that time, had become associated with Cobra and were included in this show. Stephen Gilbert's simple sinister insects and vegetative mandalas belonged within 'the Cobra language', but William Gear's vivid colours were stretched over black armatures of lines reminiscent of the headstocks of the Fife coalmines of his youth. The works of most of the other artists in the show could be characterized as epiphenomena of Surrealism.

Two days after the opening, the Dutch poets arranged a session of experimental poetry at the museum. Dotremont was supposed to read one of his poems, but began instead reading a long manifesto in French that he had just written. As most of the Dutch audience did not understand French, but picked up the words 'Soviet' and 'Russian', there was a misunderstanding that he was endorsing the Communist Party line on art. Scuffles broke out and then continued on the street outside and Dotremont finally declaimed his original poem to an empty room. In a press statement the following day, some of the Dutch painters and poets dissociated themselves from Dotremont's speech and resigned from the Dutch Experimental Group, leaving only Appel, Constant and Corneille. The Dutch press was delighted and attacked the exhibition on the usual grounds, one journalist unfavourably comparing a drawing by Theo Wolvecamp with one by his three-year-old daughter. The reports of the 'poetry session' were equally sensational. Predictably, this media attention intrigued the public, and people streamed to the exhibition until it closed on 28 November. On the day before the press attacks, eight copies of the fourth issue of *Cobra*, which also served as the catalogue, were sold, and, on the following day, eighty. In Holland, at least, Cobra had made its mark.

Scattered through this fourth issue of *Cobra* were ten provocative slogans by Corneille (for example, 'An art without politeness – art comes from raw desire/ art has nothing in common with beauty/ realism is the negation of reality') in a curious Gothic font. Some of the other contents, however, revealed contradictions in Cobra thinking. Although published in Amsterdam, edited by Corneille and containing some poems and texts in Dutch, the main polemical essays were in French. Half of the text of Dotremont's misunderstood public manifesto was in both languages. However, the more explicit second half, published later in the sixth issue of *Cobra*, appeared only in French. Dotremont made a straightforward attack upon 'formalist bullying' and 'the three flags of formalism' – 'the old Surrealism of Magritte, Dalí or Léonor Fini', abstract art and Naturalism. He wrote: 'The painters who make up Cobra completely give themselves to the complete expression of complete reality [sic]. This is to say that *spontaneity* is their weapon: that it is all they have against formalism.'[5] However, his statement that, 'the researches of the experimental artists do not present an *immediate* interest in *the transformation of the world*, but they are no less indispensable'[6], completely contradicted Constant's manifesto, 'Our desire makes the revolution', which opened the fourth issue of *Cobra*. Constant *did* envisage such 'an *immediate* interest'. Indeed, he went further. In a letter written to Jorn slightly later, he insisted that the Cobra artists should create a Social Realist art that was superior to the accepted bourgeois style of officially sanctioned Social Realist art.[7] Subsequently, Dotremont and Constant bitterly attacked each other in letters to Jorn, who, not without some duplicity, attempted to keep the dispute at the level of a dialectic, committing himself to neither side. He believed that such unresolved conflicts were useful to creation. It is clear, however, that Constant (and Jorn) believed that their spontaneous pictorial language based on primitive impulses had deep and universal social resonances. This ideological dialectic went on against a background of deep personal disturbance, as Constant's wife had left him for Jorn some months earlier, thus causing Constant to contemplate abandoning Cobra.

Liège, 1951

In September 1948, even before Cobra, Dotremont and Jorn had attempted in vain to organize an exhibition of like-minded artists at the Palais des Beaux-Arts in Brussels. Three years later, however, Dotremont was given the chance in Belgium to demonstrate his wider perception of the concept of experimentation and include works that did not necessarily involve the element of spontaneity. Another *International Exhibition of Experimental Art*, much larger than the first, was crystallizing.

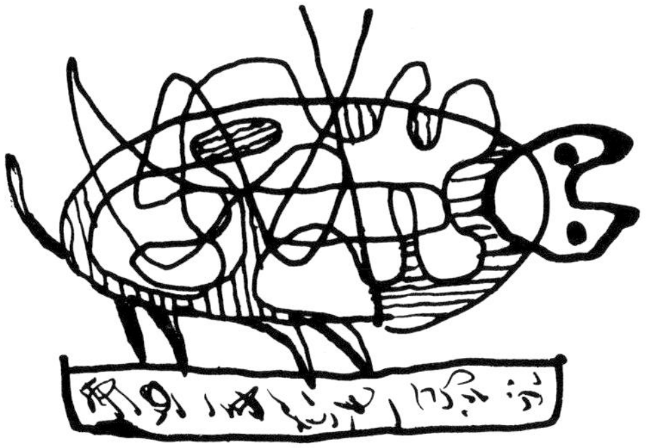

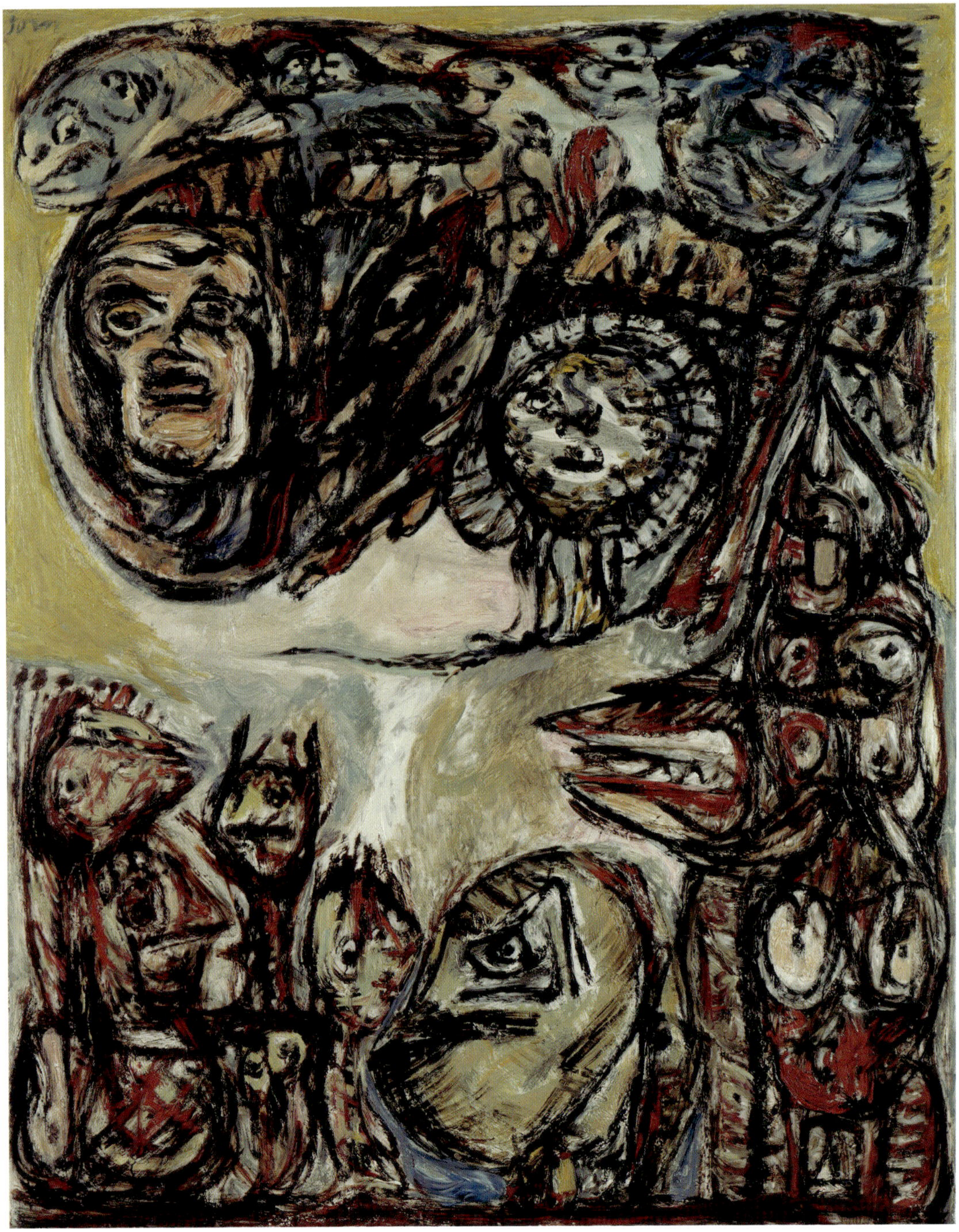

92 Asger Jorn
(Return to) the Detested Town, 1951

In 1949, two prominent Belgian collectors, François Graindorge and Ernest van Zuylen, who had growing interest in Appel and Corneille, received permission from the cultural authorities for an exhibition of young Dutch artists at the Palais des Beaux-Arts in Liège. Gradually these plans grew into a much larger project scheduled for late 1951, financed by van Zuylen, and the organization of the show was taken over by Dotremont and Alechinsky, who had a desire for a broader context, including artists from countries other than Holland.

There were nearly 200 works by thirty-three artists from eleven countries, some of whom had little discernible connection with Cobra, and, as usual, the catalogue was organized to emphasize the national origins of the participants. A group of works by artists considered to be precursors to Cobra was displayed in the show and included two canvases by Joan Miró and two sculptures by Alberto Giacometti, each artist in his own way an influence on some Cobra members. Also part of this group were six works by Wifredo Lam, Jorn's friend since the late 1930s, works by Raoul Ubac, whose inscribed slates had been reproduced in *Cobra*, and by Pol Bury, who had contributed articles to that publication. Several artists in this precursor group belonged to the Galerie Maeght stable, to which Alechinsky also had an attachment via his participation in their annual exhibition *Dazzling Hands* (*Les mains éblouies*) in 1948 and 1950. Other artists in the exhibition were related only to the outer fringes of Cobra. Alechinsky saw a certain Cobra resonance in a dragon by Étienne Martin fashioned from a tree-root. The Belgians Louis van Lint and Jan Cox had contributed illustrations to various issues of *Cobra*, whilst Georges Collignon was the founder of the loose local group *Cobra Libre*. Two sculptors, Reinhout d'Haese and Corneille Hannoset, and an artist-craftsman, Olivier Strebelle, who were involved with Alechinsky's International Cobra Research Centre in Brussels also took part.

There were only four Dutch (Appel, Constant, Corneille and Wolvecamp) and five Danish (Heerup, Jorn, Ortvad, Pedersen and Thommesen) participants included in the show, their work representing less than a third of the total exhibition. The previous year, Jorn had complained that 'Corneille and Appel [...], are about to swing over towards the classic abstract tendency. Constant is the only one going forward [...].'[8] The contributions of Appel and Corneille did display more formal concerns than previously, but not enough to justify Jorn's misgivings. While Wolvecamp's work was still predominantly explosively abstract, Constant exhibited no less than six paintings entitled *The War* from 1950–51 (cats. 58 and 59). The onset of the Korean War in June 1950 had deeply affected both Constant and Jorn. Constant employed some of Picasso's motifs – the wounded horse, the broken wheel, the wounded dove, etc – as a received anti-war language in his 'Social Realist' response, whilst Jorn made a series of *War Visions*, 1950, based on universal symbols such as predatory animals and burning towns, in raging turmoil or sardonic caricature (for example, *The golden swine*, 1951 (cat. 84), *The burning city*, 1951 (cat. 90) and *The eagle's share II*, 1951 (cat. 91)). Yet Jorn exhibited only one war-related work here, a paraphrase of Théodore Géricault's *Raft of the Medusa*, 1819, his three other oils being in a more whimsical style (for example, *The moon and the animals*, 1950 (cat. 85)). Pedersen's lyrical gold and blue works had a wall to themselves overlooking a group of Heerup's small stone sculptures. Ortvad was represented by more abstract works of soft geometrical figures and there were five of Thommesen's wood sculptures.

Alechinsky had developed considerably since Amsterdam and now exhibited six large abstracts with repetitive forms, somewhat akin to the work of the Frenchman Jean Bazaine (who was also represented in the exhibition). However, as Alechinsky himself writes, giving some idea of the atmosphere of the time: '[…] myself, already a painter before and during Cobra, but above all a Cobra activist, rushing off to the printers, writing and typing out letters to potential patrons in the hope of getting them to untie their purse-strings, seeking advertisements so as to be able to 'balance' the budget and doing the rounds of the bookshops with the review, well […] it would be more accurate to consider me as a post-Cobra painter, for my finished works were done after the fifties […].'[9] He also contributed a leading article to the tenth number of *Cobra*, which was also the catalogue for the show. In this article, Alechinsky writes that the possibilities and limitations of the material of the work of art can only be realized ' […] if one keeps the hands free, being struck by a certain dose of amnesia […]. For the time being, it is through spontaneity that painting is advancing, stepping on hardly seen preceding pictures, without re-traversing terrain already explored.' This '*abstraction faite*' (abstraction accomplished) is contrasted in the article to Piet Mondrian's successors and their '*abstraction froide*' (cold abstraction), the result of which Alechinsky sees as 'a maniacally ordered painting, a cupboard with closed compartments, as if there were treasures hidden behind its coloured doors,' as a metaphor for 'a bourgeois heritage' and as 'a totalitarian discipline'.[10] Neither Constant nor Jorn, nor indeed any other non-francophone Cobra member, contributed to this number, which thus lacked that flavour of the anti-aesthetic that characterized their polemics. Perhaps they were present in spirit, for, in his introductory apologia to this issue of the magazine, Dotremont seemed to be defending himself against unnamed critics.[11]

With its pompous neo-Louis XVI interior, the Palais des Beaux Arts is a far more monumental building than the Stedelijk Museum. Aldo van Eyck, again responsible for the design of the exhibition, spread the pictures, now generally somewhat larger, wider along the walls and was more restrained in his hanging. The many sculptures were placed on long and low oblong plinths, some of which were covered with cobbles of Liège coal, in a reference to the raw material that had created Liège's prosperity. The two Giacomettis, from 1950, were placed side by side, each on its own elongated plinth – *The Chariot* posed at the top of a long black ramp, the other, *Place, Neuf Personnages*, on a lower flat white plane.Whilst not as provocative as in the Amsterdam exhibition, van Eyck was still following his principles of allowing art and architecture to exist on complementary planes. However, from photographs, the variety of idiom that he had to juxtapose with the huge spaces forced him into a much more well-mannered presentation than in Amsterdam. The exhibition lasted from 6 October to 6 November 1951. A photograph exists of a formal opening ceremony by the authorities. Nevertheless, the Belgian press was almost uniformly hostile.

Far away in his Danish sanatorium, it became clear to Dotremont that Cobra had disintegrated. He wrote to Alechinsky, who had been holding the fort in Brussels for some months, directing him to make a formal announcement of Cobra's demise. The last page of the tenth edition of *Cobra* carried an announcement that it was to be the final number of the magazine.

'...a splintered ruin'

The Amsterdam exhibition, financed by municipal funds and containing only artists seen to have an affinity with Cobra principles, presented the idealistic initial explosion of Cobra ideas.

Two years later, the Liège exhibition, although impressive, had compromised with the gallery system and had also broadened the scope of experimentation to include the work of artists incompatible with Cobra. This was Cobra in decline, with Appel, Constant and Corneille settled in Paris, and Jorn and Dotremont seriously ill in Denmark, and no real cohesive spirit remaining.

Nevertheless, Jorn was surely correct when he later wrote of '[...] that artistic tendency we called COBRA, which at that point lay a splintered ruin whilst Christian Dotremont and I, despairing and mutually distrustful in the extreme, lay side by side in the beds of Silkeborg Sanatorium, discussing what had happened. Neither of us dreamt that, despite everything, we had realized something unique.'[12]

1 Aramis (pseudonym for Otto Gelsted), 'Vi vil ikke skille skønhed og liv...', in *Land og Folk*, Copenhagen, 3 December 1948.
2 Pierre Alechinsky, 'Souvenotes', in *Alechinsky. Paintings and Writings*, Pittsburgh, Museum of Art, 1978, p. 194.
3 Francis Strauven, *Aldo van Eyck. The Shape of Reality*, Amsterdam, Architectura & Natura, 1998, p. 125.
4 Anton Rooskens, *'de a van cobra'*, in catalogue *Anton Rooskens, 1949 cobra 1951*, Rotterdam, Galerie Delta, 1964, unp.
5 Christian Dotremont, 'Le grand rendez-vous naturel', in *Cobra* 6, (Brussels), April 1950, p. 5.
6 Ibid., p. 3.
7 Constant: letter to Asger Jorn, (early 1950), Silkeborg Kunstmuseum Archives.
8 Asger Jorn: letter to Pedersen & Alfelt, (Paris 1950) in Troels Andersen and Aksel Evin Olesen (eds), *Erindringer om Asger Jorn*, Silkeborg, Galerie Moderne, 1982, p. 90.
9 Pierre Alechinsky, op. cit. (note 2), p. 196.
10 Pierre Alechinsky, 'Abstraction faite', in *Cobra* 10 (Brussels), November 1951, pp. 4–8. The second half of this article, 'a pamphlet against social realism', remains unpublished.
11 Christian Dotremont, 'L'expérience de Holbaek' in *Cobra* 10 (Brussels), Autumn 1951, 3.
12 Asger Jorn, *Held og hasard*, Copenhagen, Borgen, 1963, inside back cover.

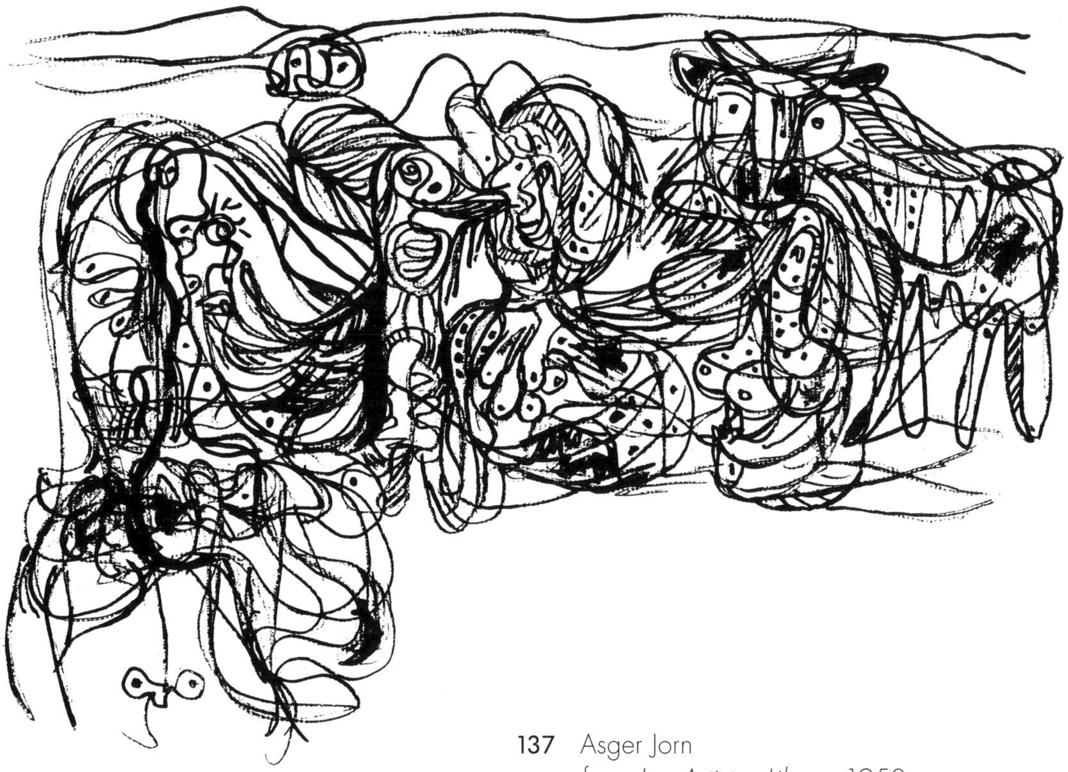

137 Asger Jorn
page from *Les Artistes Libres*, 1950

next page:
2 Pierre Alechinsky
Les Métiers, 1948
The occupations

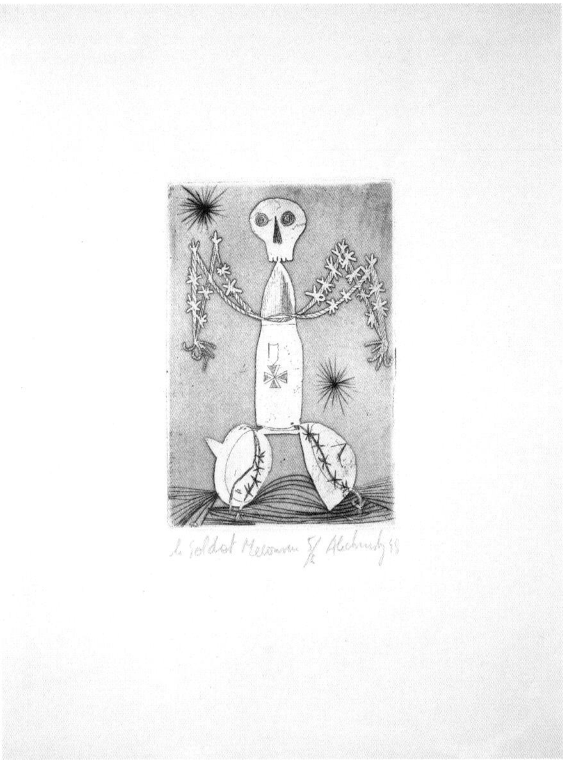
le Soldat Meconnu 5/6 Alechinsky 48

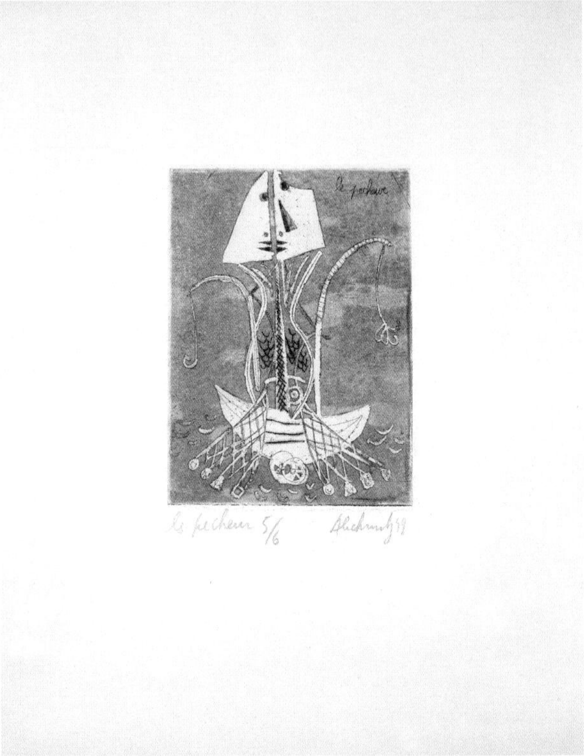
le pecheur 5/6 Alechinsky 48

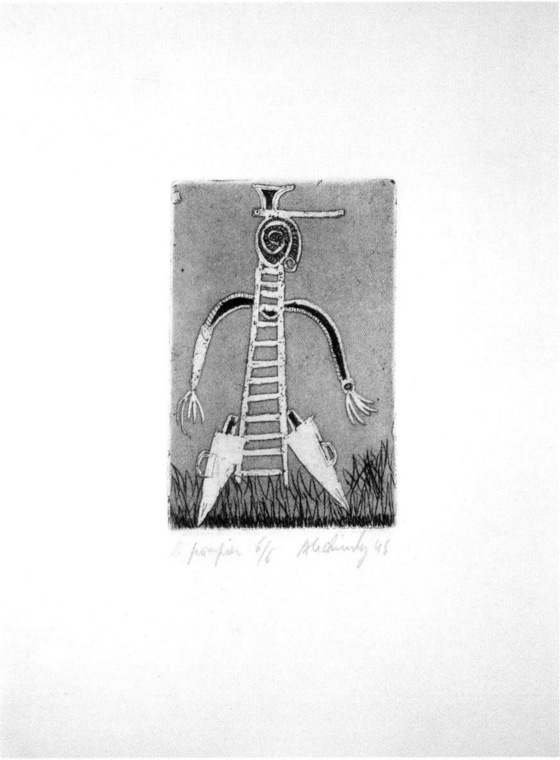
le pompier 6/6 Alechinsky 48

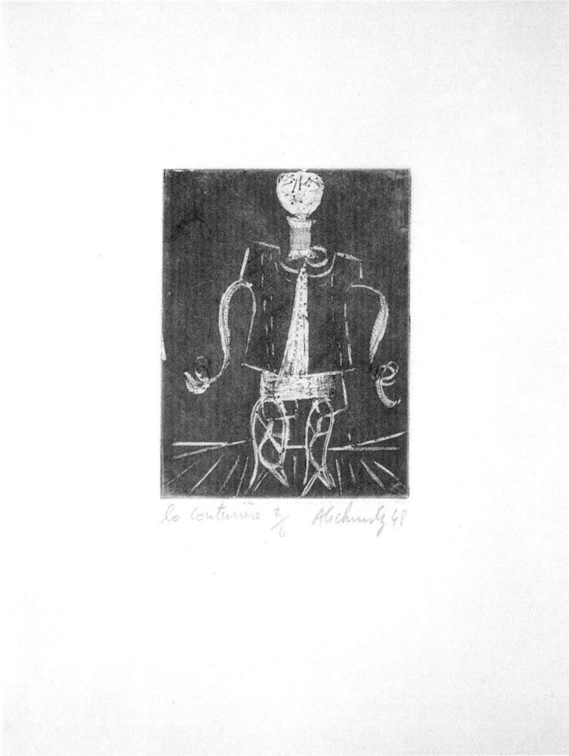
la couturière 2/6 Alechinsky 48

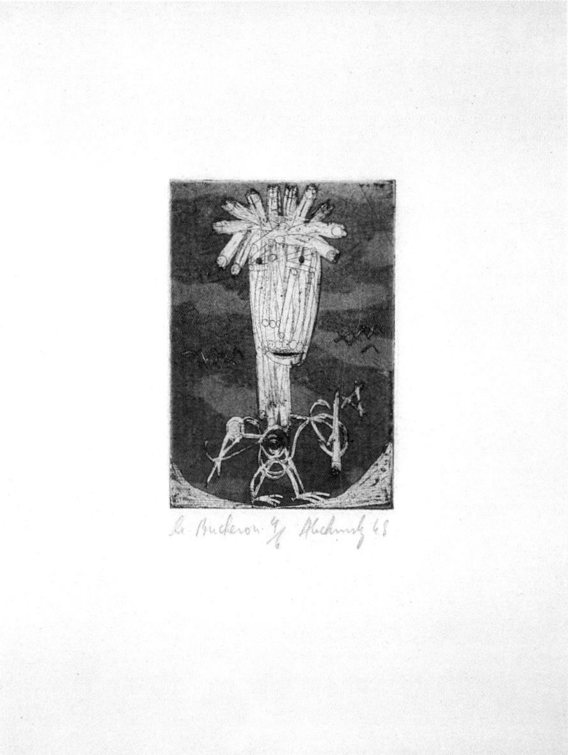

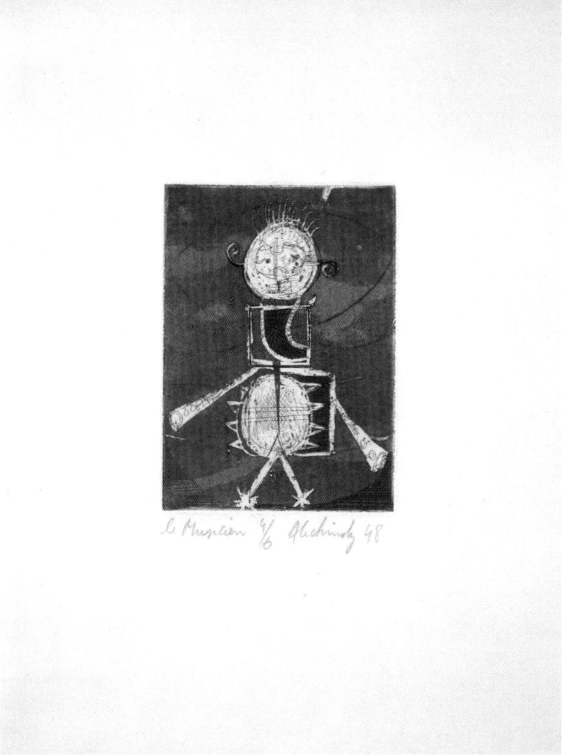

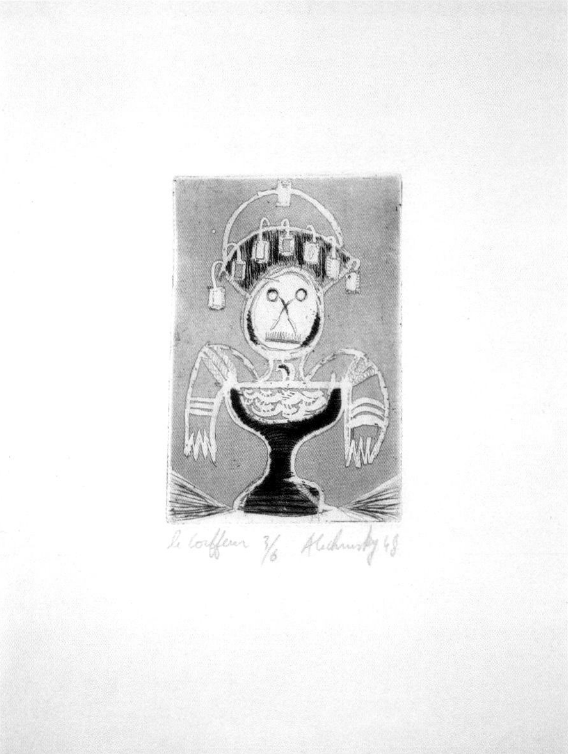

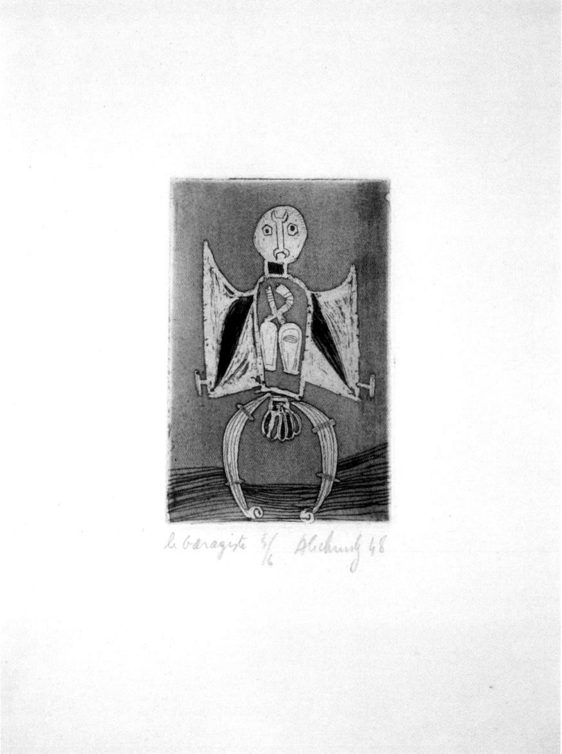

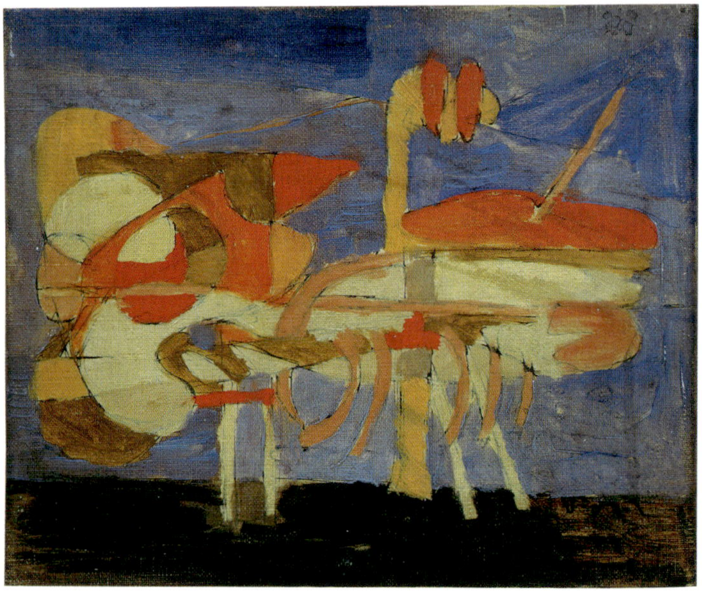

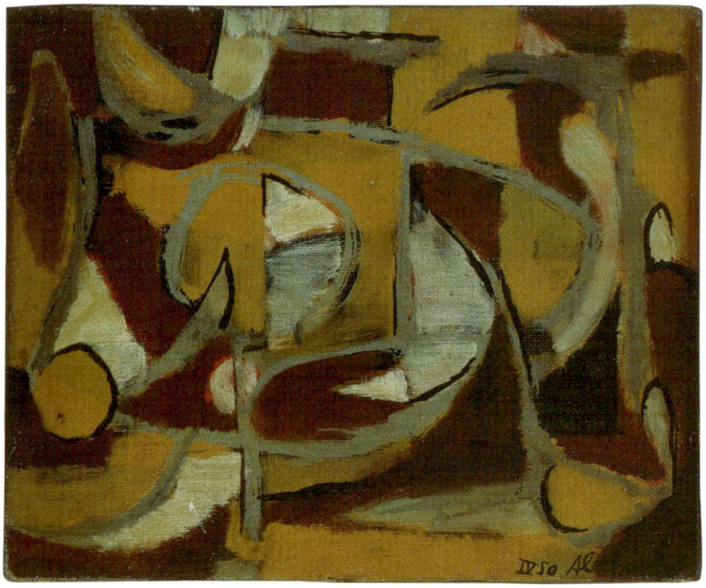

top:
7 Pierre Alechinsky
Épaves, 1950
Flotsam

bottom:
9 Pierre Alechinsky
Terre, 1950
Floor

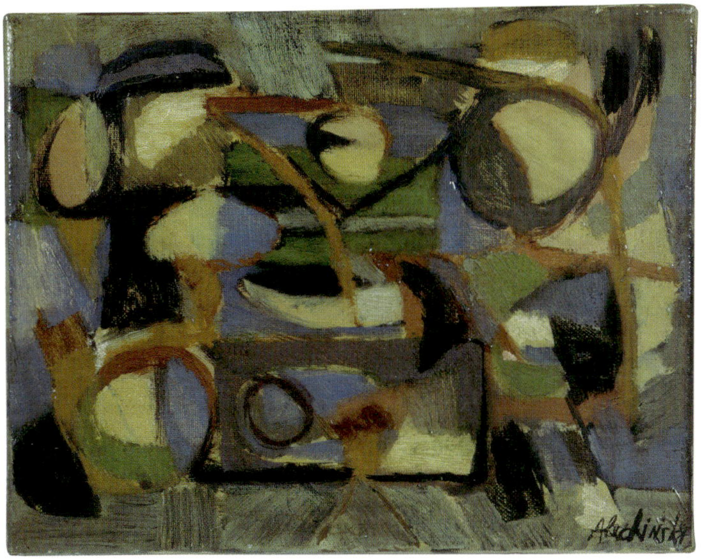

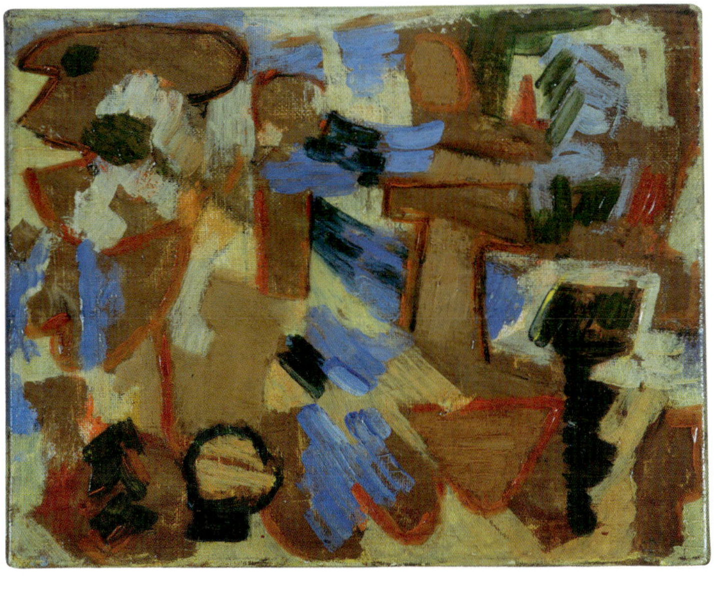

top:
13 Pierre Alechinsky
Panoplie, 1951
Panoply

bottom:
14 Pierre Alechinsky
Promenade des épaves, 1951
Procession of flotsam

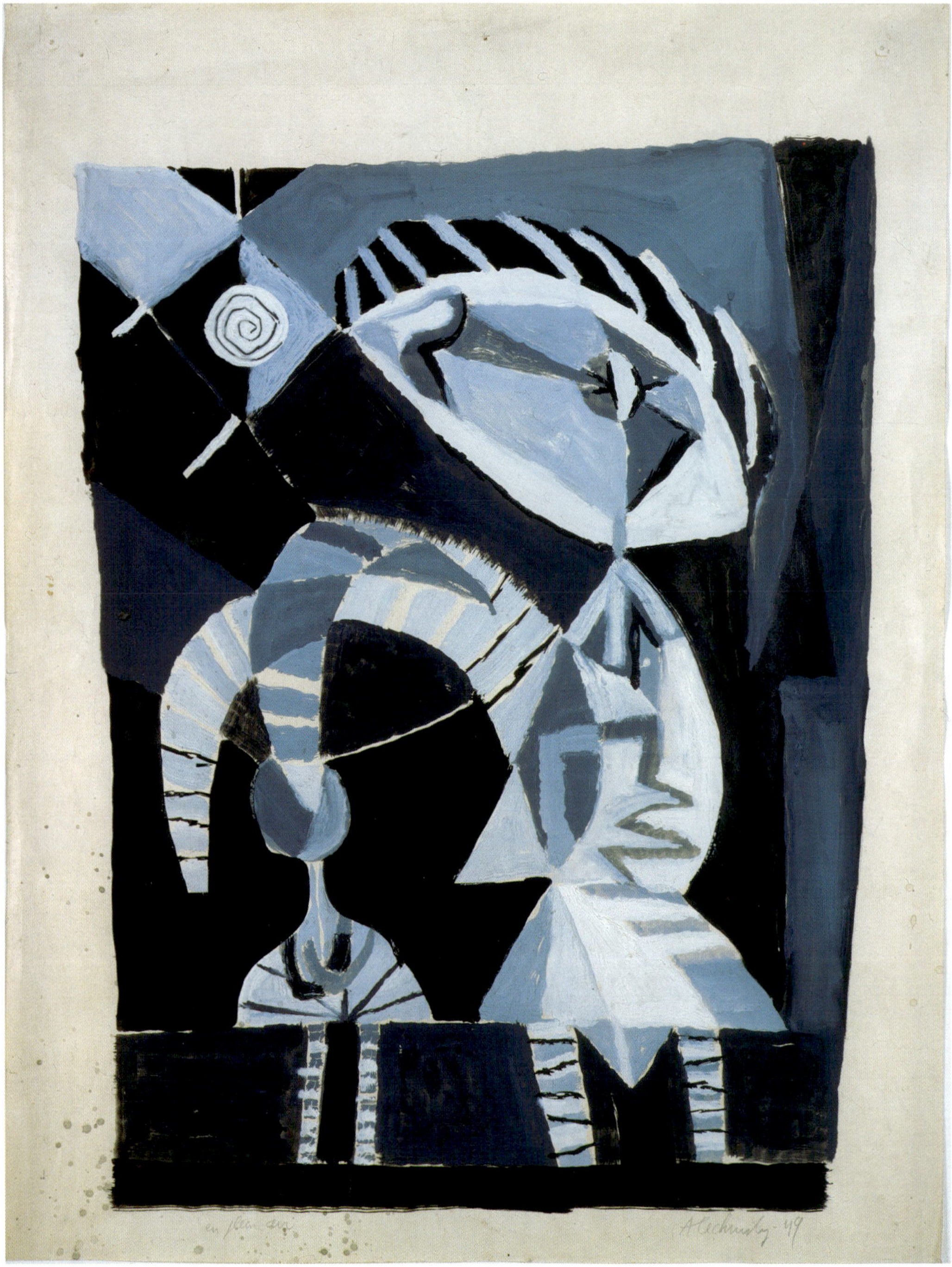

3 Pierre Alechinsky
En plein air, 1949
In the open air

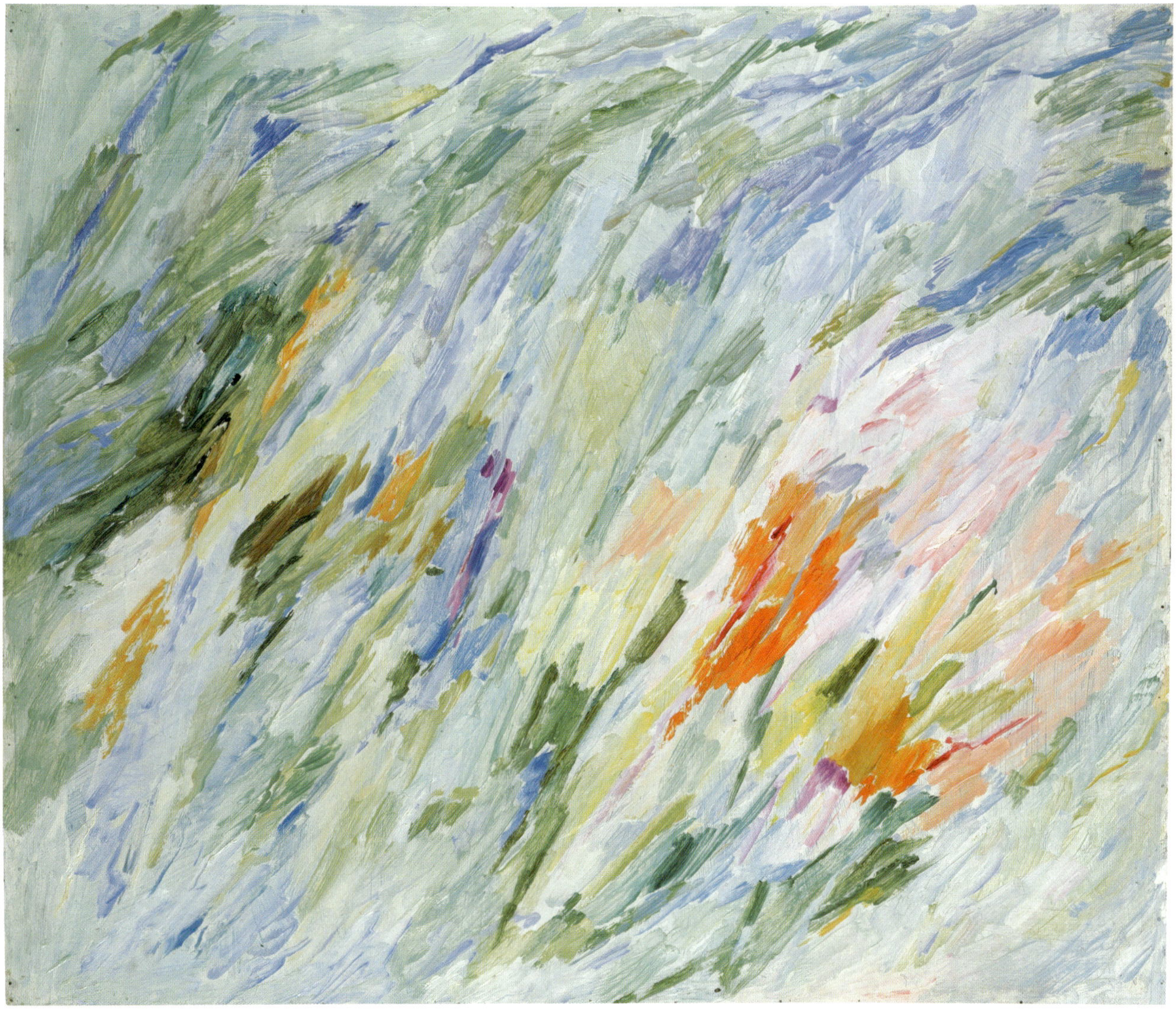

16 Else Alfelt
Regnbue-variation 1, 1948
Rainbow variation I

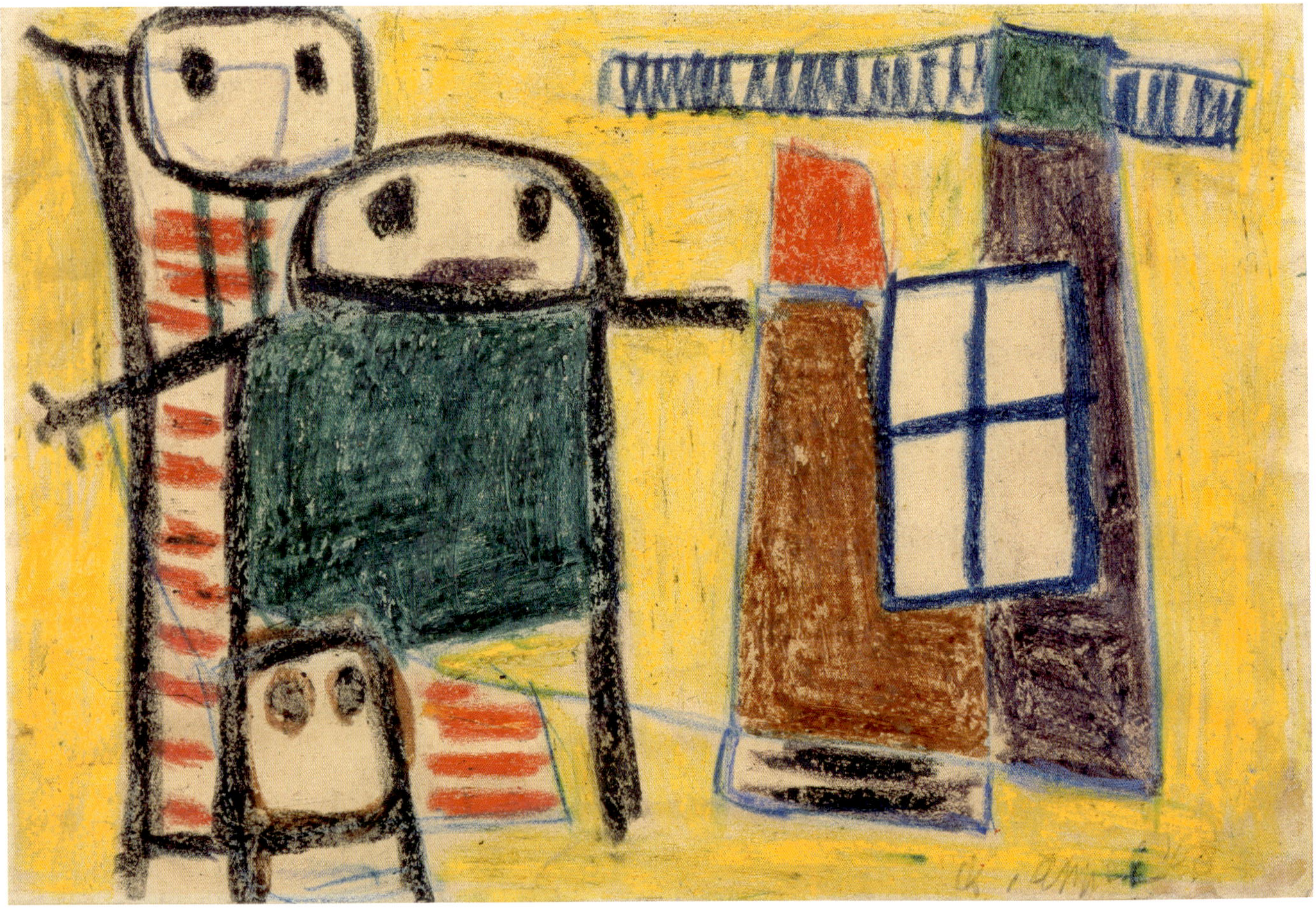

24 Karel Appel
Vragende kinderen, 1948
Questioning children

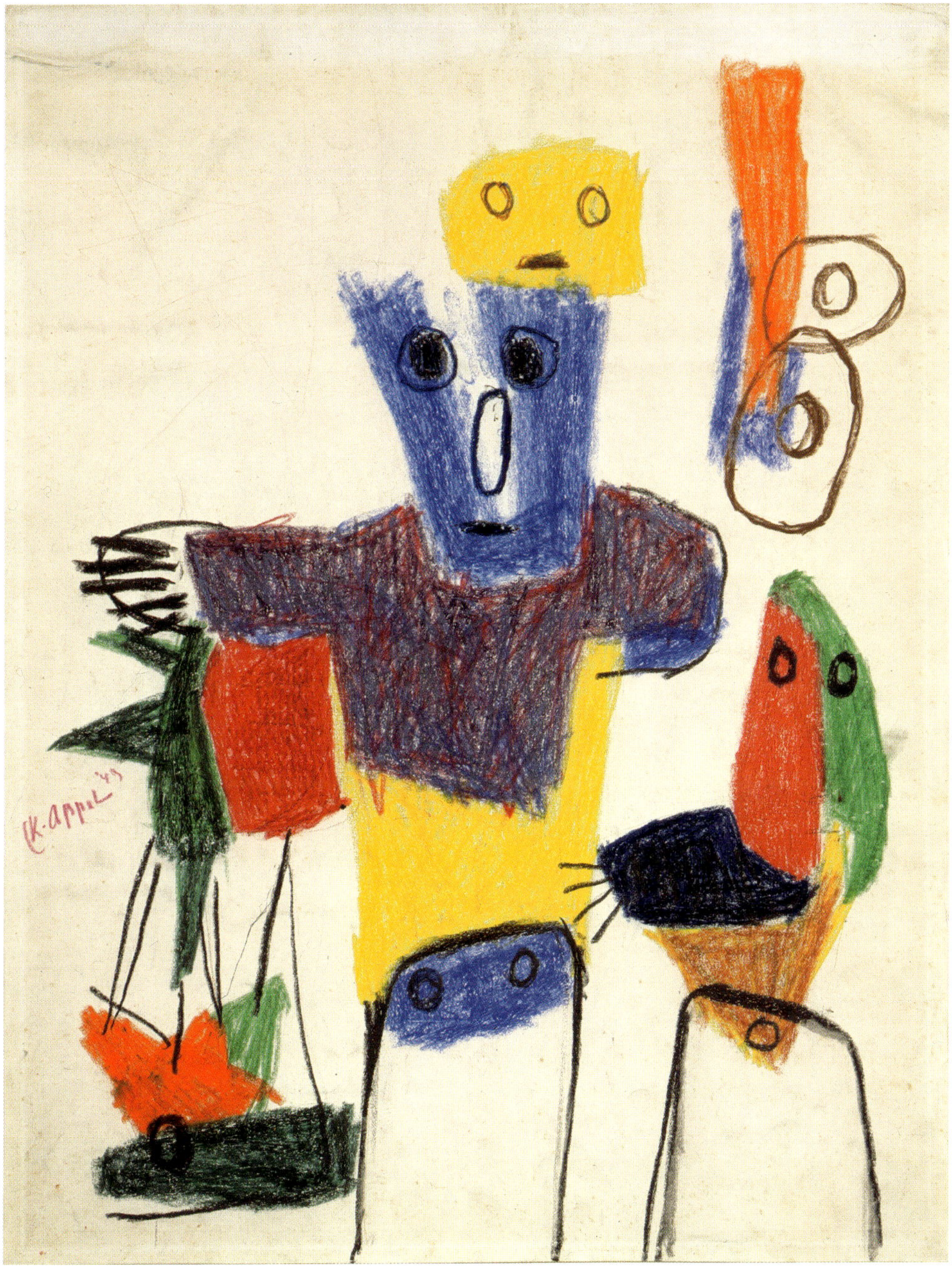

32 Karel Appel
Vragende kinderen, 1949
Questioning children

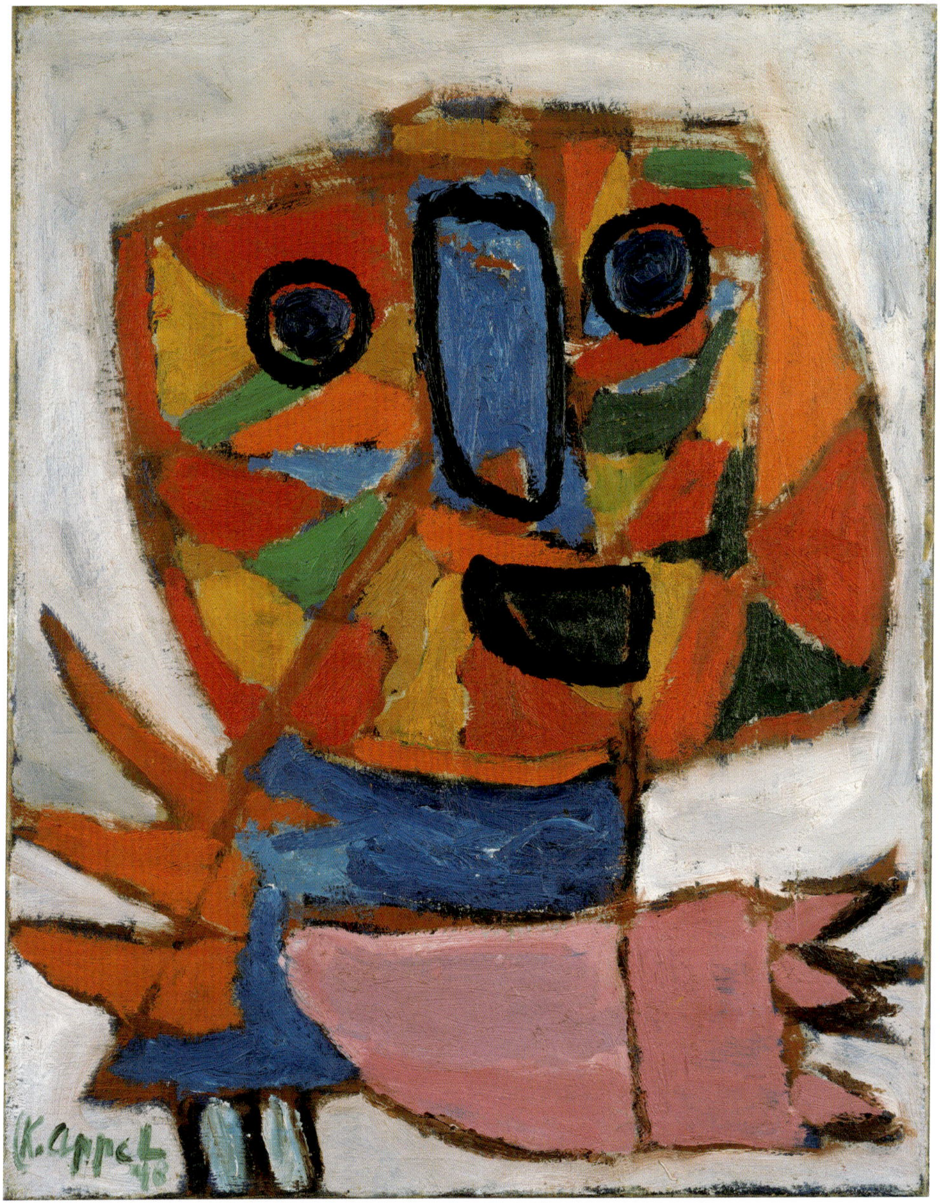

25 Karel Appel
Vrijheidsschreeuw, 1948
Cry of freedom

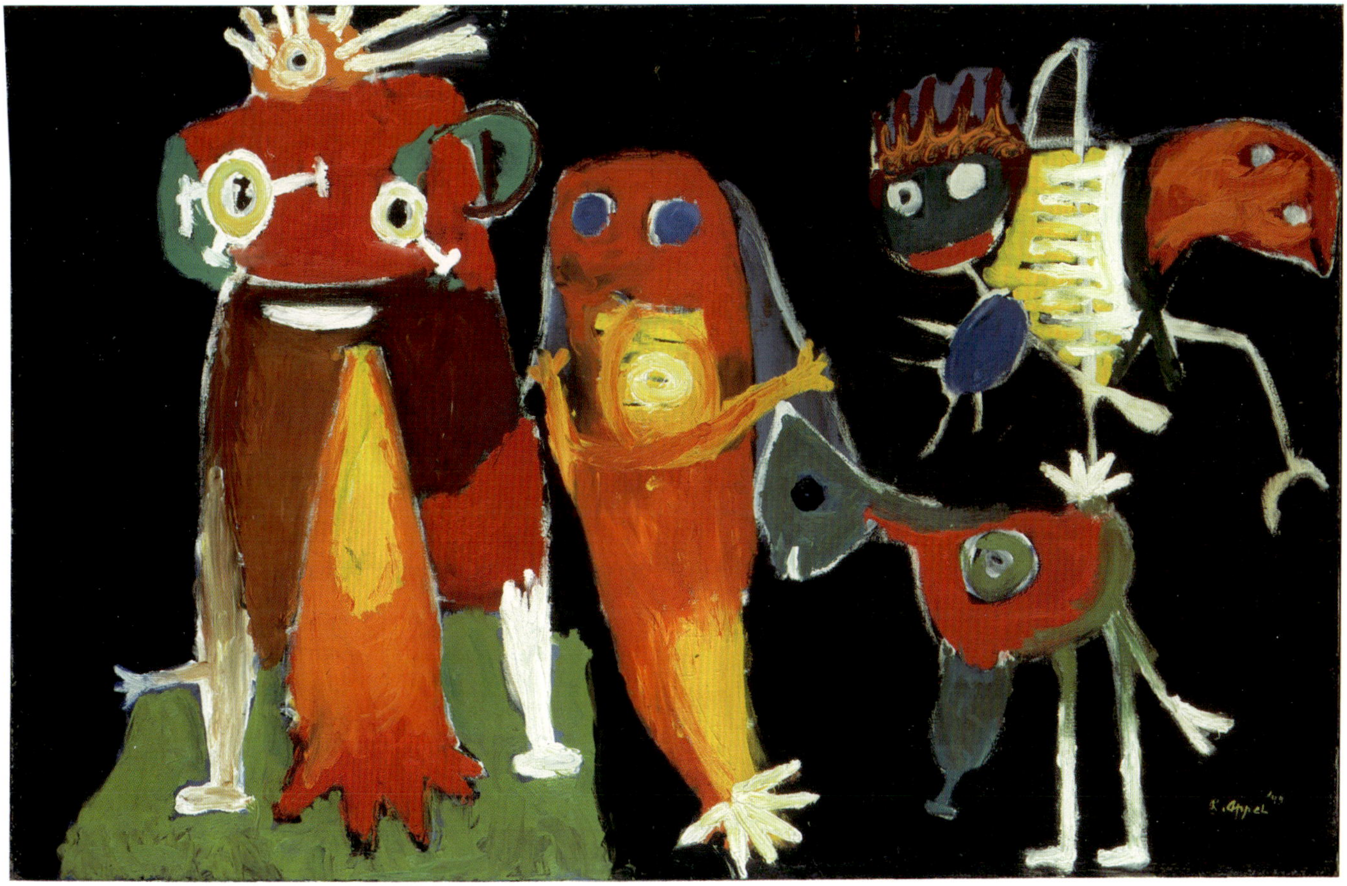

28 Karel Appel
Hiep, hiep, hoera!, 1949
Hip, hip, hooray!

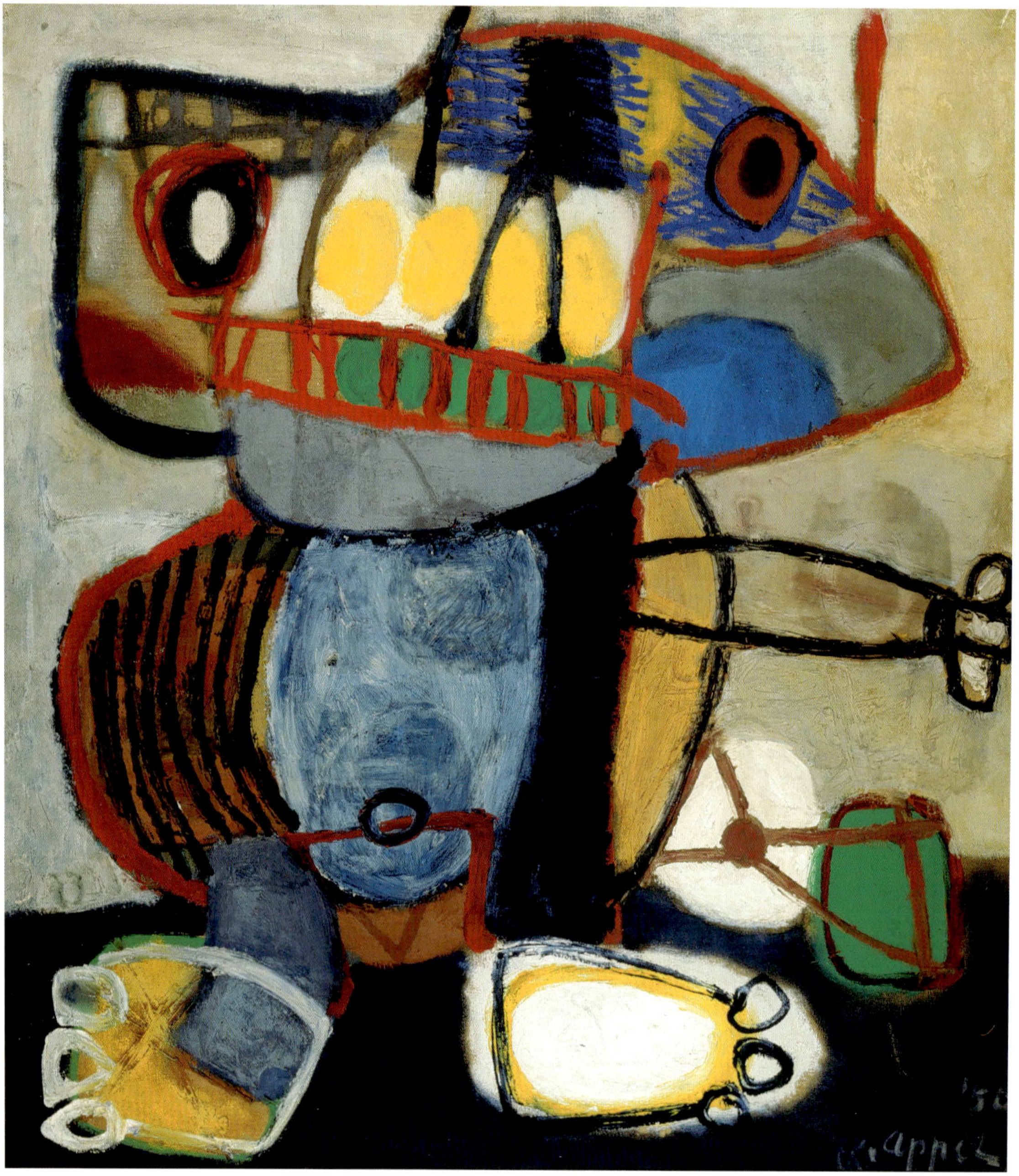

40 Karel Appel
The Look, 1950

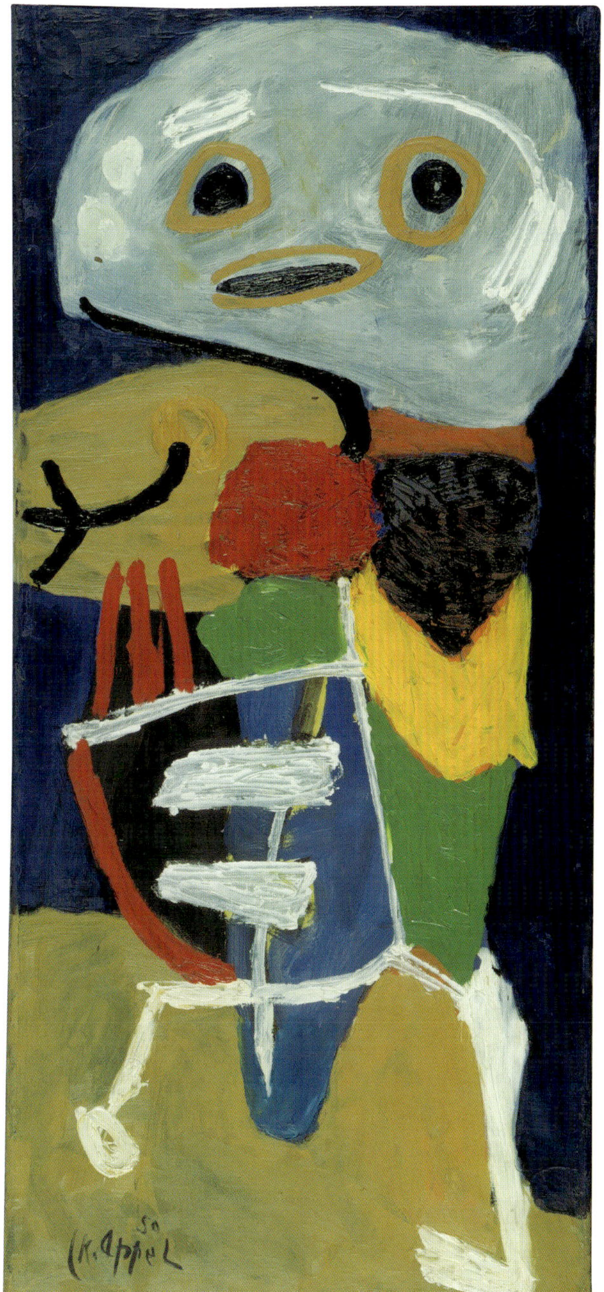

35 Karel Appel
Petit Garçon, 1950
Young boy

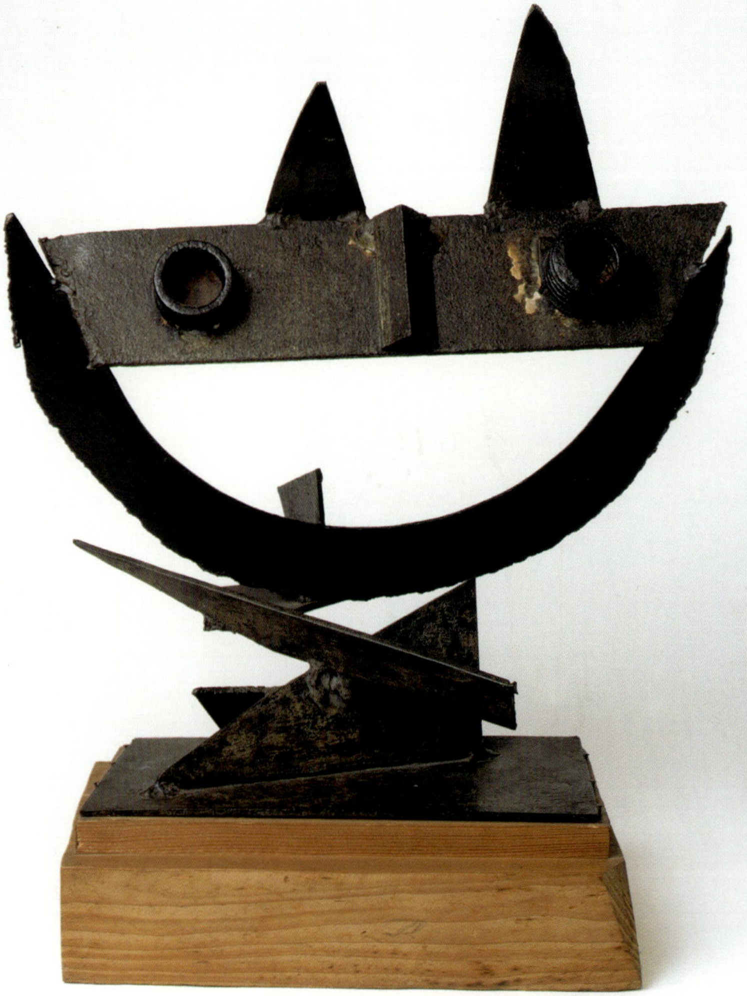

34 Karel Appel
Glimlach, 1950
The smile

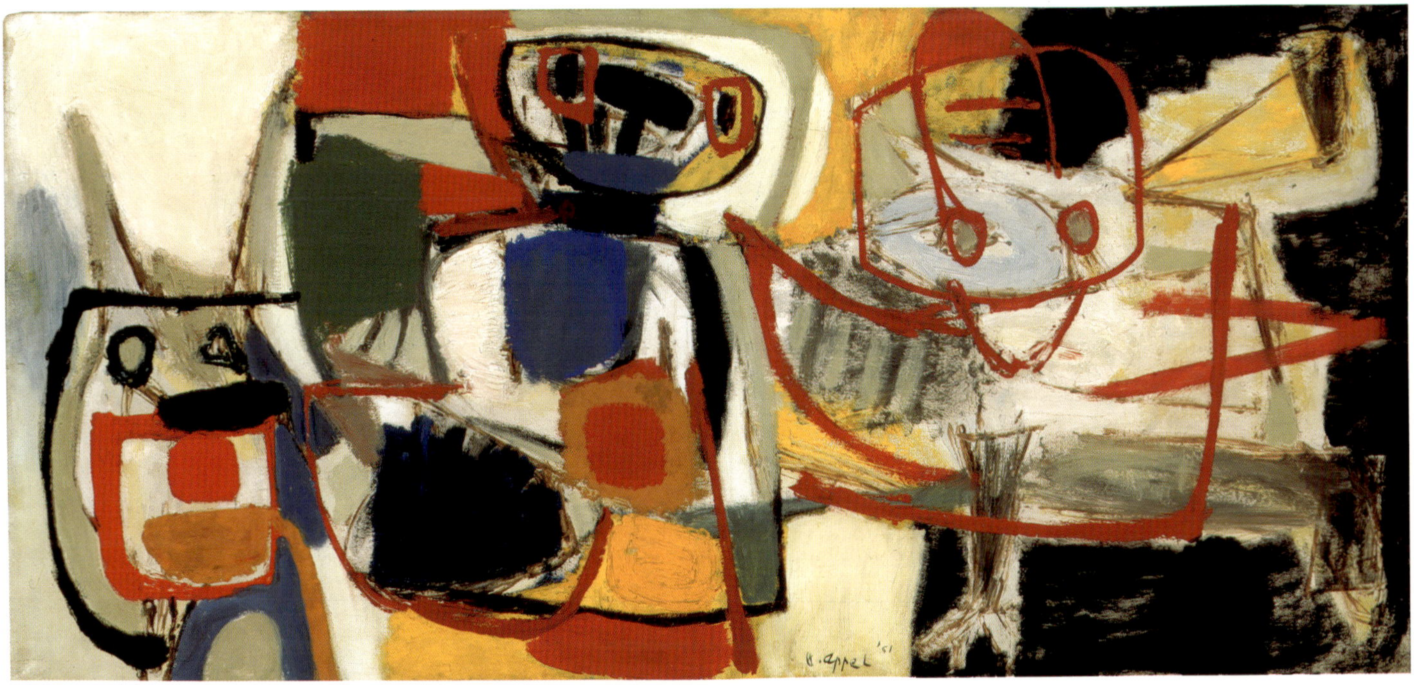

43 Karel Appel
Composition with animal figure, 1951

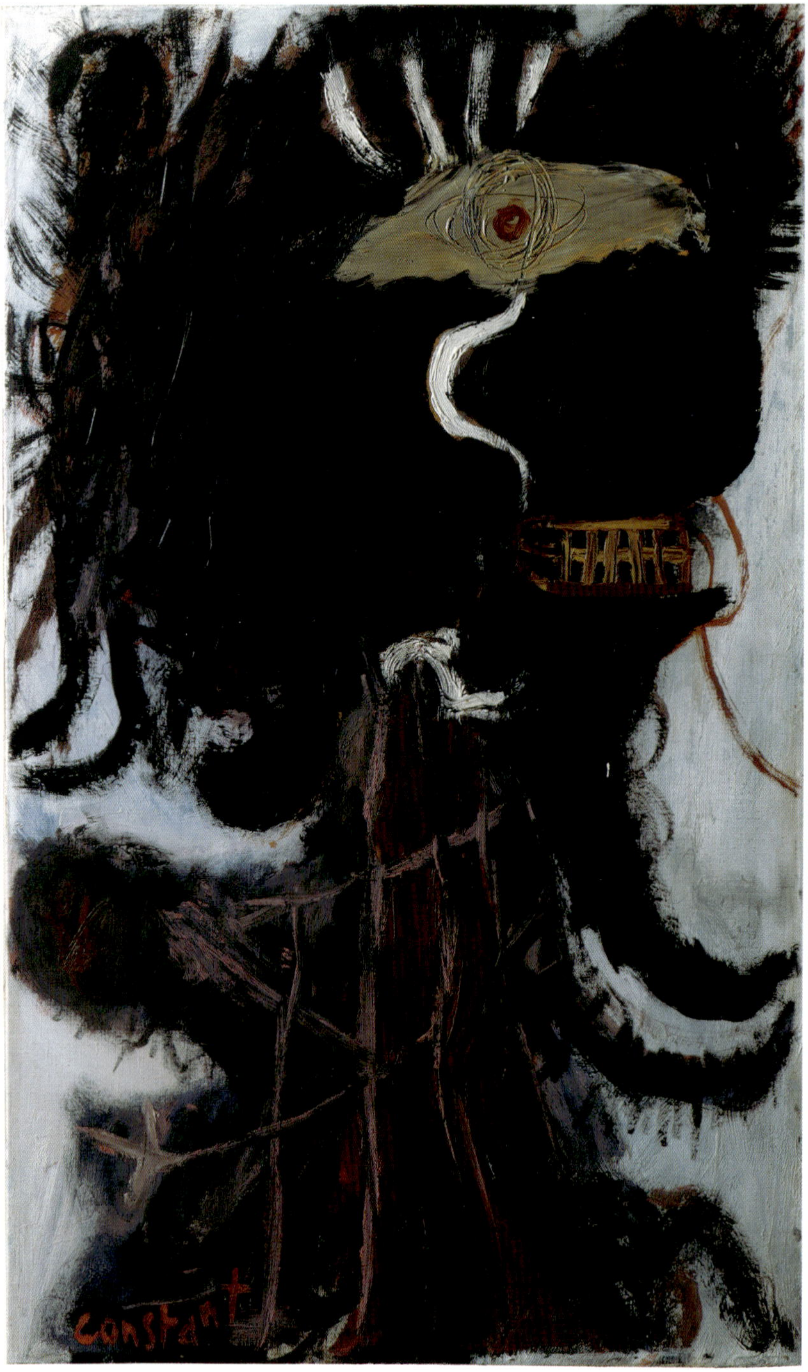

51 Constant
Satyr, 1948

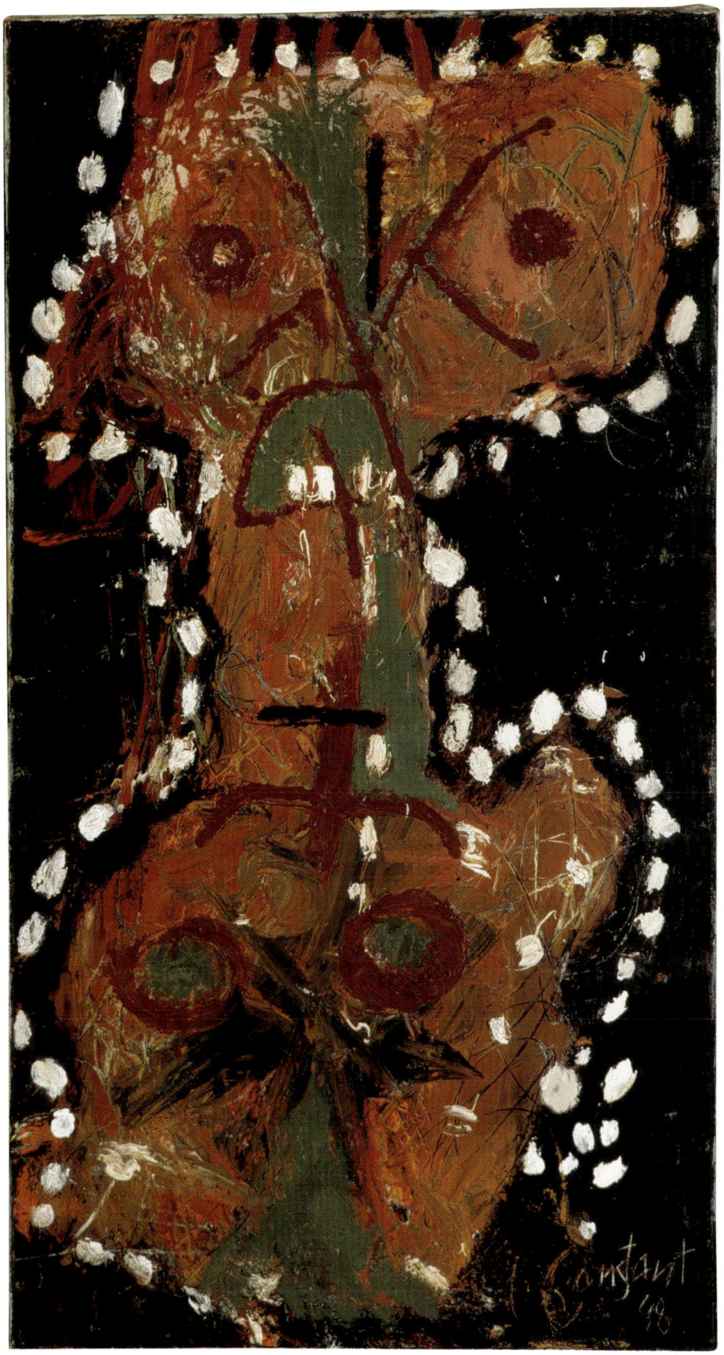

50 Constant
Parelvisser, 1948
The pearl fisher

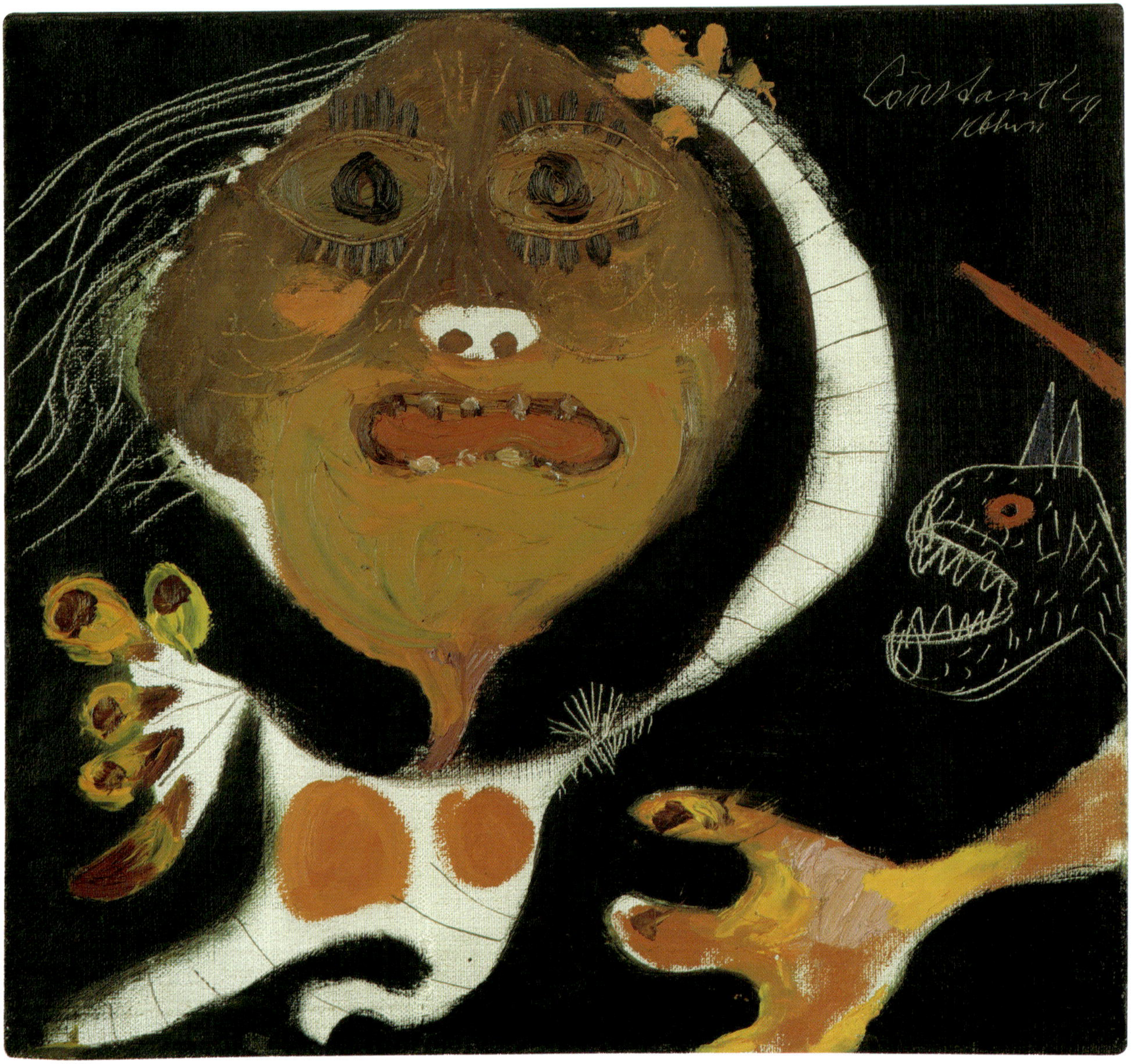

56 Constant
Untitled (Copenhagen) "KBHVN", 1949

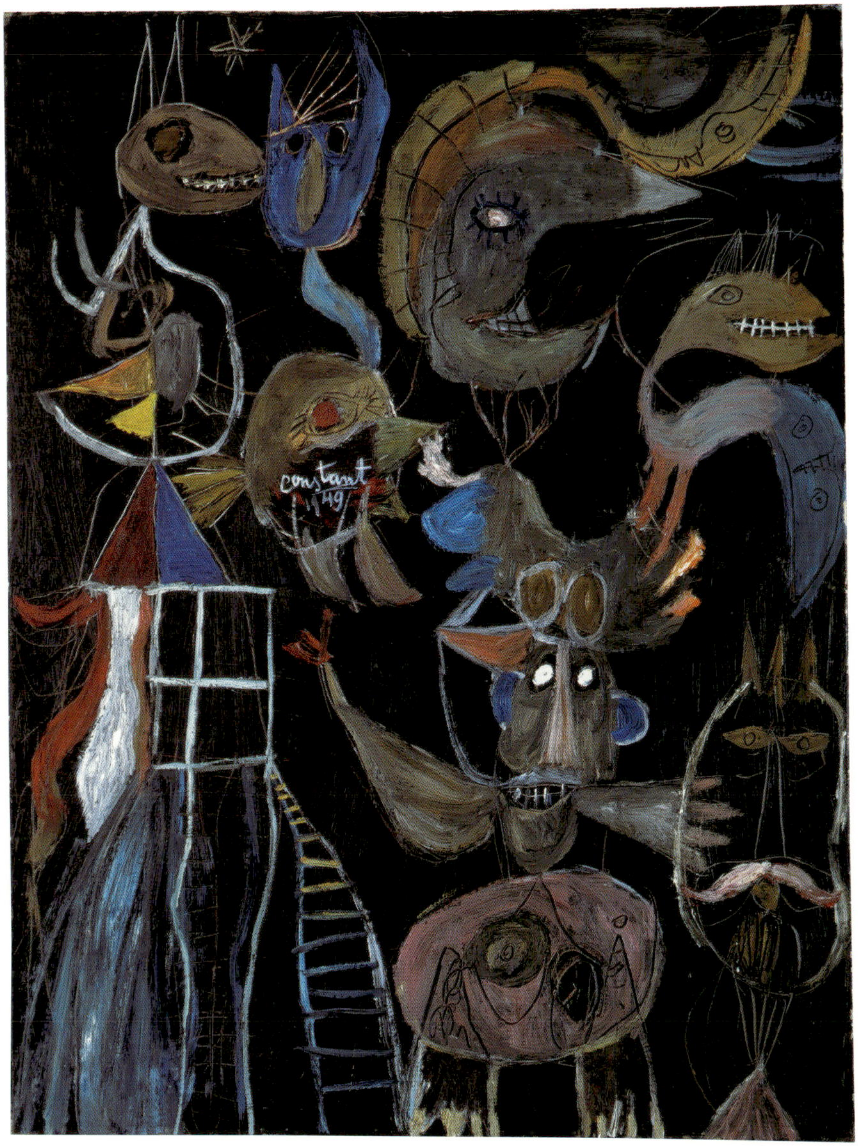

53 Constant
Après Nous la Liberté, 1949
After us liberty

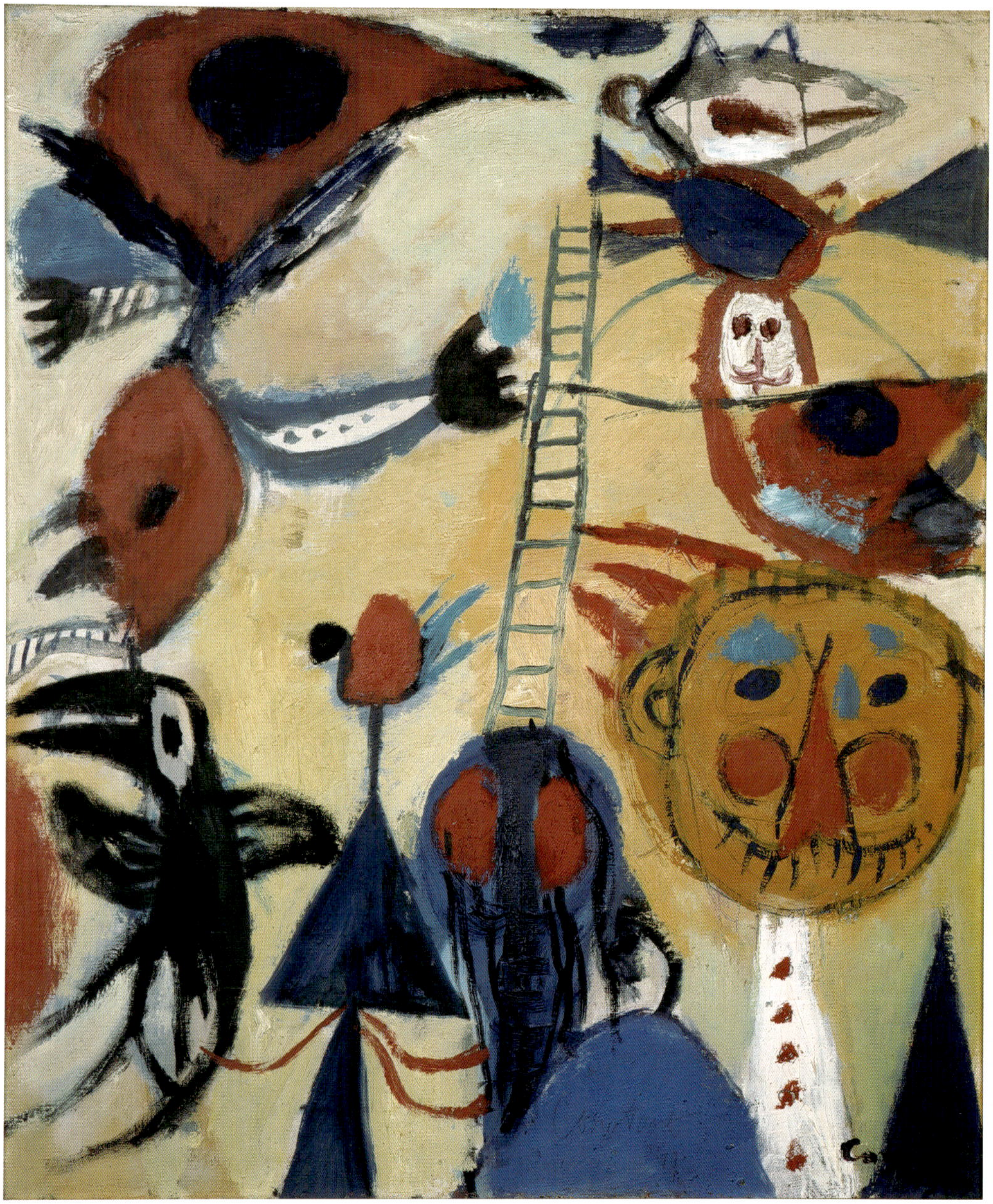

54 Constant
Het laddertje, 1949
The little ladder

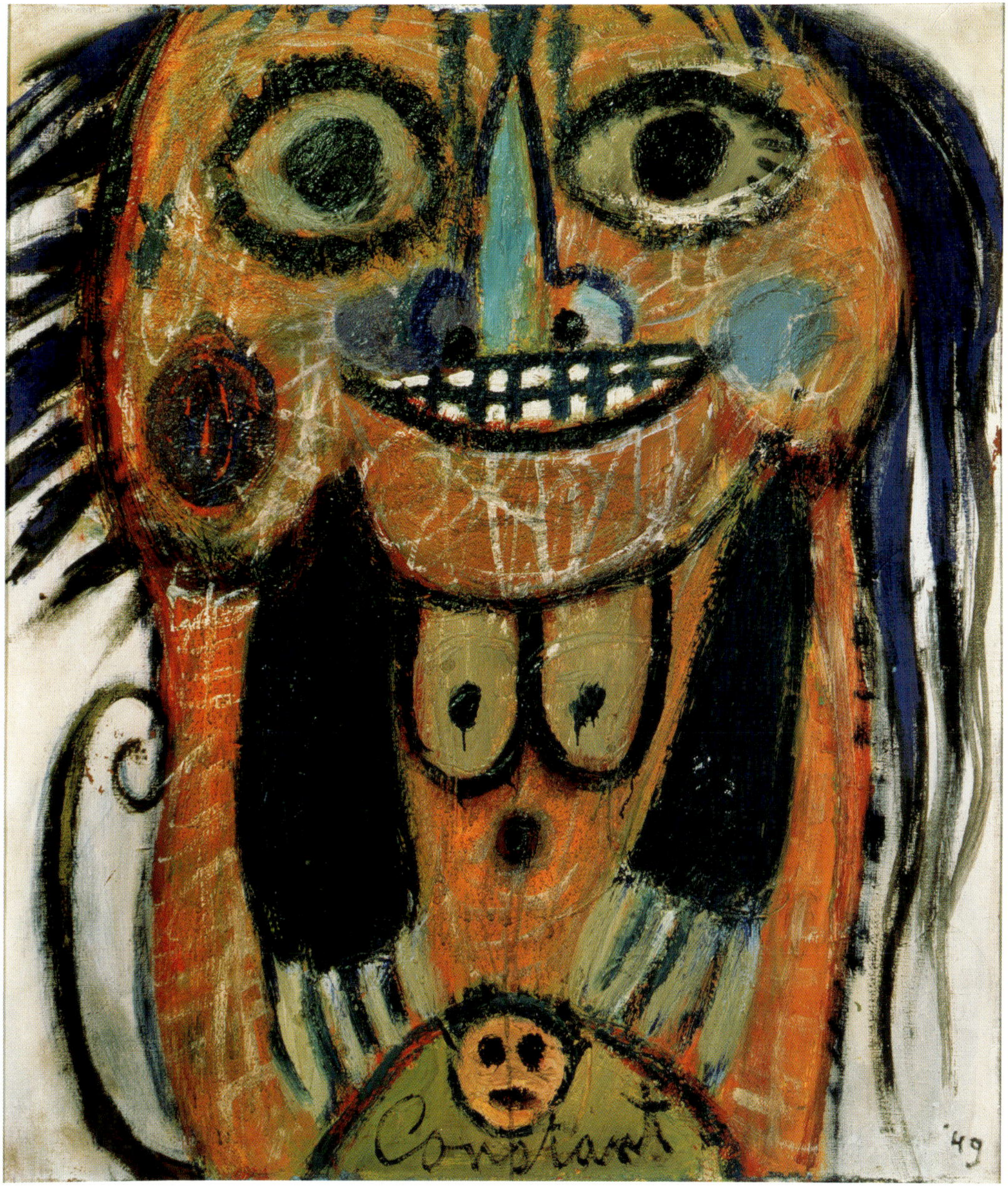

55 Constant
La femme terrible, 1949
The terrible woman

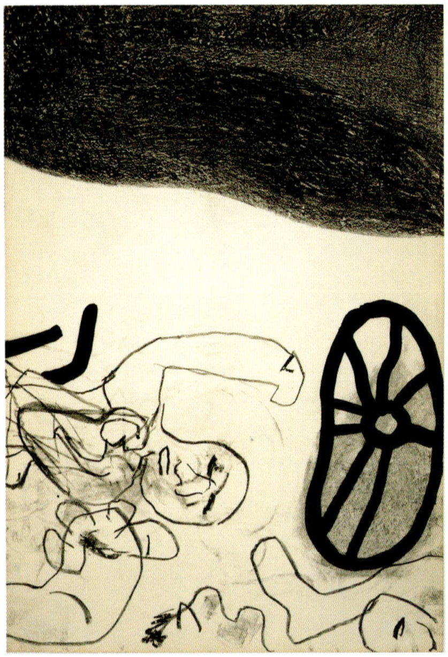
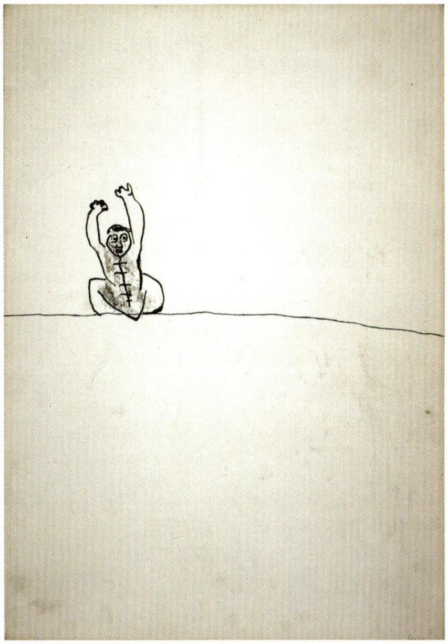
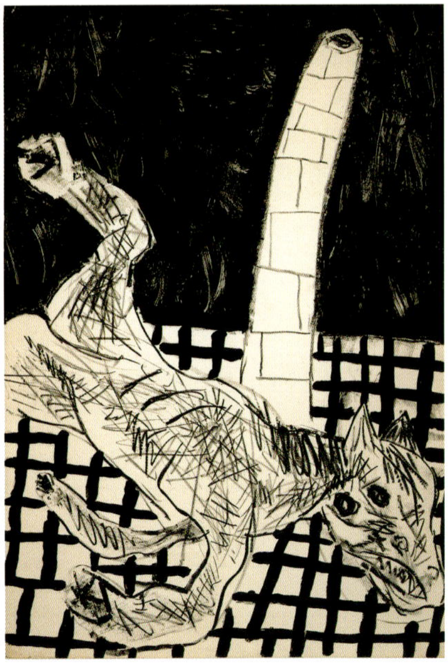
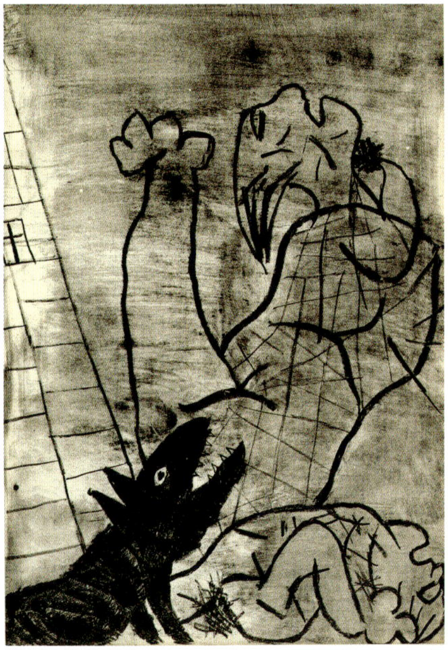

59 Constant
8 x la guerre, 1951
8 x the war

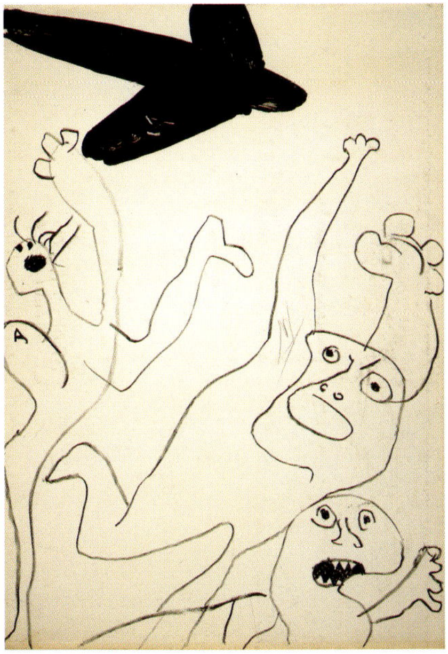

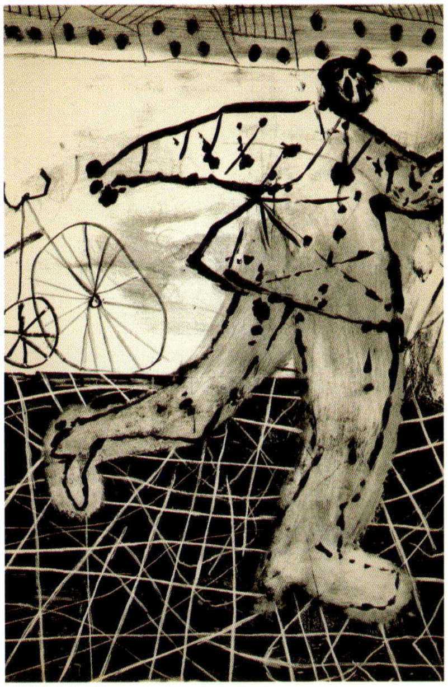

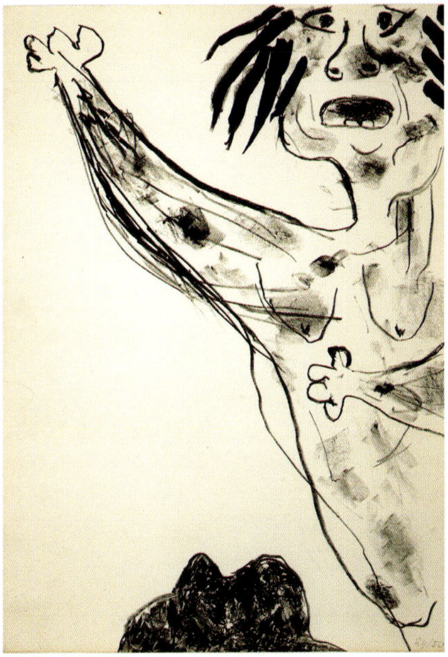

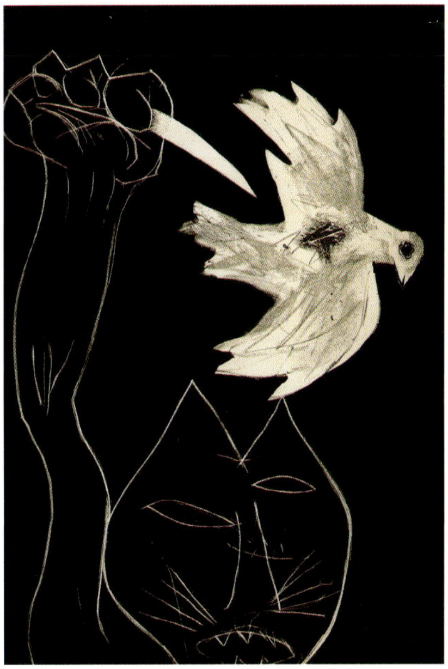

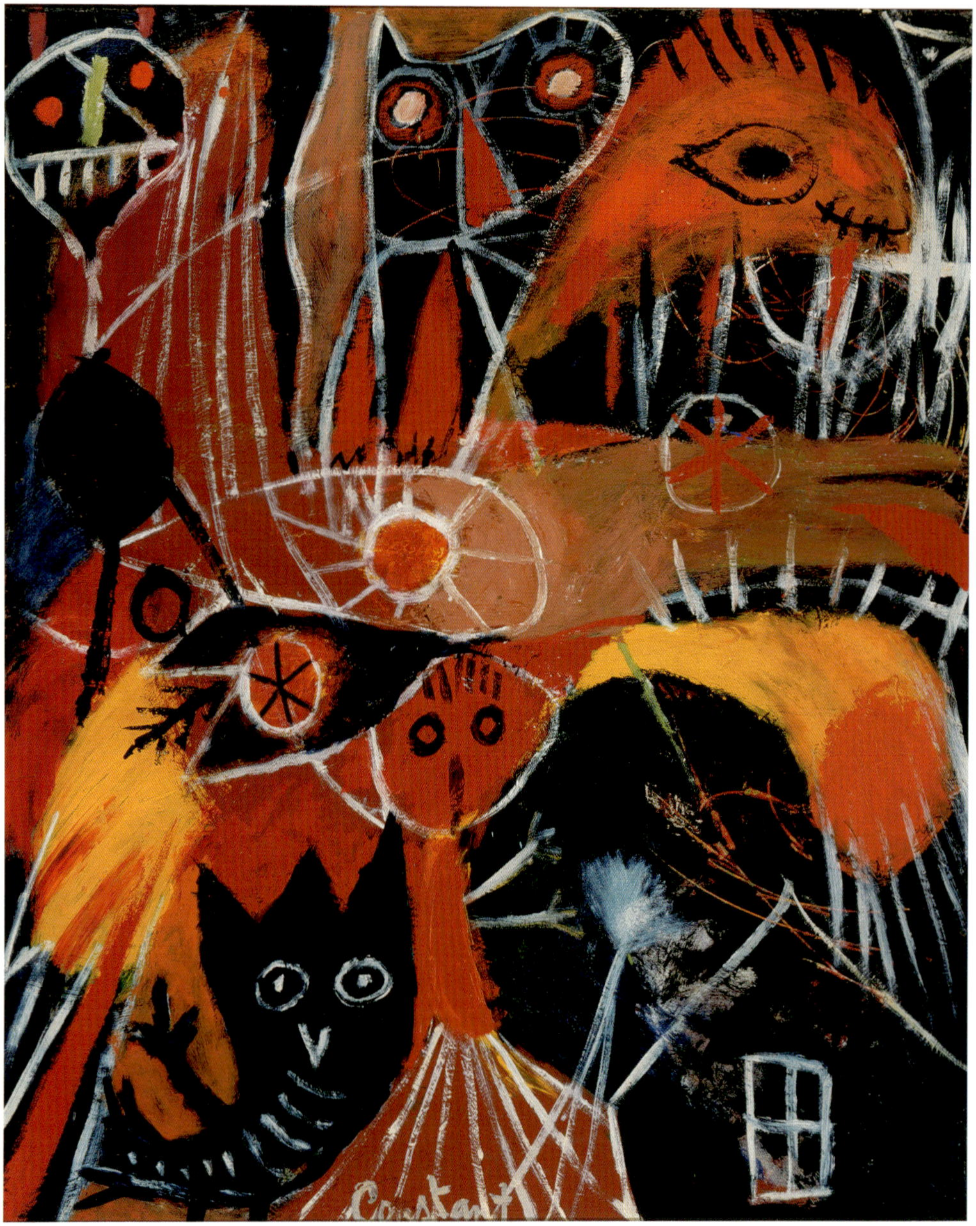

52 Constant
Animaux, 1949
Animals

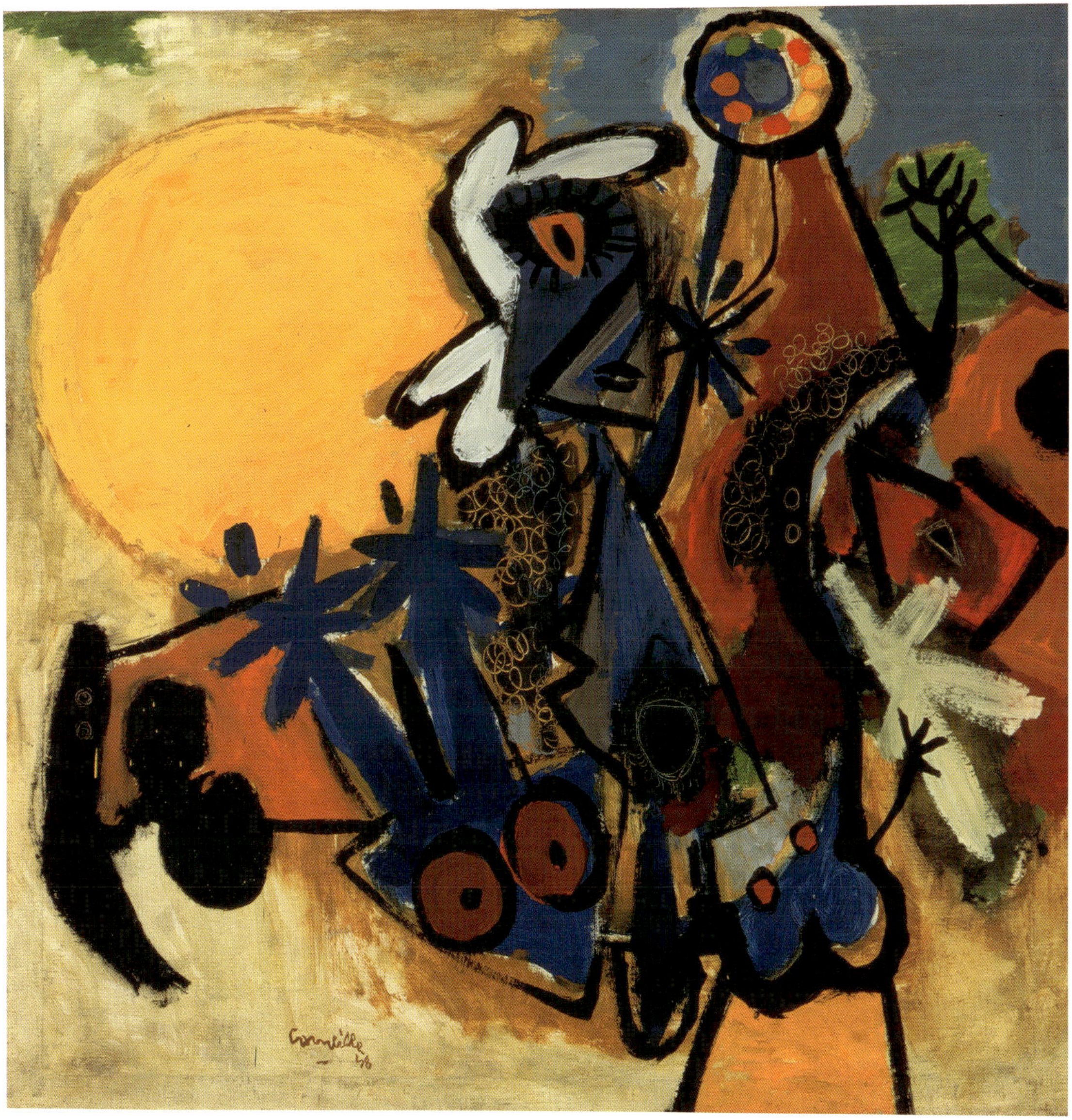

62 Corneille
Zomer, 1949
Summer

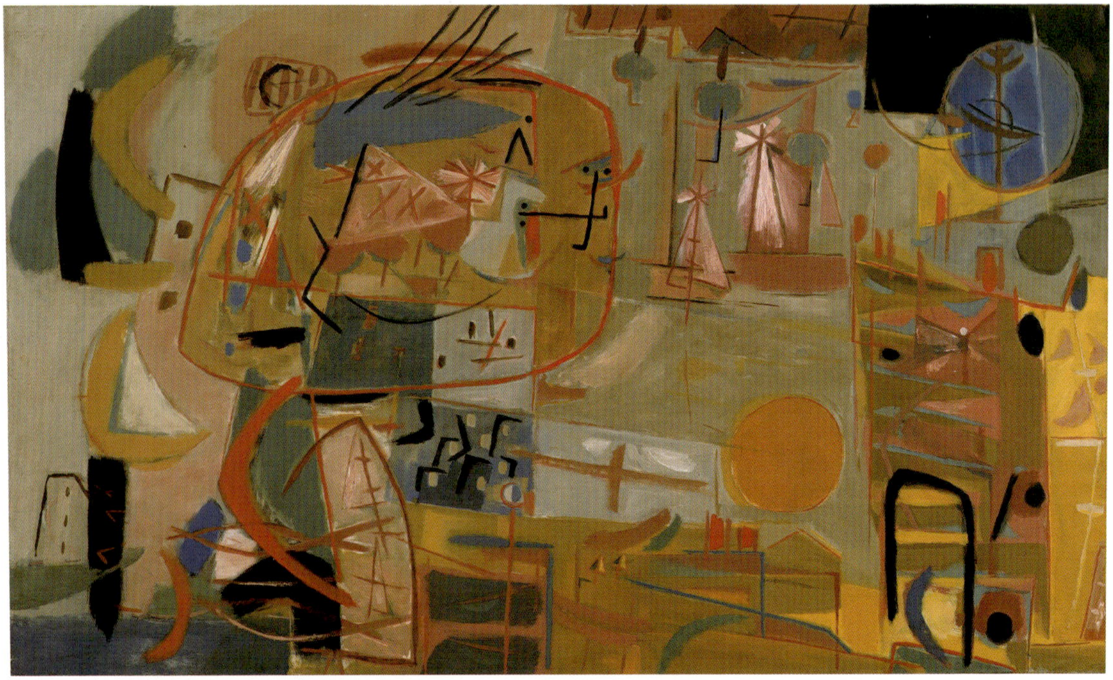

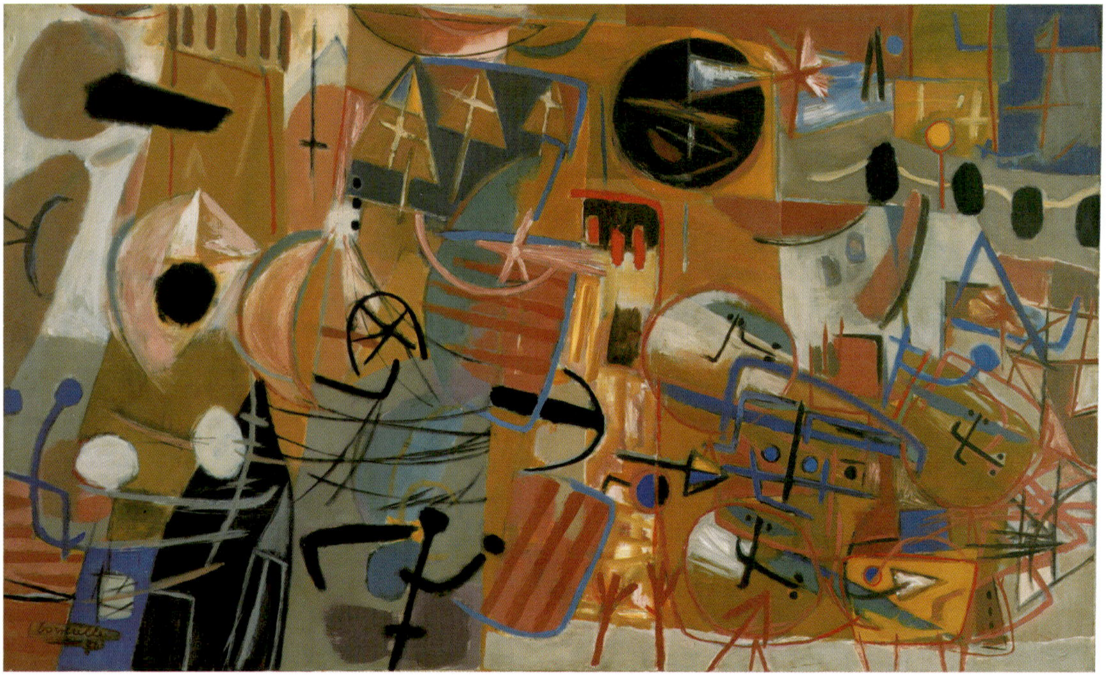

63 Corneille
La ville, 1950
The town

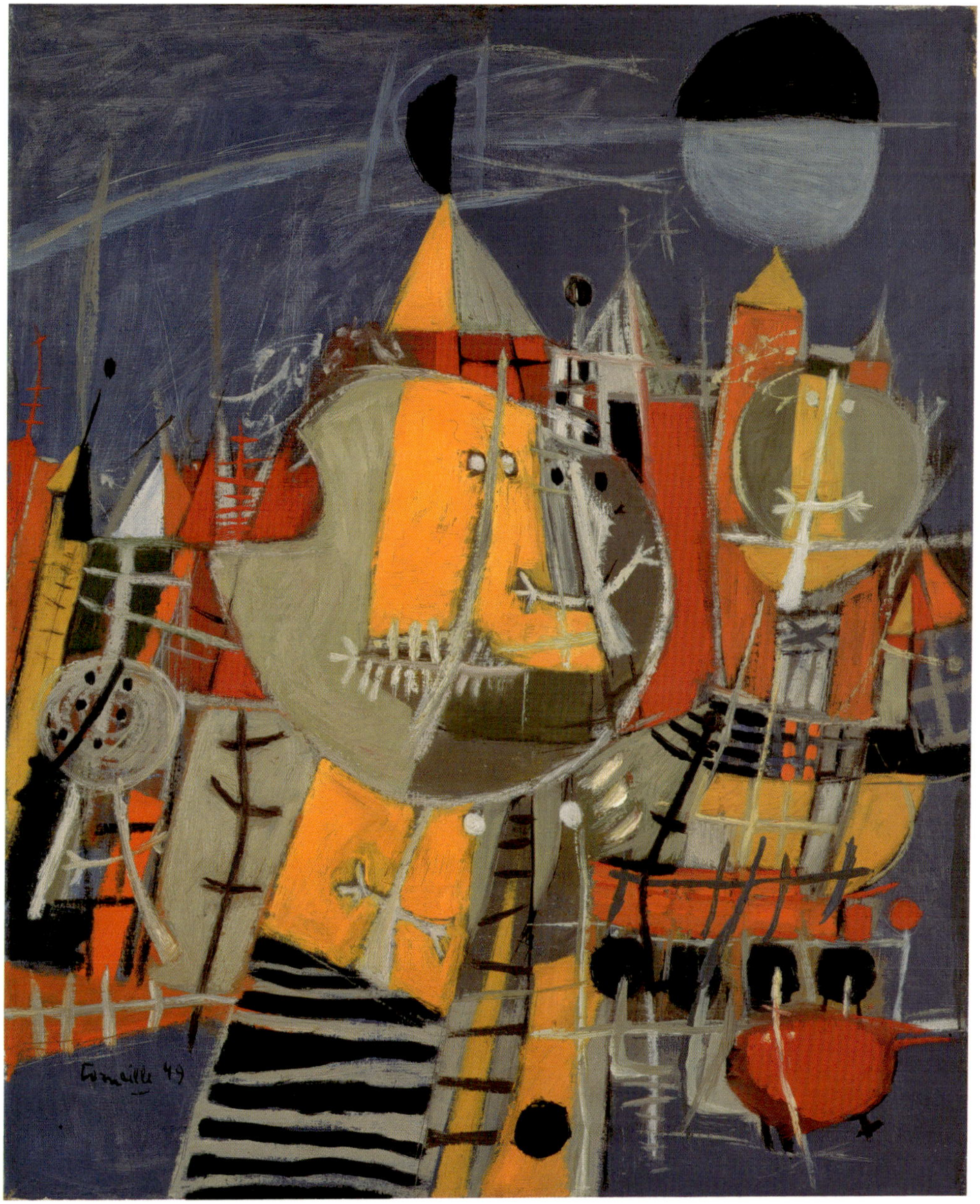

61 Corneille
Het vrolijke rythme van de stad, 1949
The joyful rhythm of the city

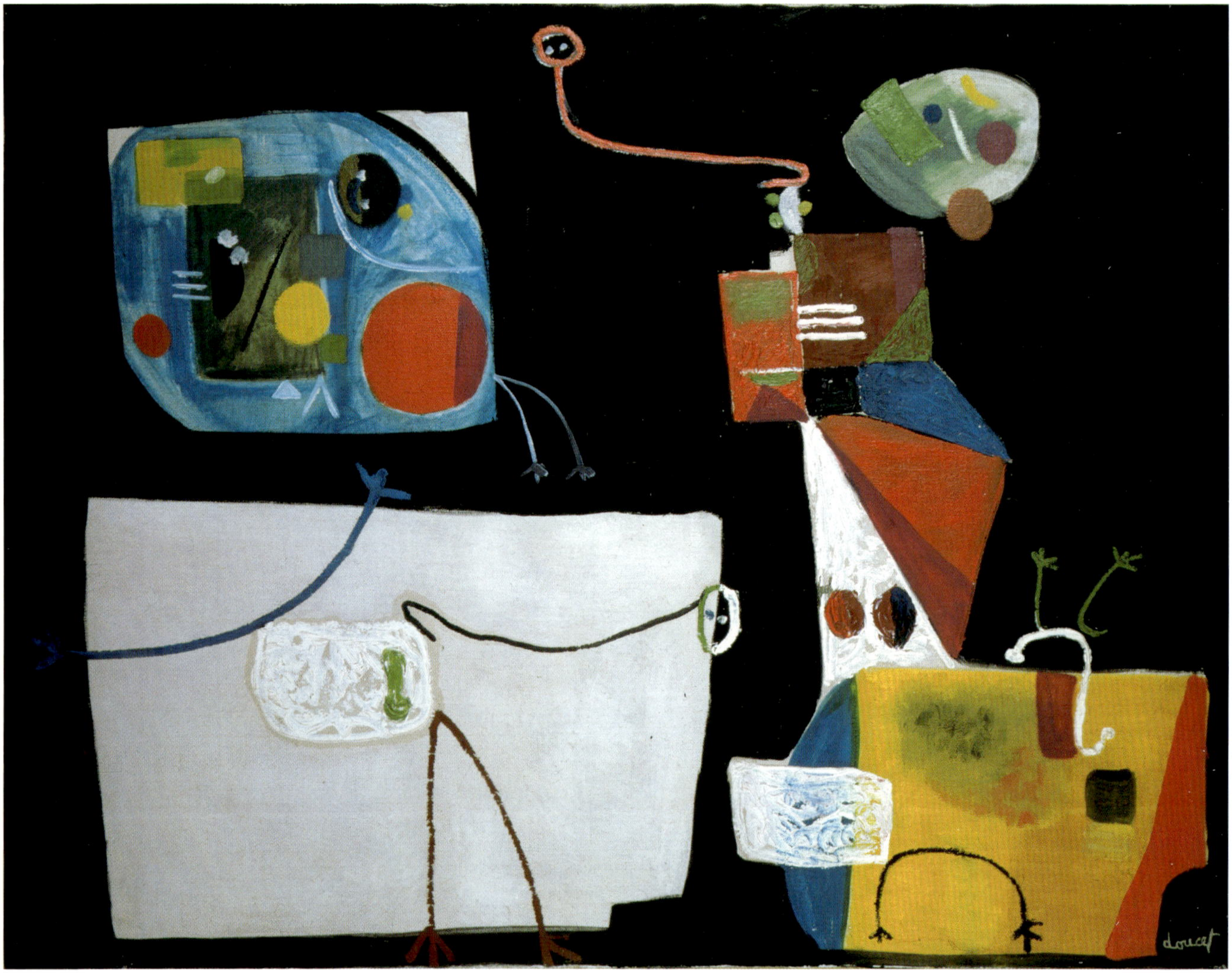

64 Jacques Doucet
Hommage à Armstrong, 1949
Homage to Armstrong

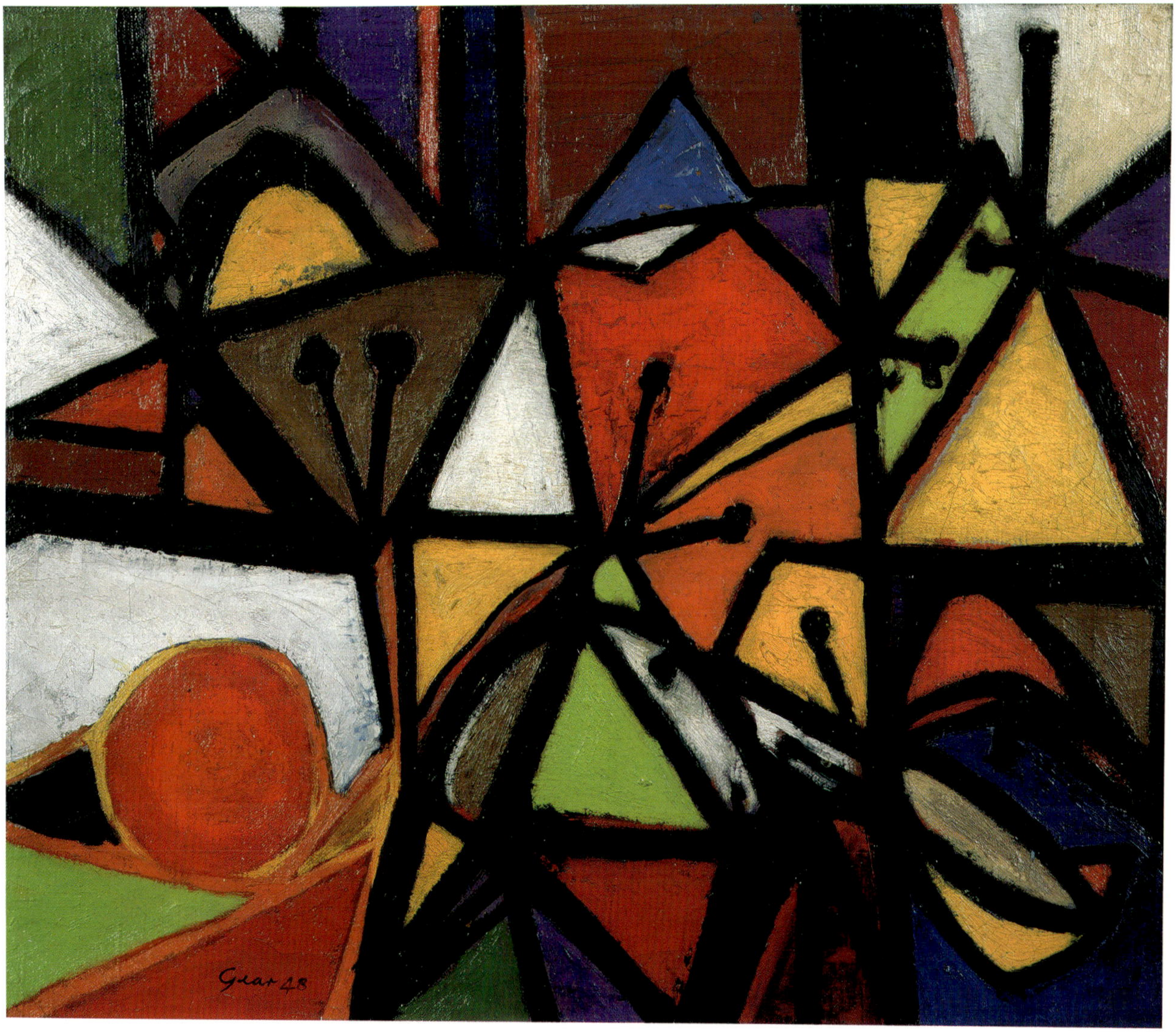

65 William Gear
Paysage au soleil couché, 1948
Landscape with setting sun

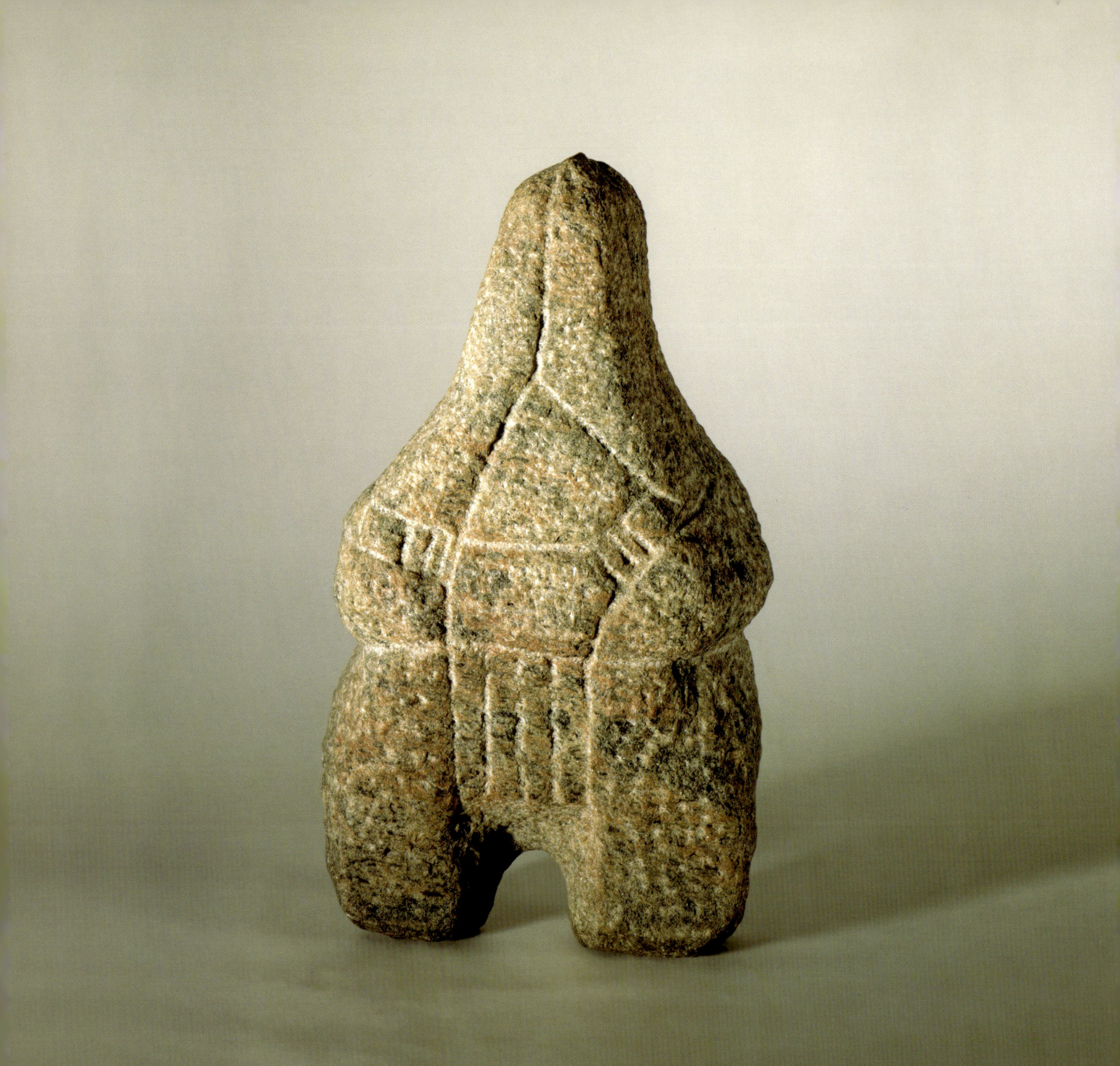

71 Henry Heerup
Kvinde som tempel, 1949–50
Woman as temple

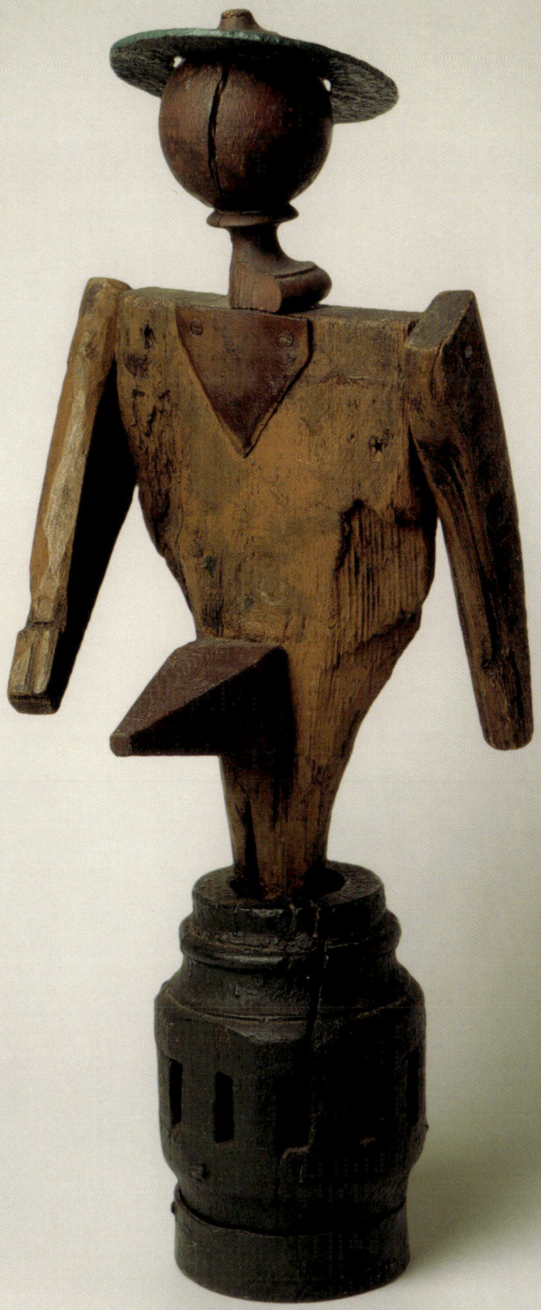

70 Henry Heerup
Nissemand, 1943
Sprite

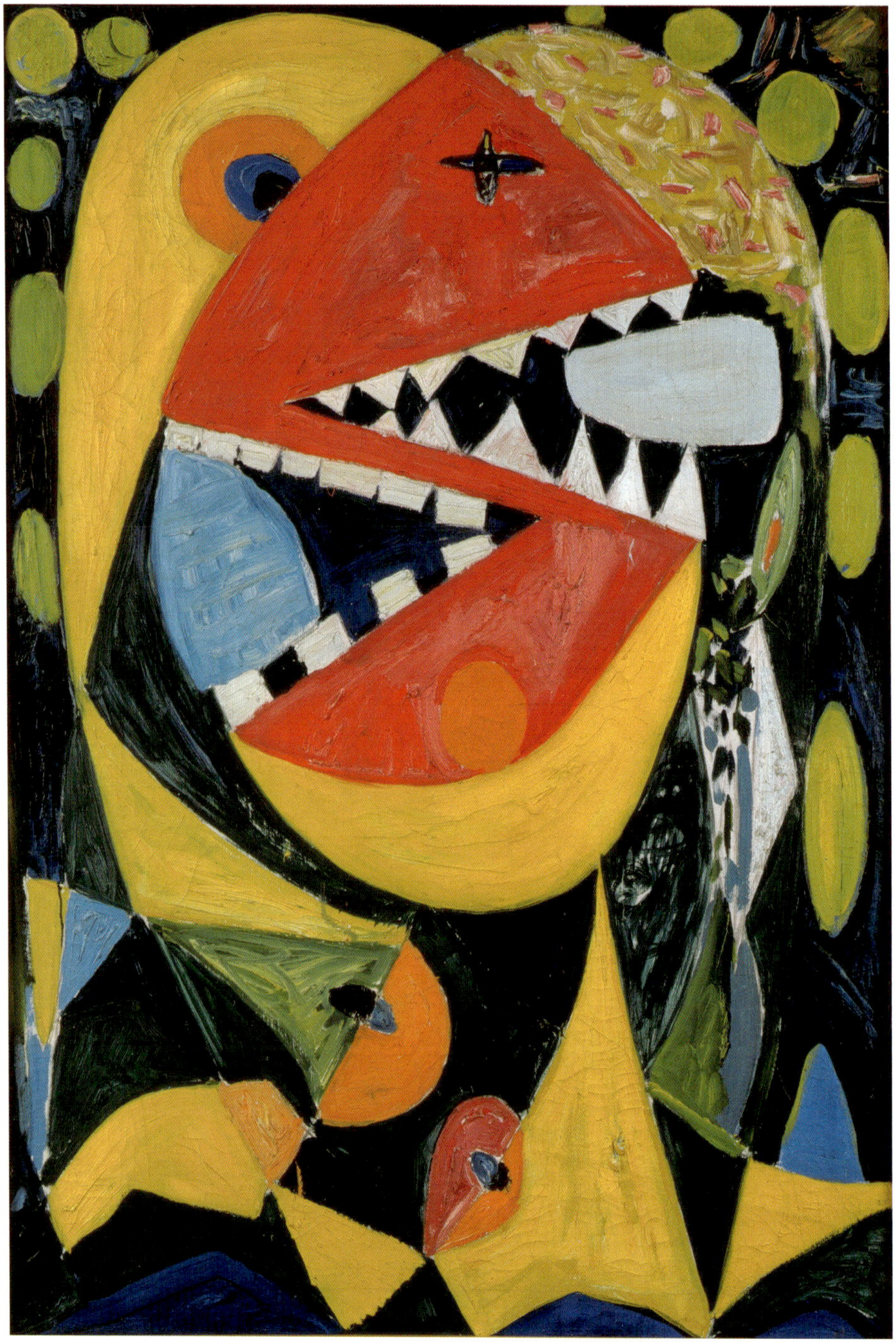

74 Egill Jacobsen
Rødt Objekt II, 1940
Red object II

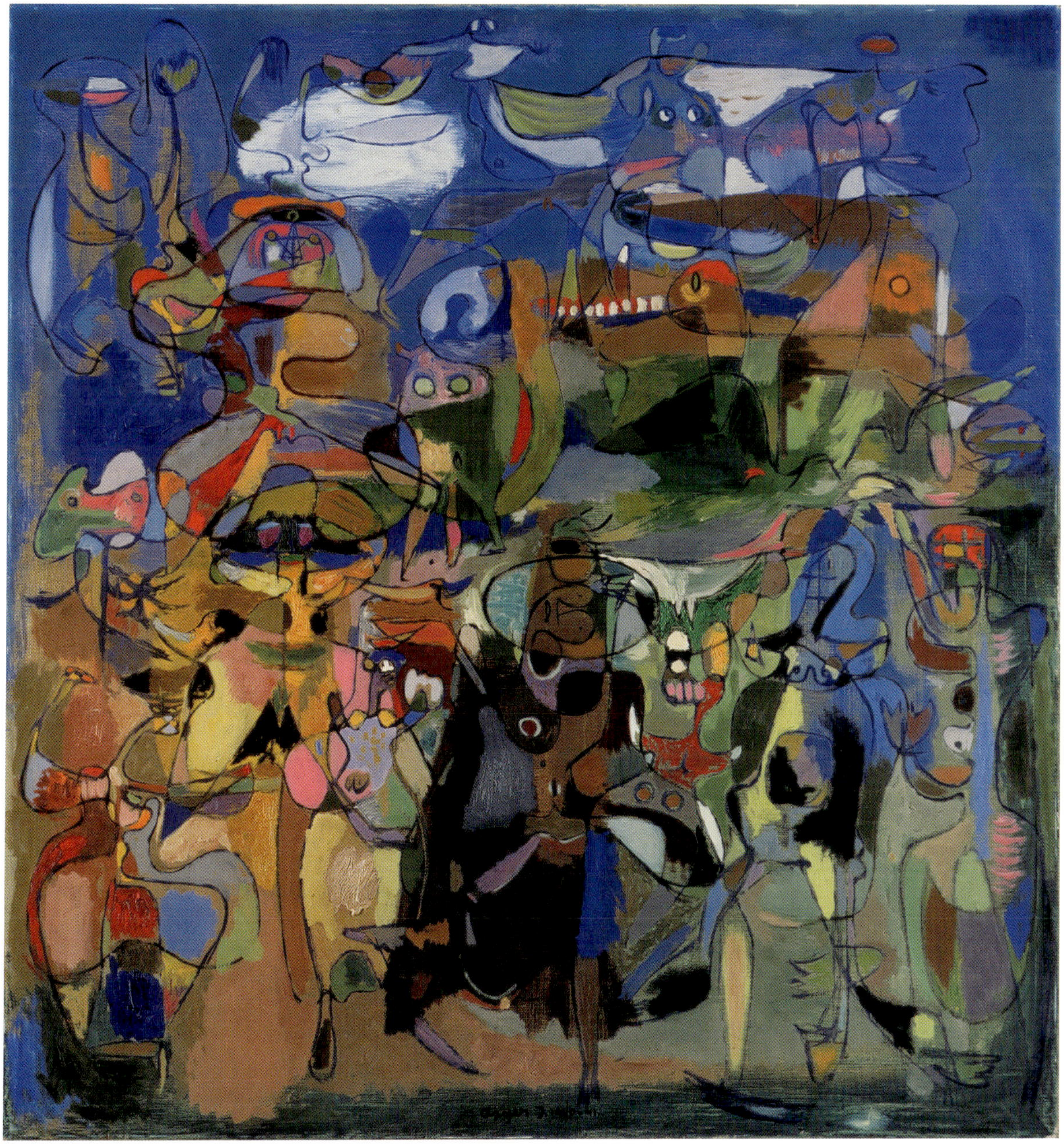

76 Asger Jorn
Titania II, 1940–41

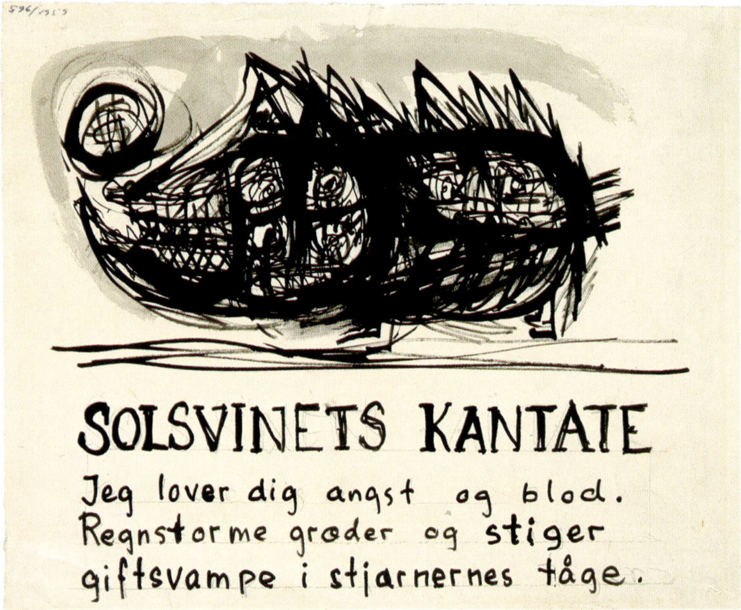

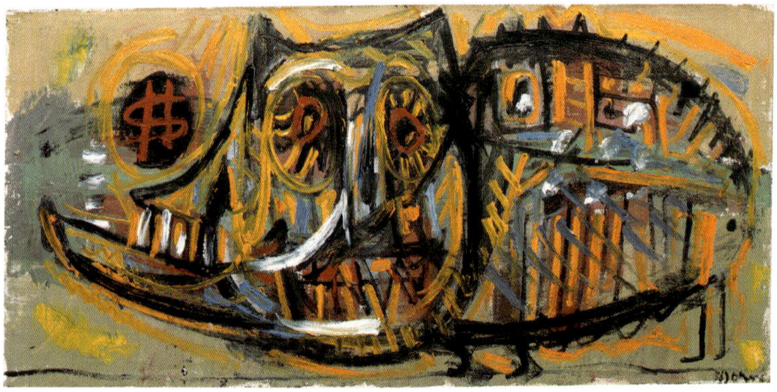

top:
87 Asger Jorn
Solsvinets kantate, 1950
The cantata of the sun swine
Drawing for *Guldsvinet,* 1950

bottom:
84 Asger Jorn
Guldsvinet, 1950
The golden swine

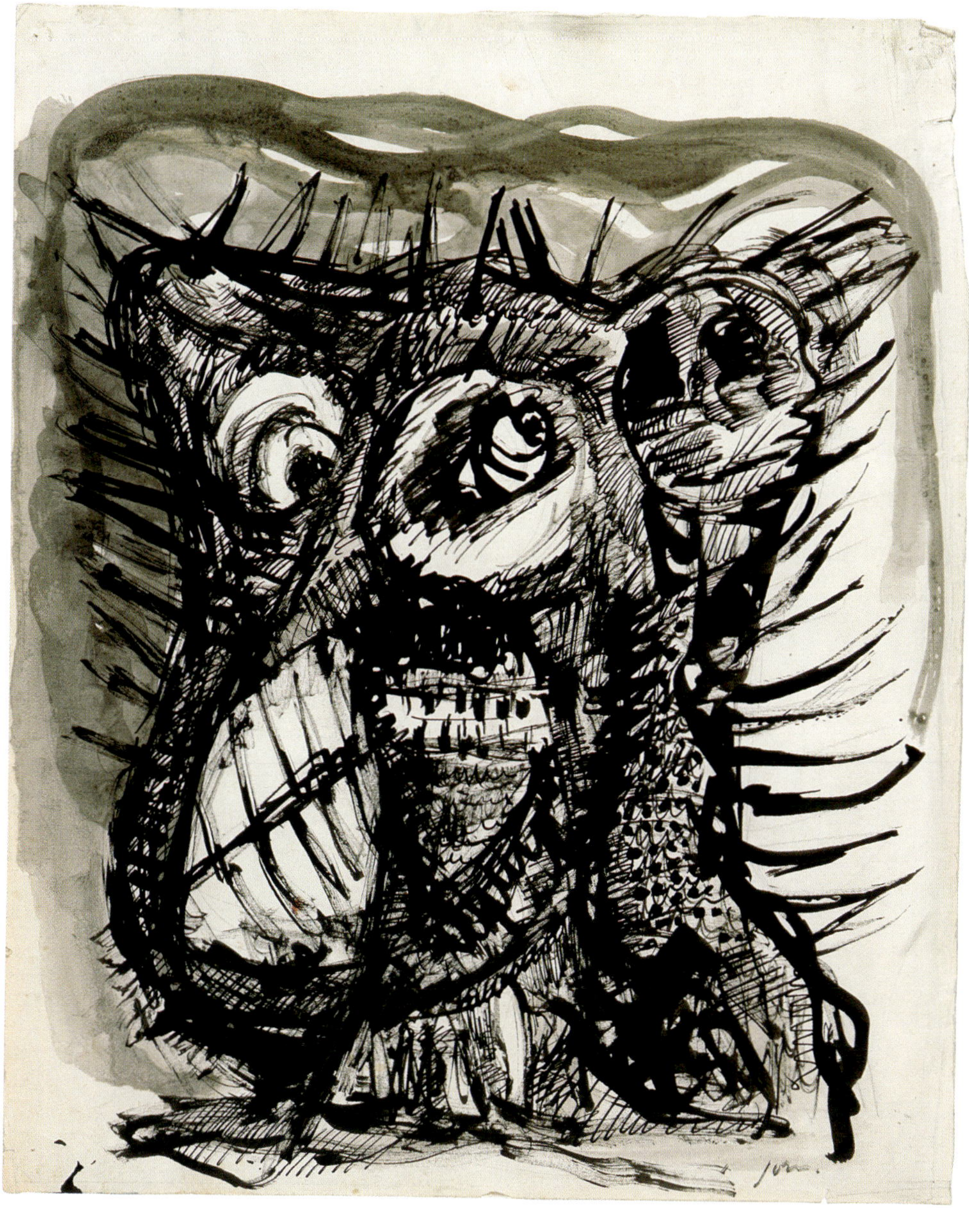

82 Asger Jorn
Drawing for *Ånden fra 48,* 1950
The Spirit of '48

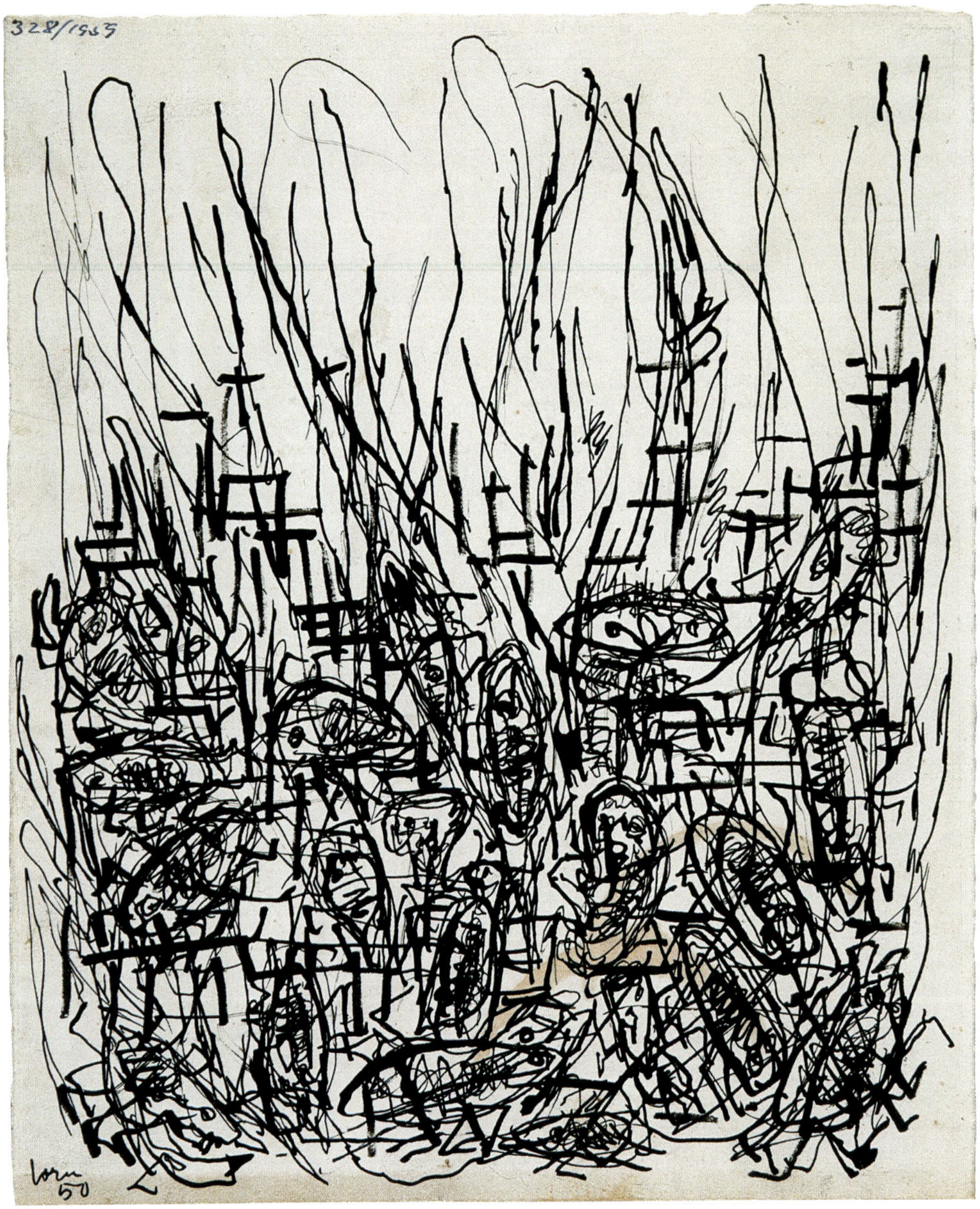

83 Asger Jorn
Dødsbranden, 1950
The burning city
Drawing for Dødsbranden, 1951 (cat. 90)

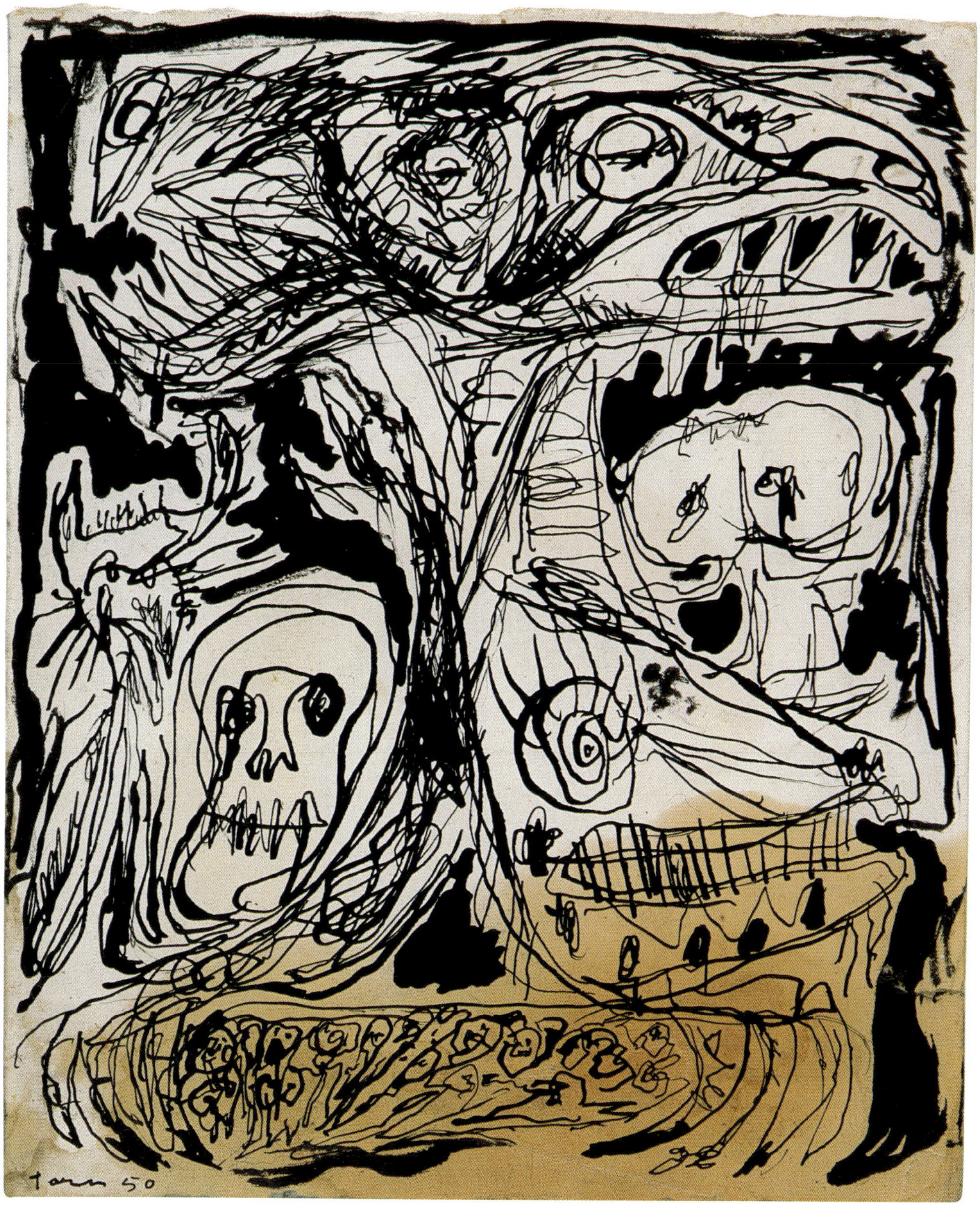

86 Asger Jorn
Drawing for *Ørnens ret,* 1950
The eagle's share

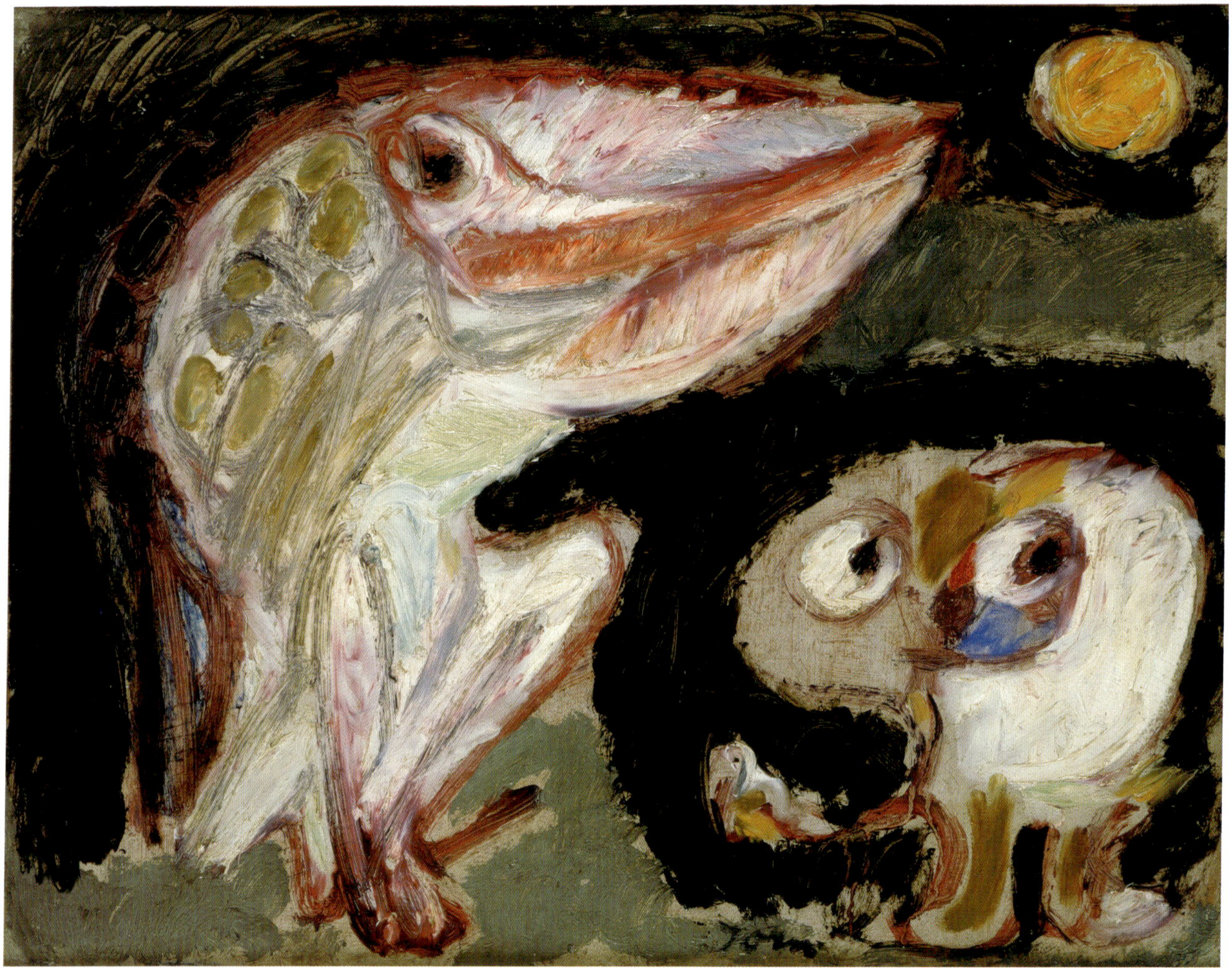

85 Asger Jorn
La lune et les animaux, 1950
The moon and the animals

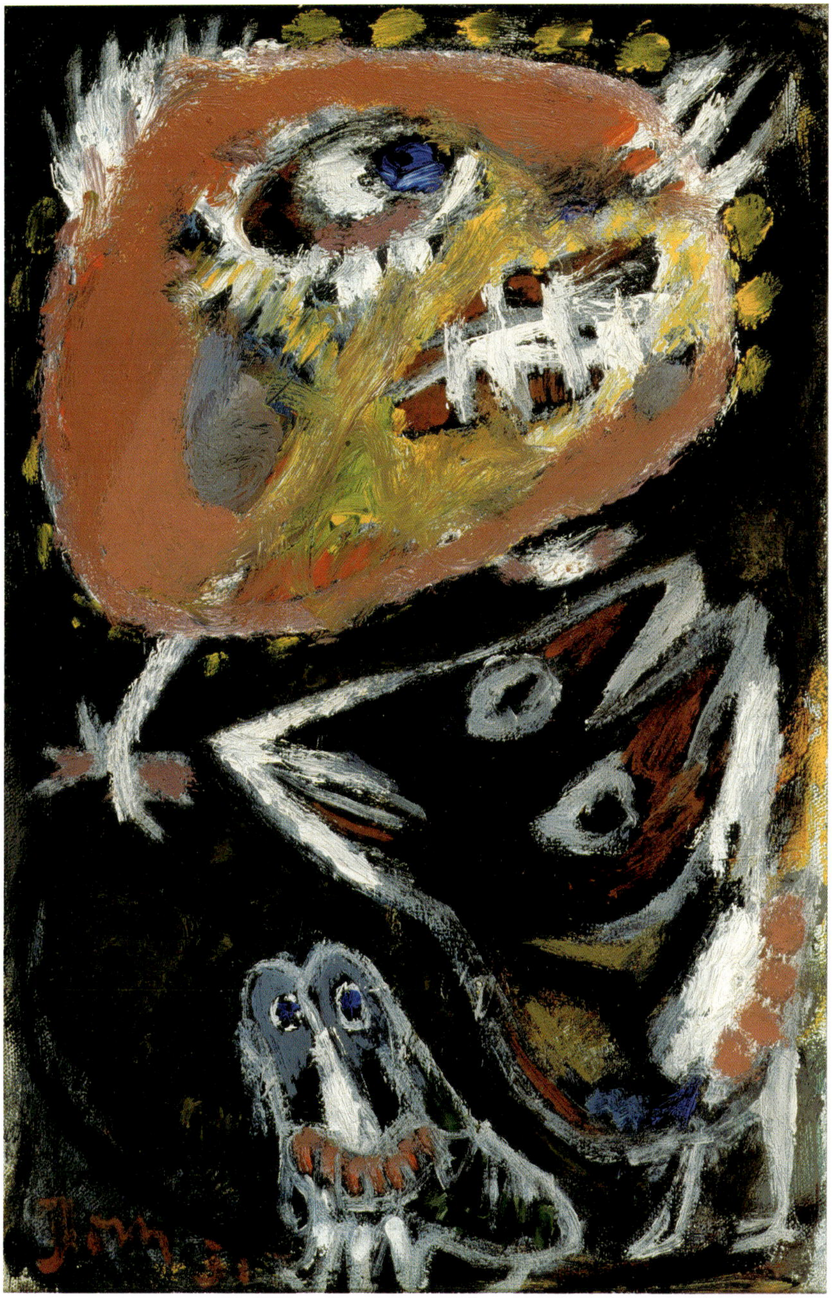

93 Asger Jorn
Sentiment d'infériorité, 1951
Inferiority complex

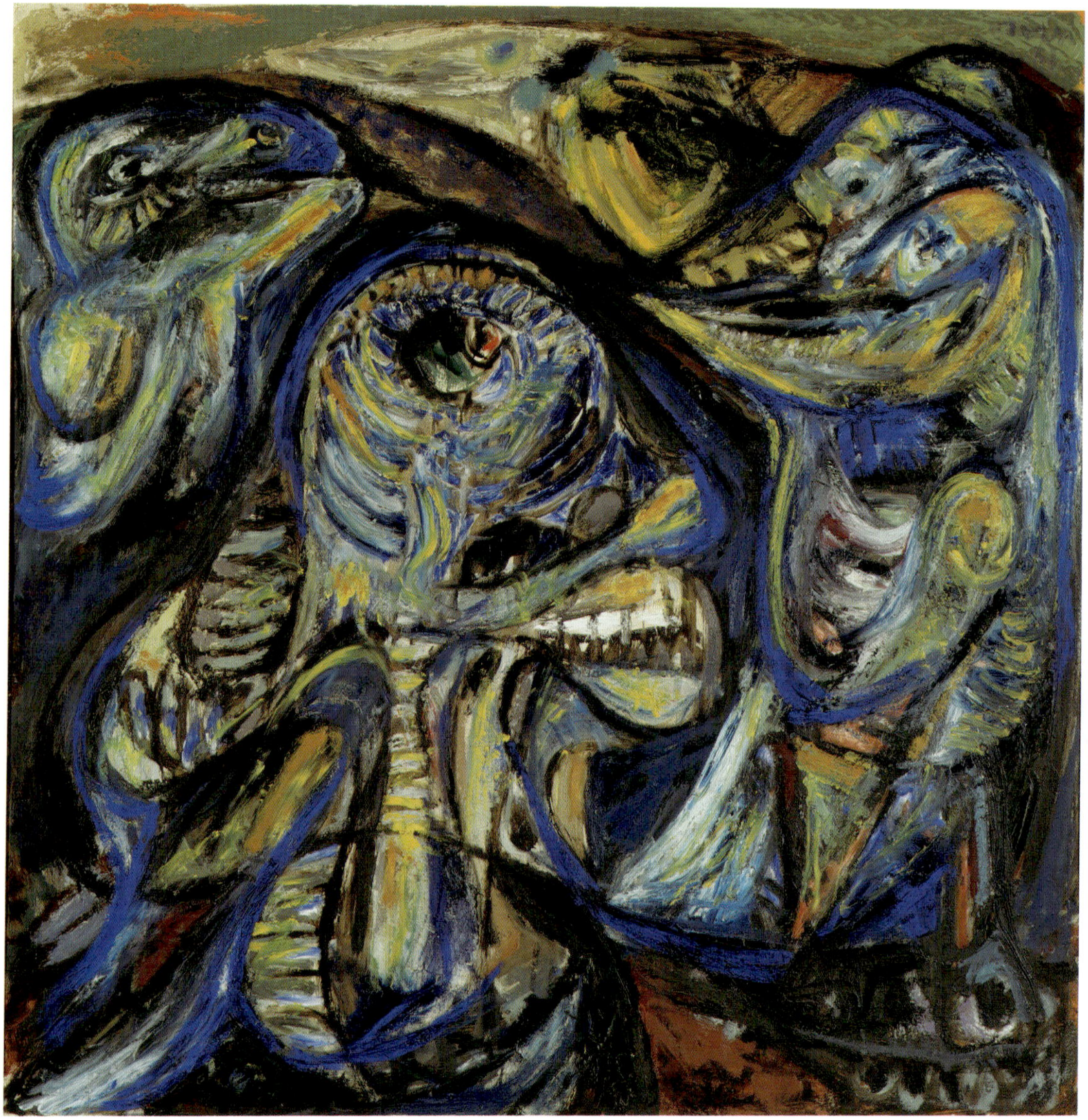

94 Asger Jorn
Sygelige fantomer, 1951
Morbid phantoms

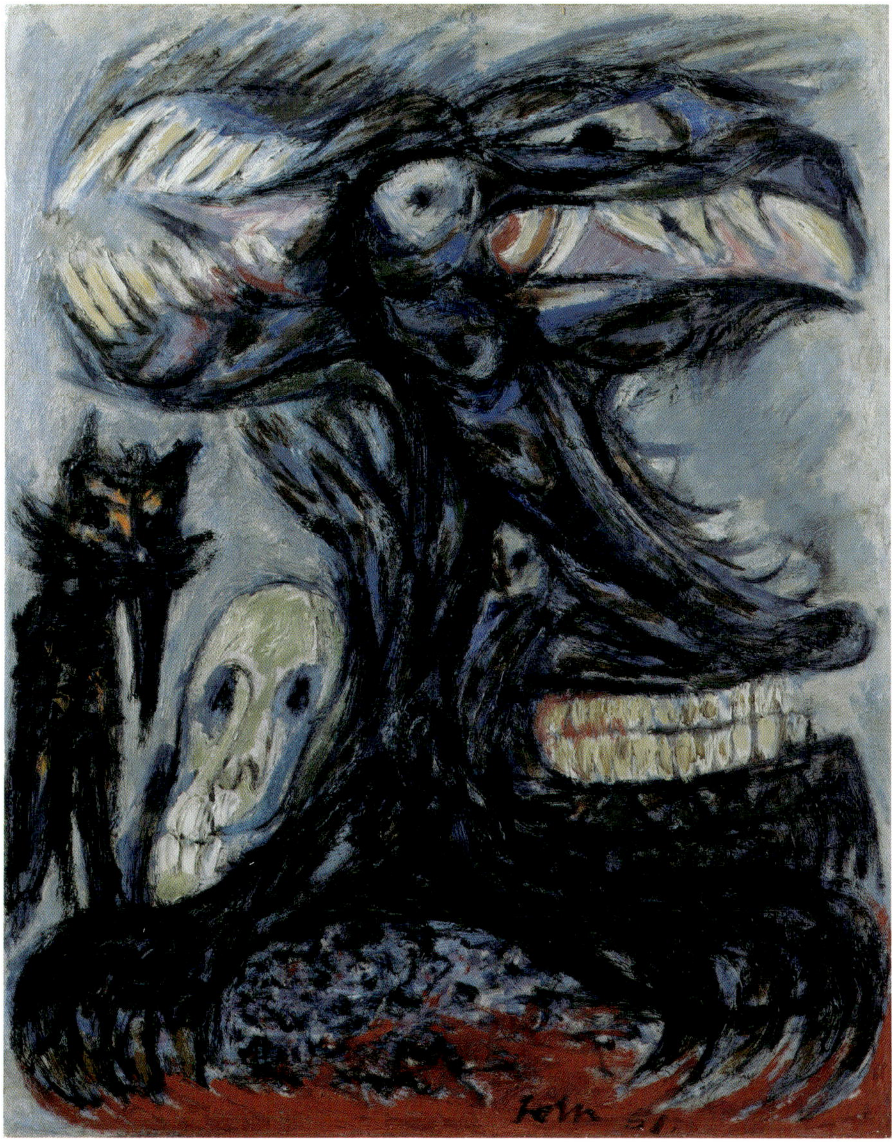

91 Asger Jorn
Le droit de l'aigle II, 1951
The eagle's share II

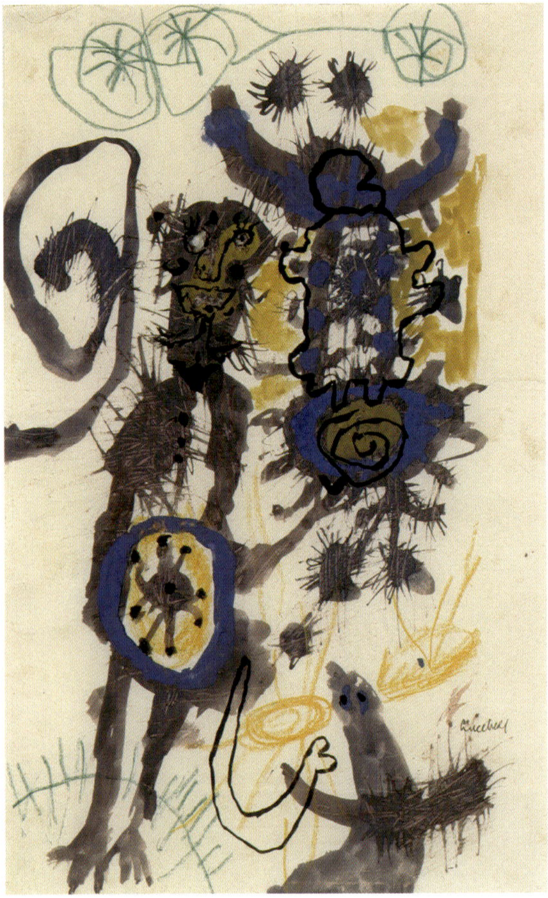

103 Lucebert
Partisans, 1952

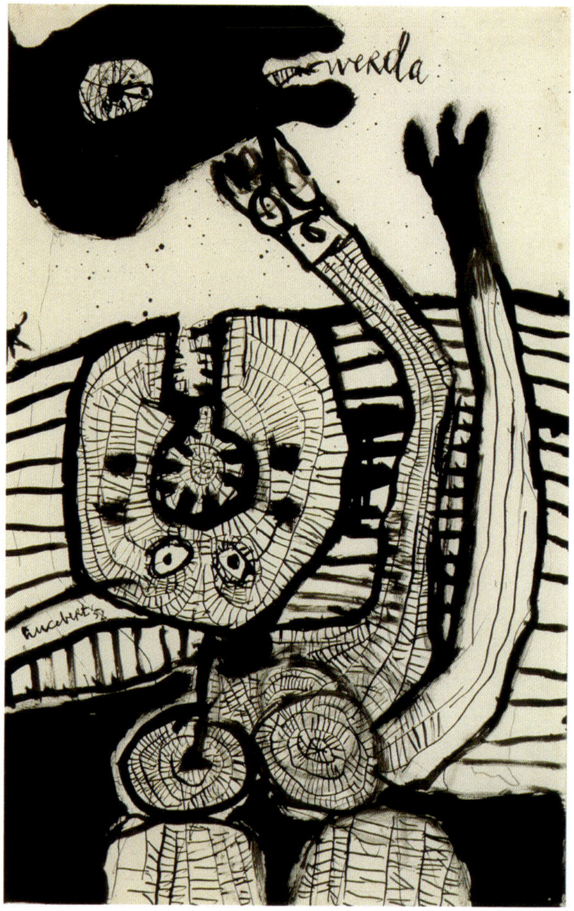

98 Lucebert
Gott mit uns I, 1952
God be with us 1

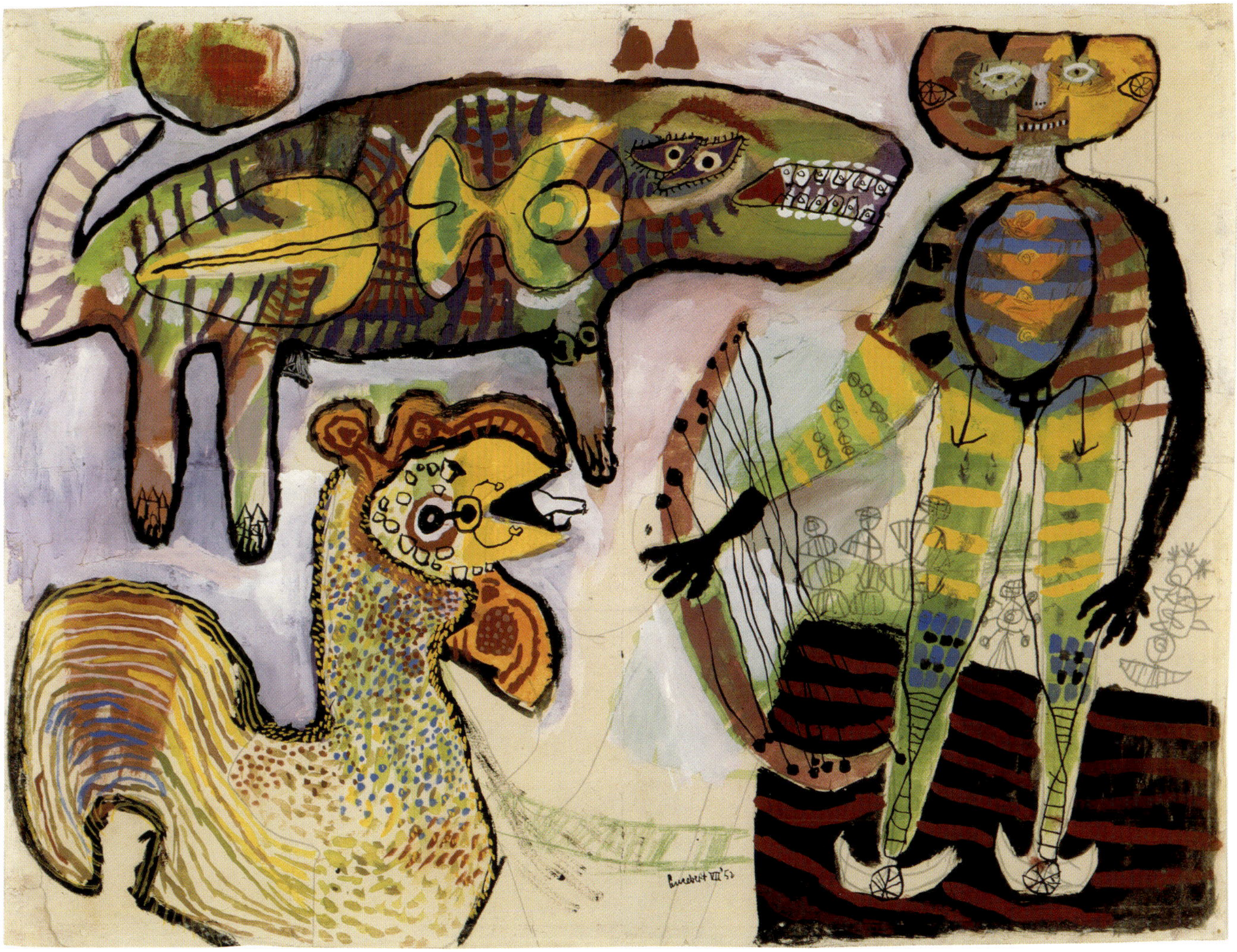

102 Lucebert
Orpheus en de dieren, 1952
Orpheus and the animals

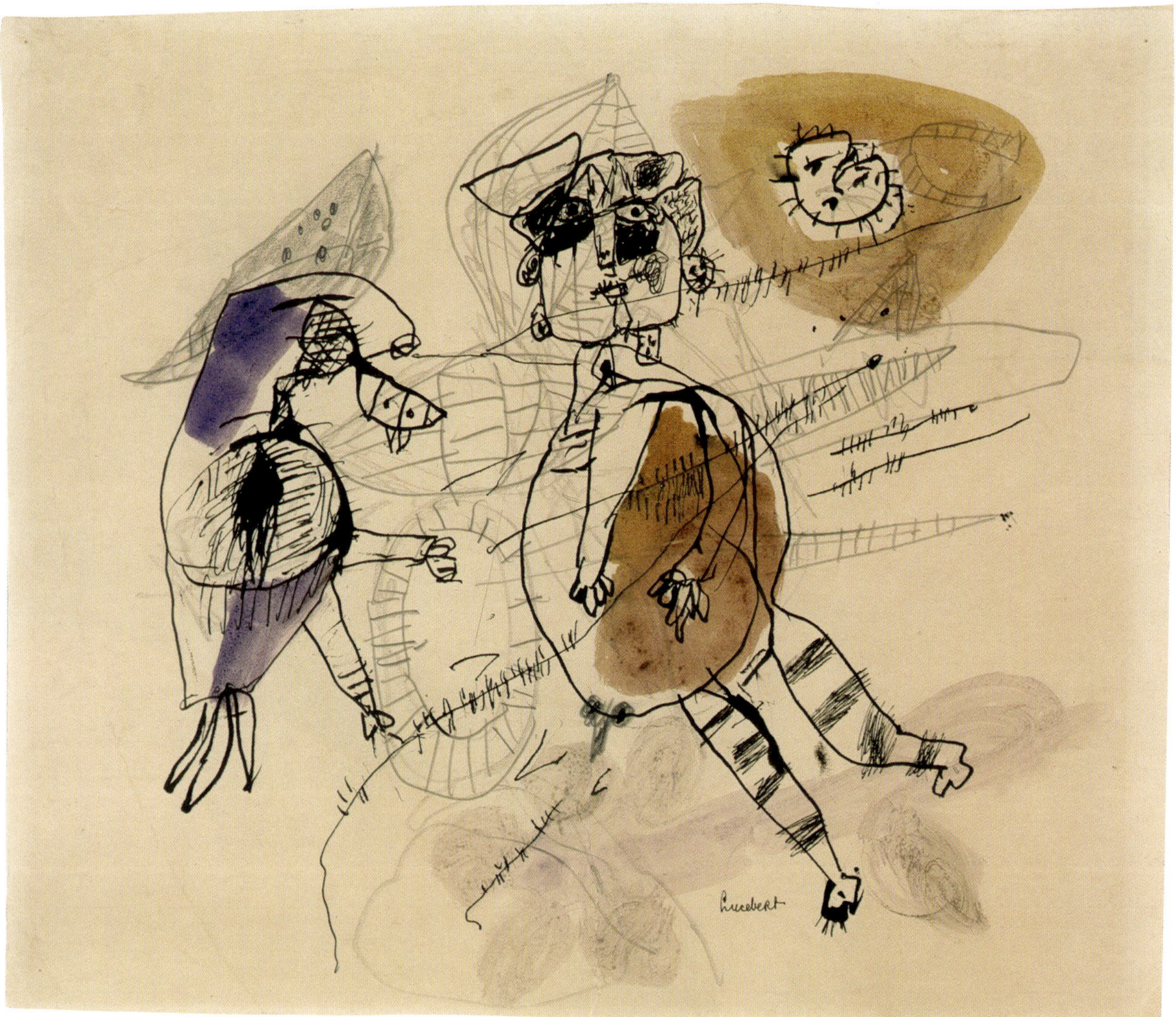

96 Lucebert
Zwevende Boer, 1951–52
Farmer floating in the air

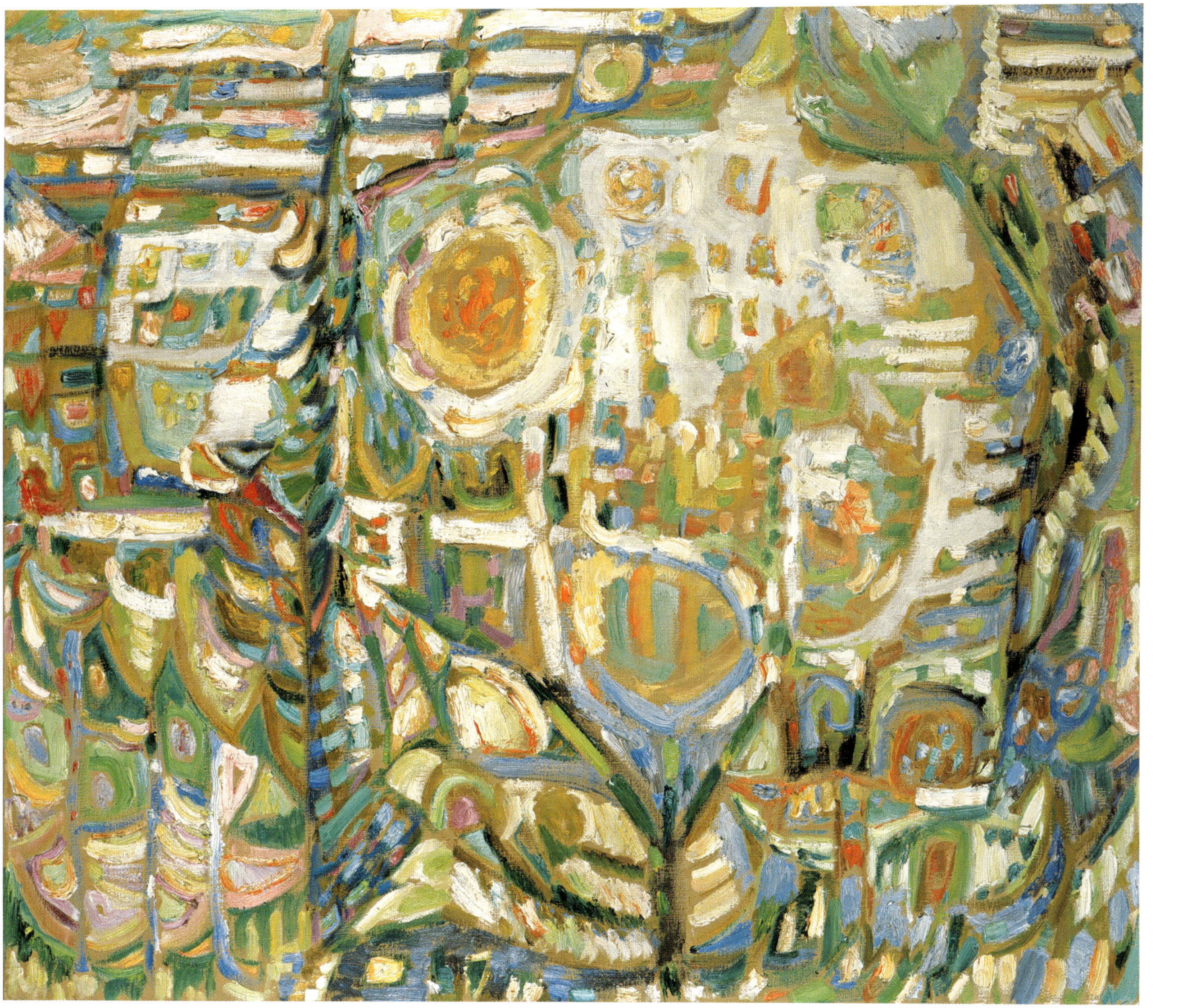

105 Erik Ortvad
Vegetation, 1948

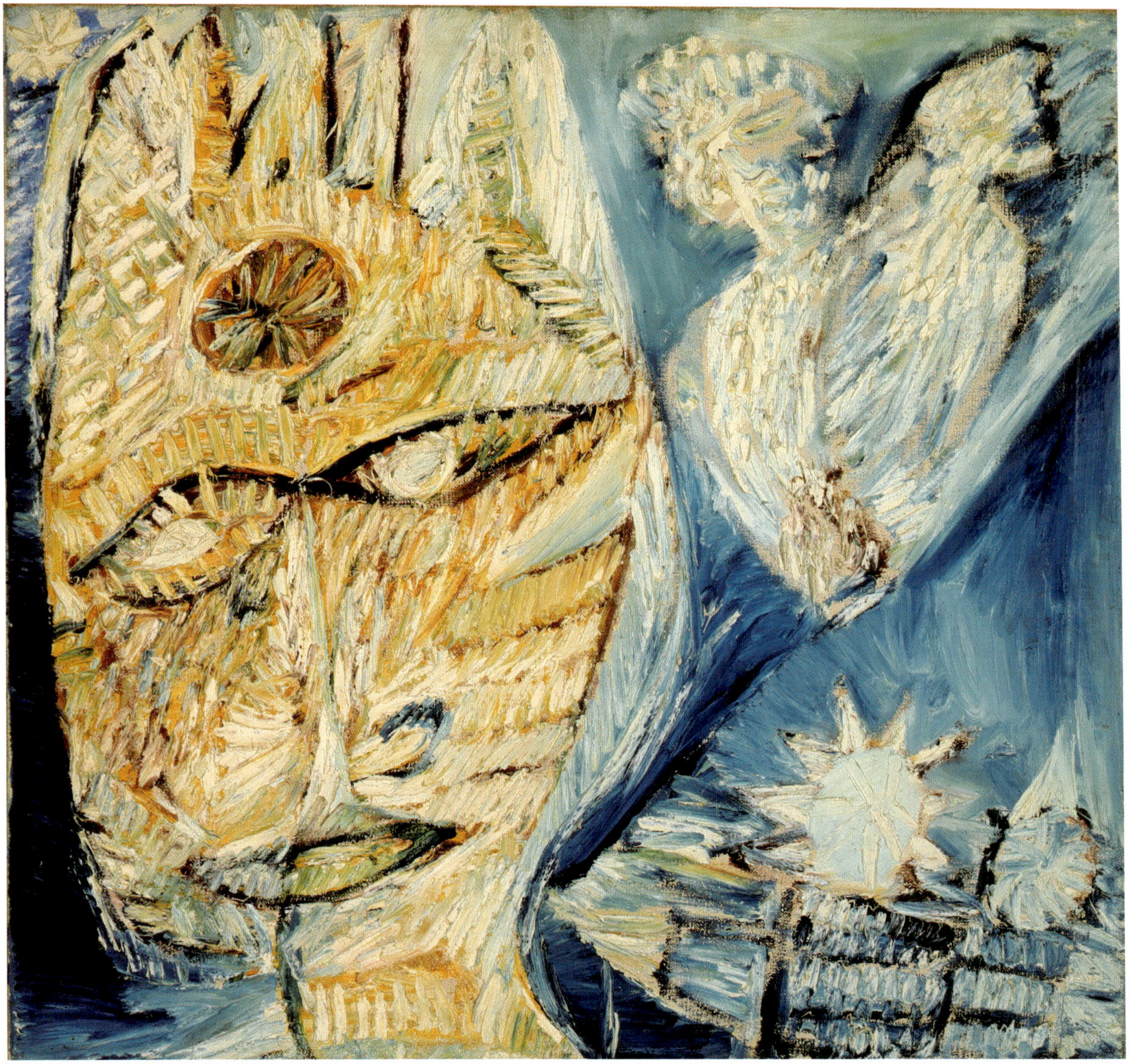

107 Carl-Henning Pedersen
Drømmen, 1947
The dream

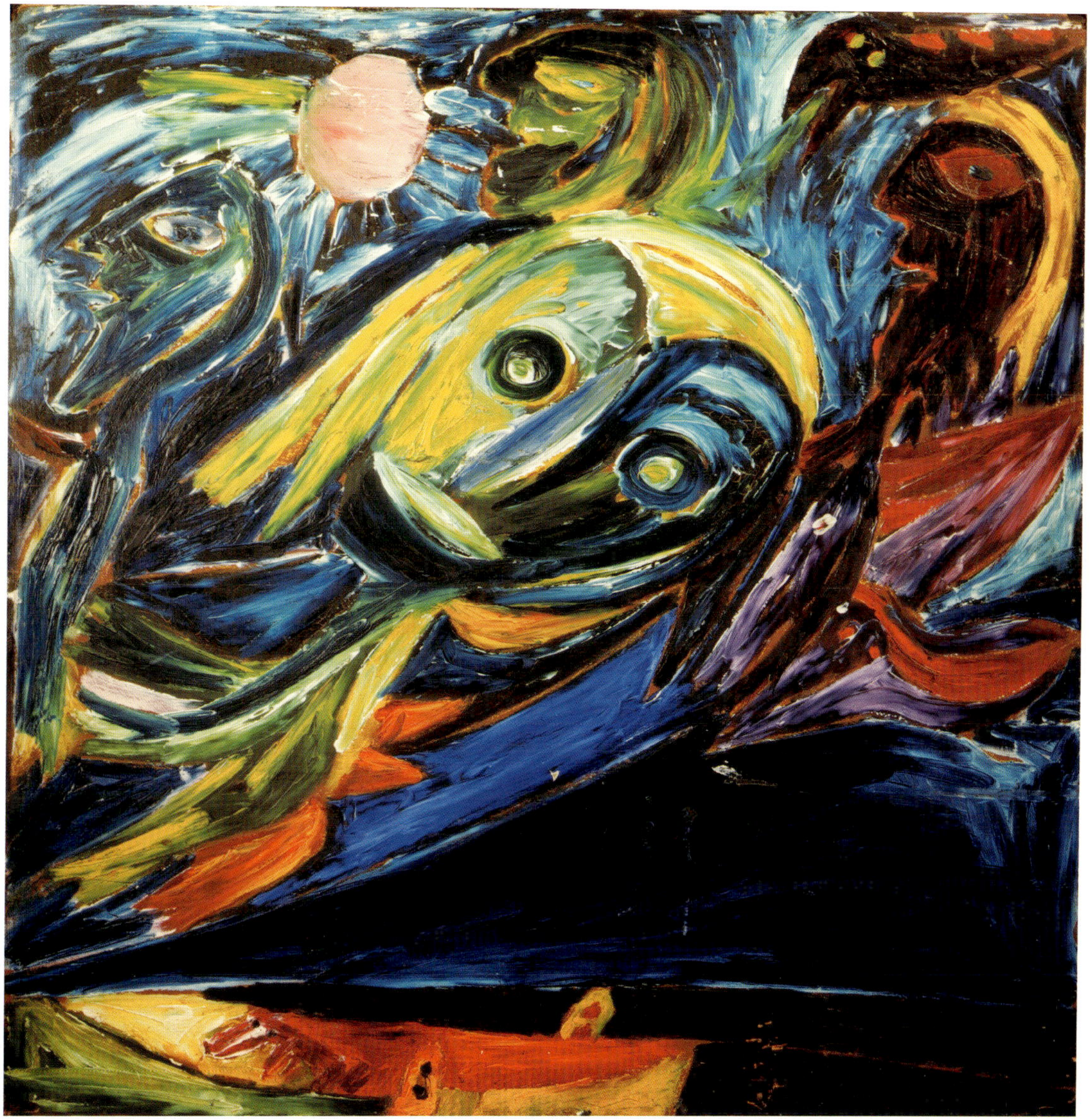

106 Carl-Henning Pedersen
Lyserød sol, 1942
Pink sun

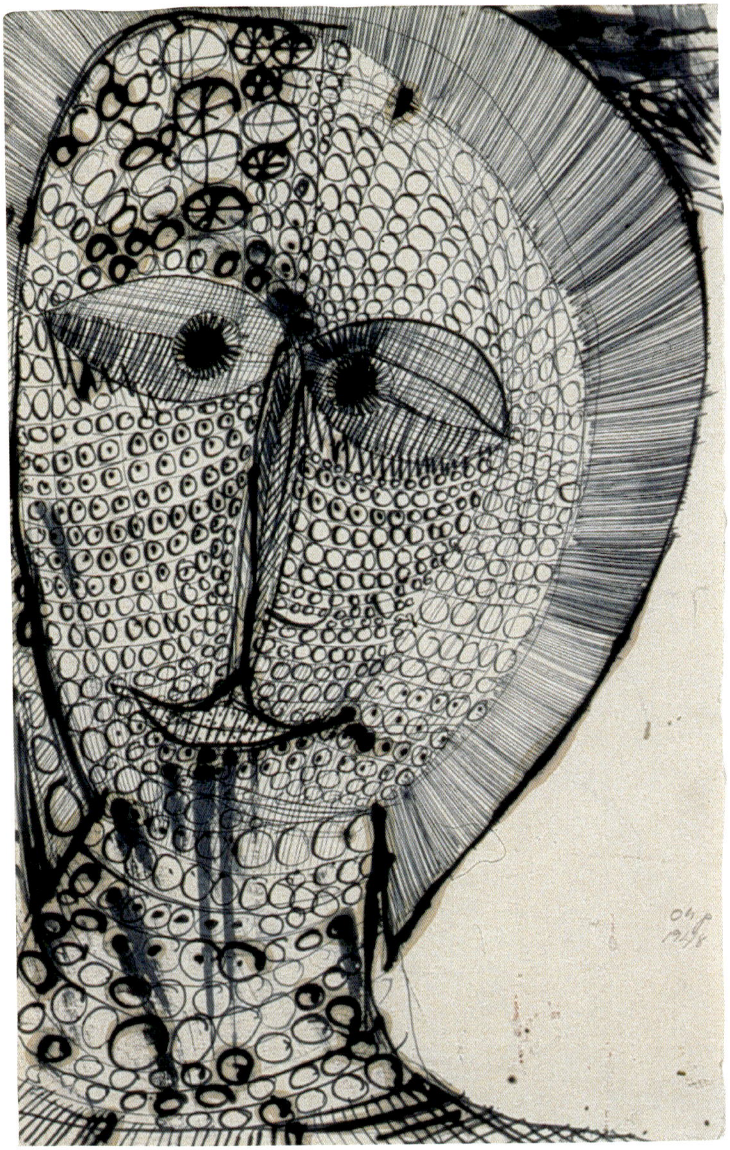

112 Carl-Henning Pedersen
Opretholderen, 1953
The upholder
from the series *Fantasifugle*, 1948–54
Birds of fantasy

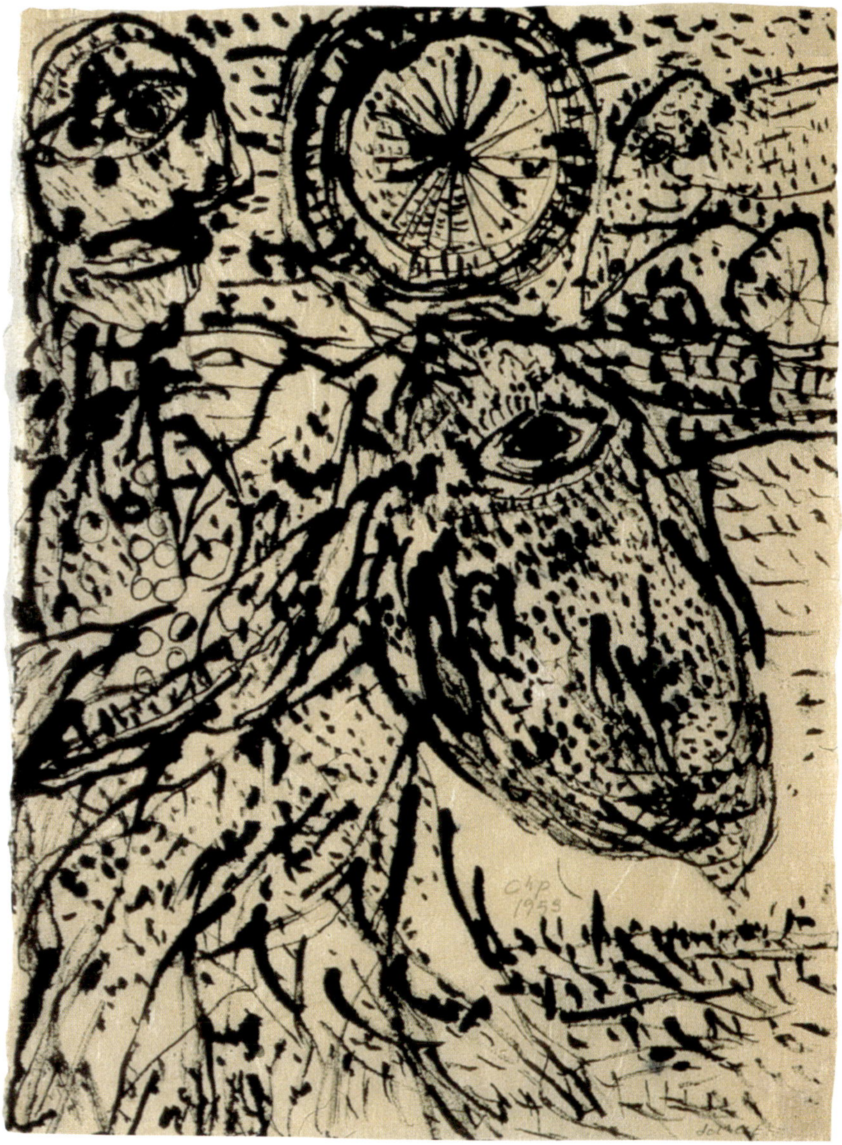

109 Carl-Henning Pedersen
De fjærne bjerge, 1949
Distant mountains
from the series *Fantasifugle*, 1948–54
Birds of fantasy

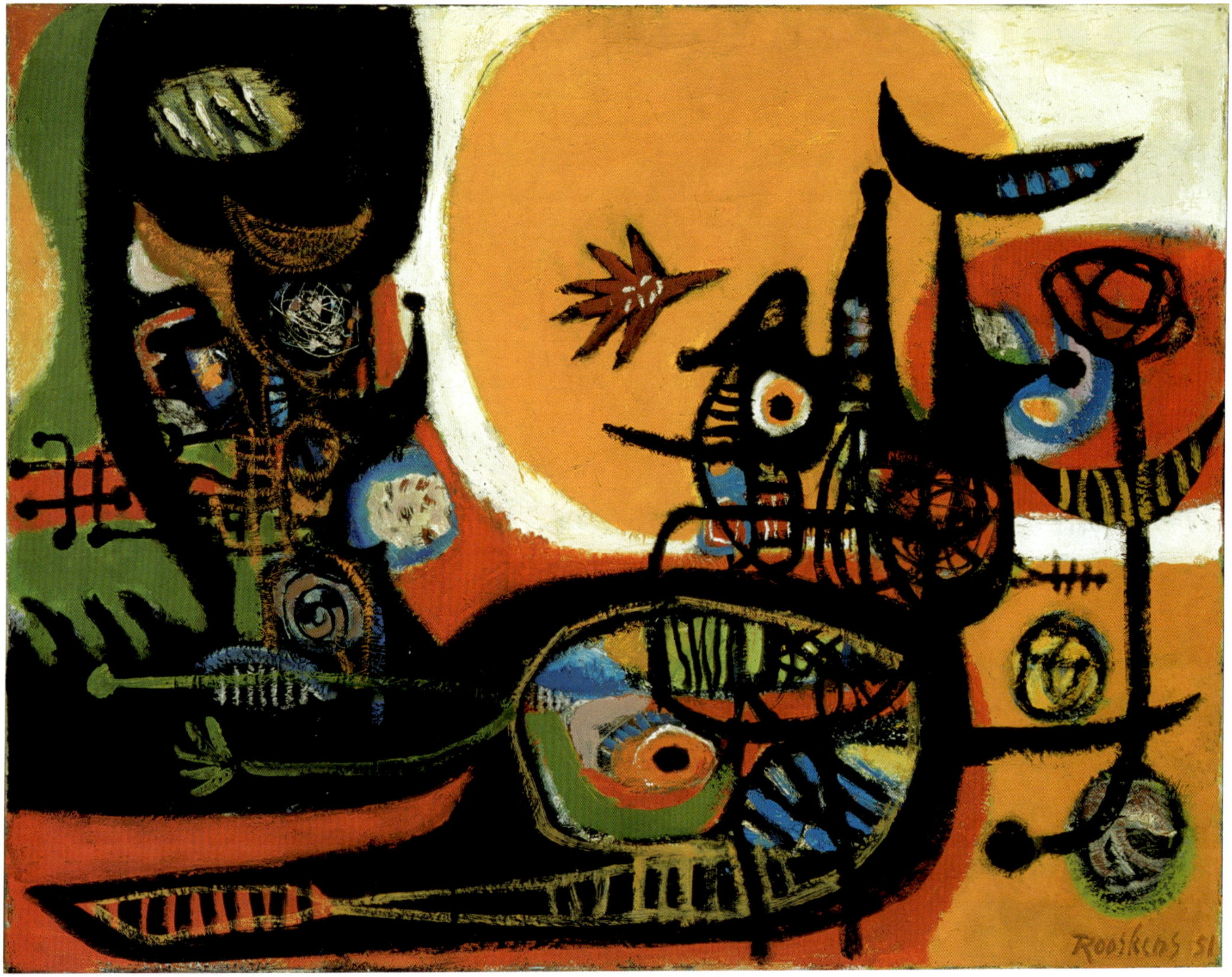

115 Anton Rooskens
Vliegende eg, 1951
Flying harrow

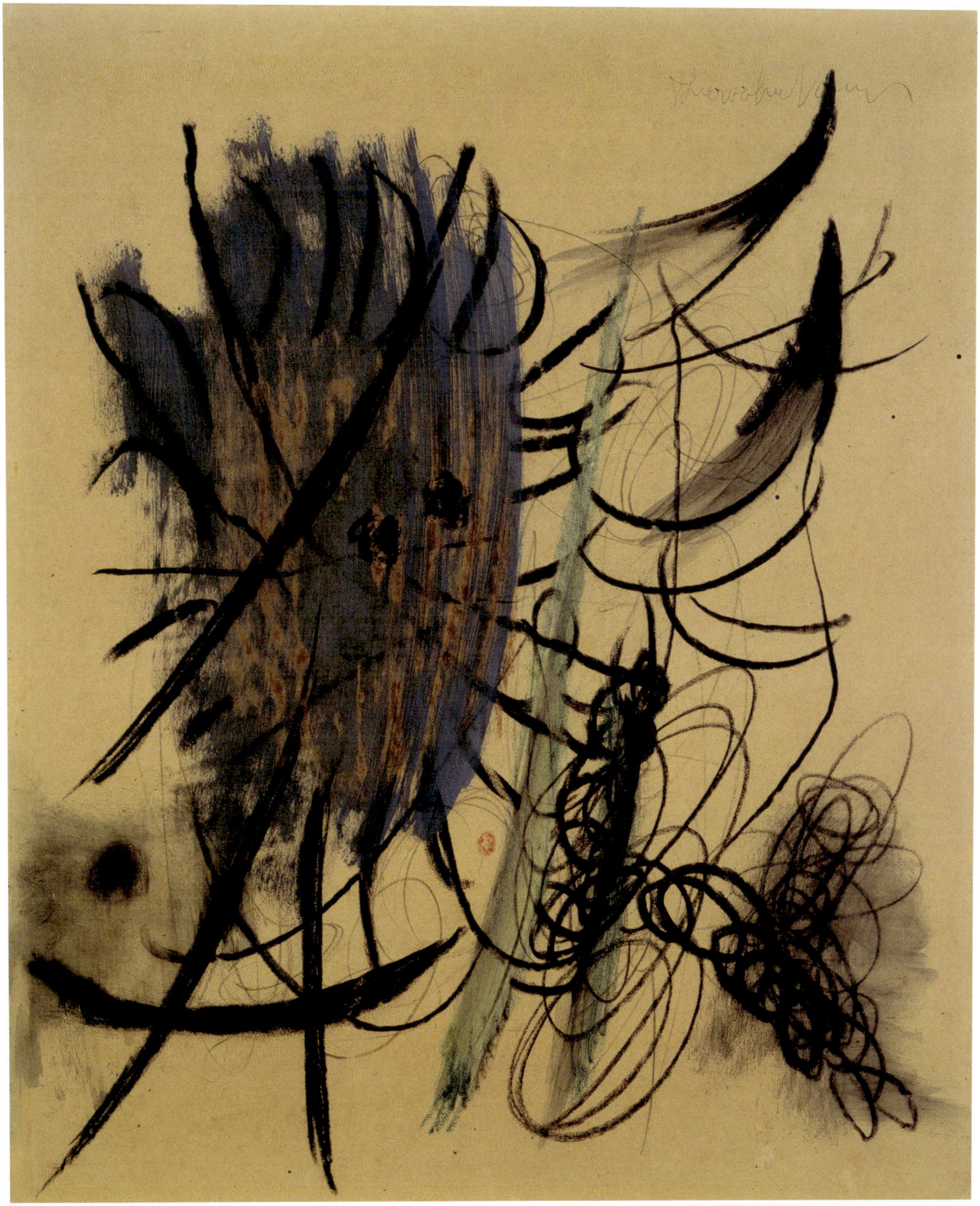

117 Theo Wolvecamp
Composition, 1949

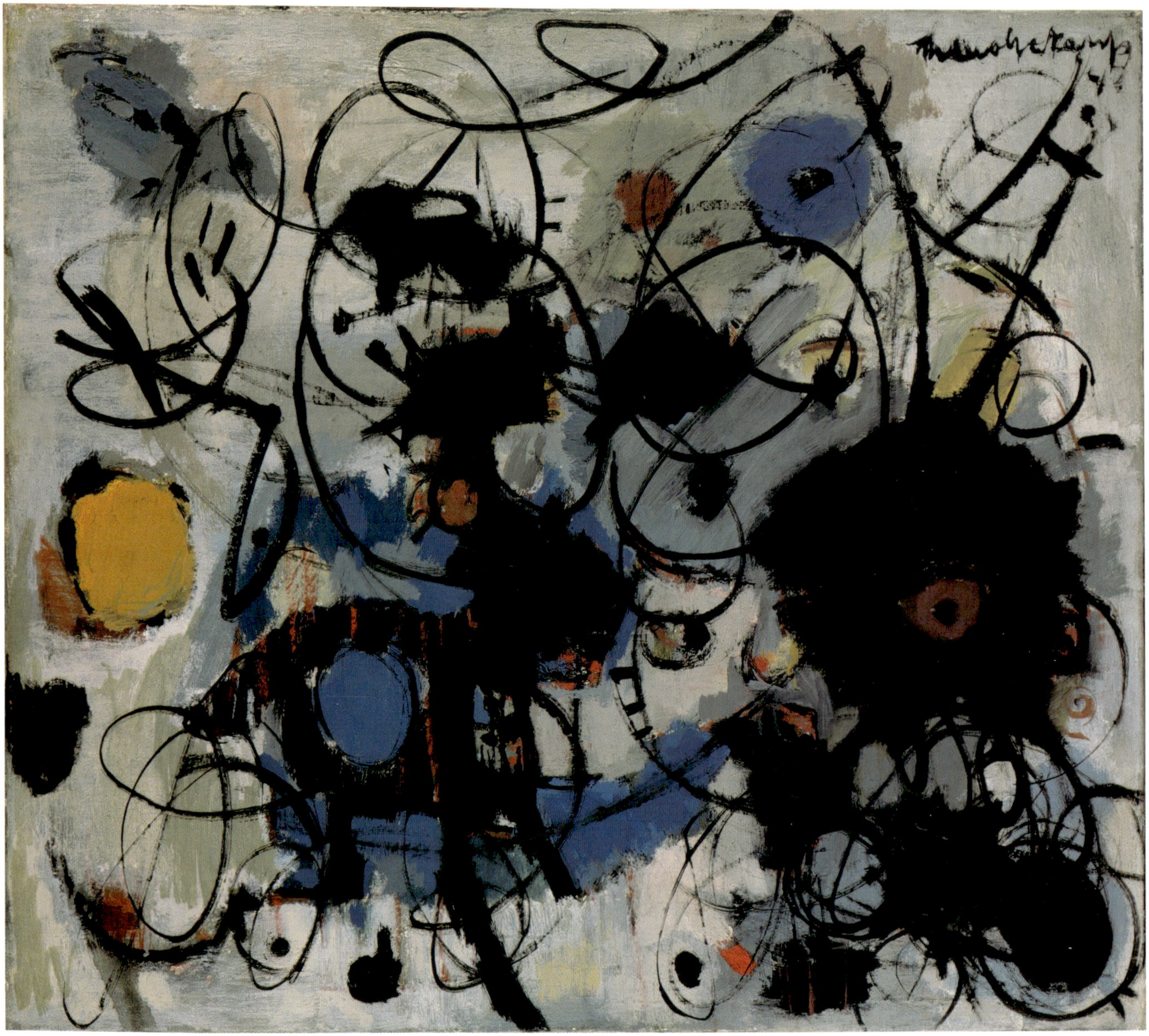

118 Theo Wolvecamp
Explosie, 1949
Explosion

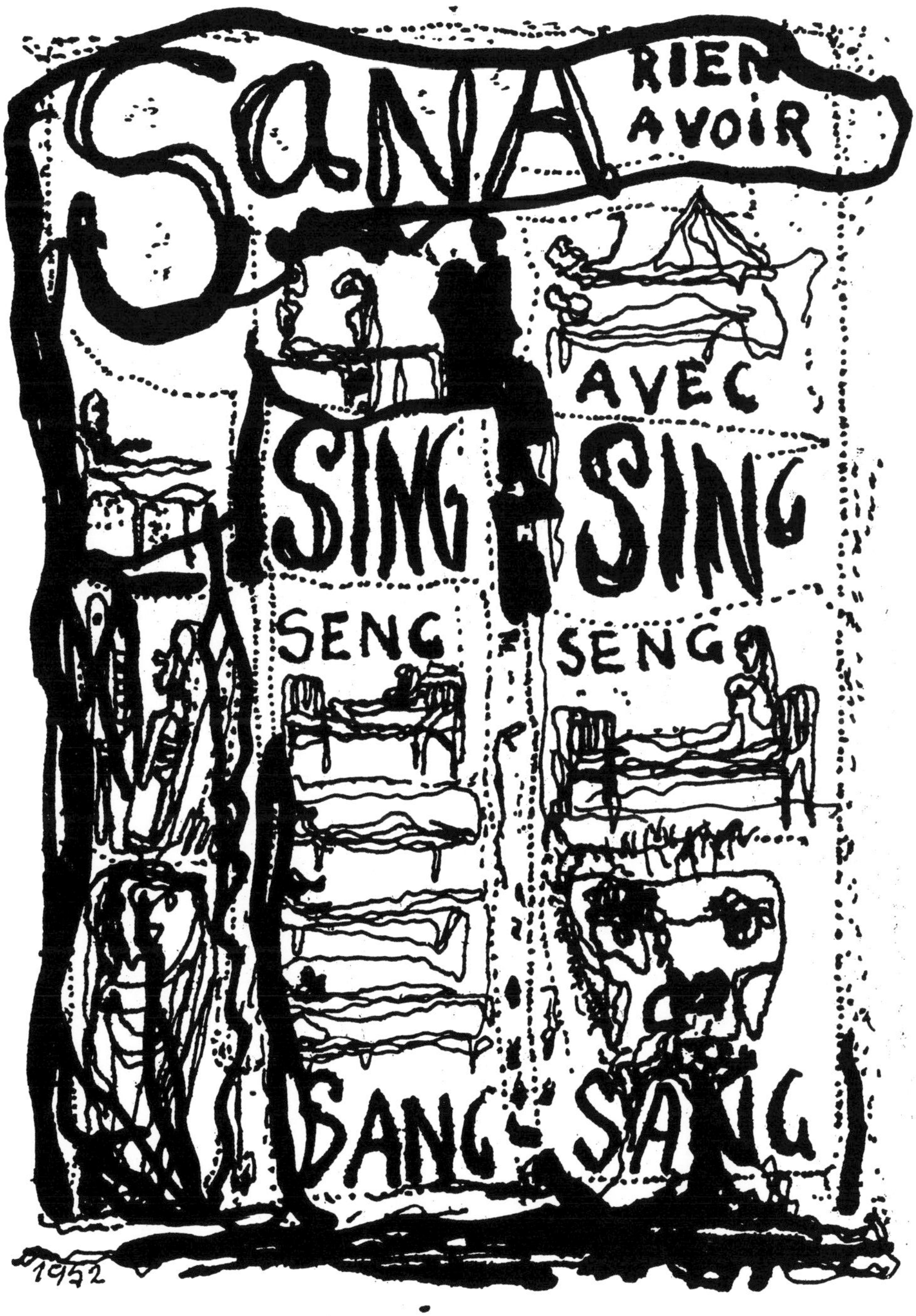

136 Christian Dotremont and Asger Jorn
Untitled drawing, 1952
page from *La chevelure des choses*, 1961
The hair-do of things

137 *Les Artistes Libres*, 1950
Artists' books
Covers:
(left to right, top to bottom)
Pierre Alechinsky; Else Alfelt; Karel Appel; Jean-Michel Atlan; Ejler Bille
Constant; Corneille; Jacques Doucet; Sonja Ferlov; Stephen Gilbert
Svavar Gudnason; Henry Heerup; Egill Jacobsen; Asger Jorn; Carl-Henning Pedersen

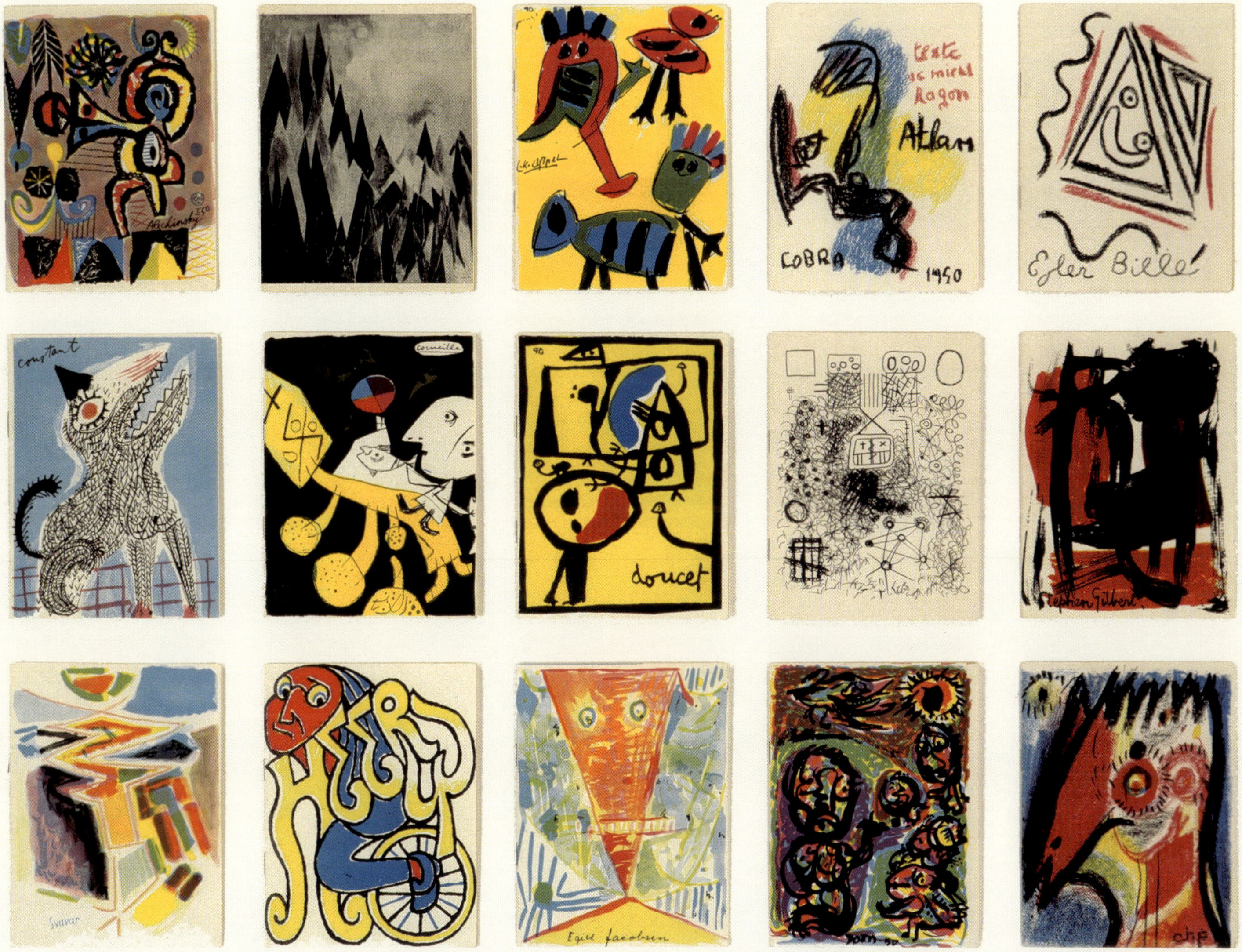
texte de michel Ragon
Atlan
COBRA
1950
Ejler Bille
constant
corneille
doucet
Stephen Gilbert
Svavar
Egill Jacobsen
chp

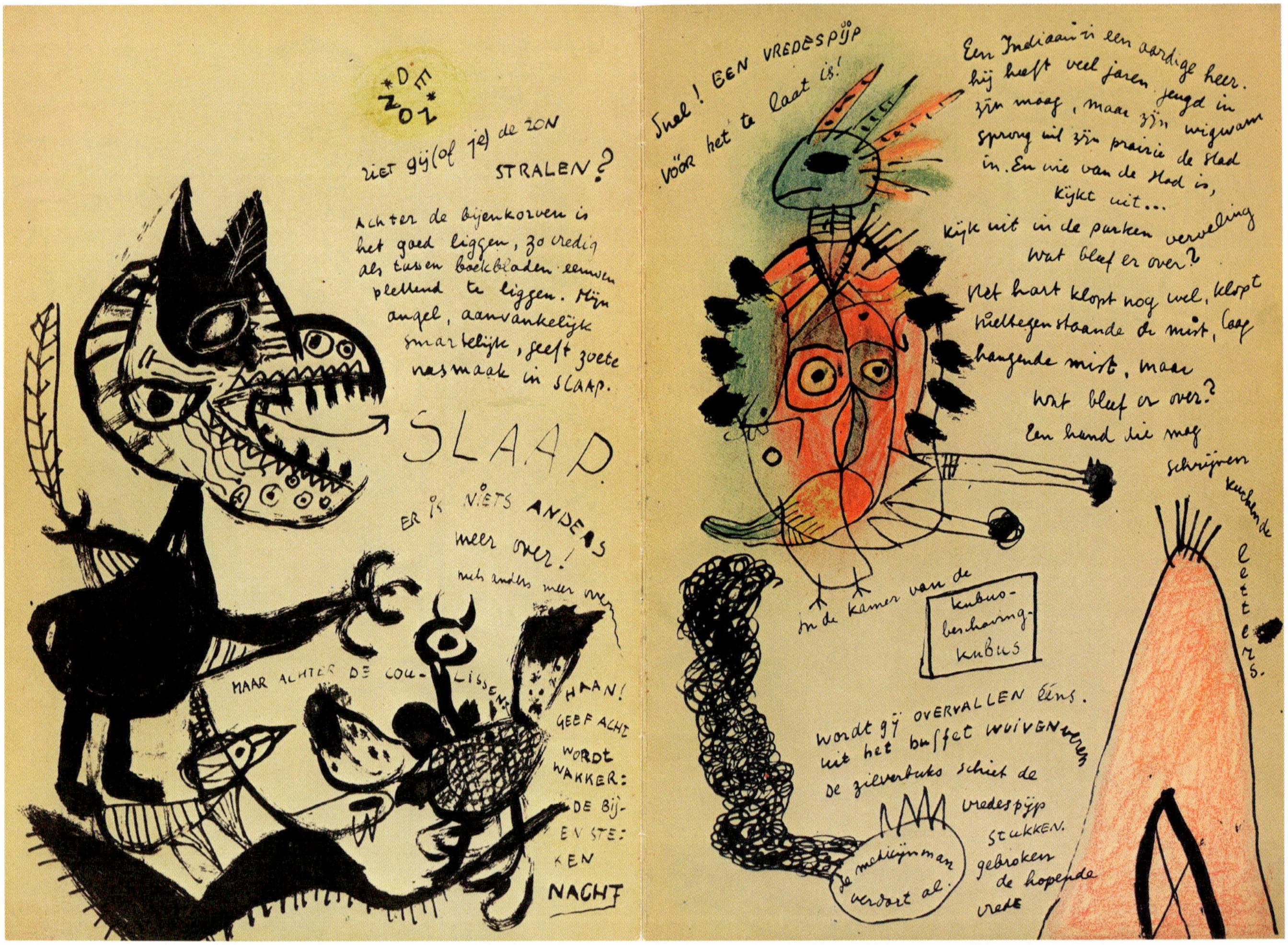

135 Constant and Gerrit Kouwenaar
Two spreads from *Goede Morgen Haan*, 1949
Good morning cockerel

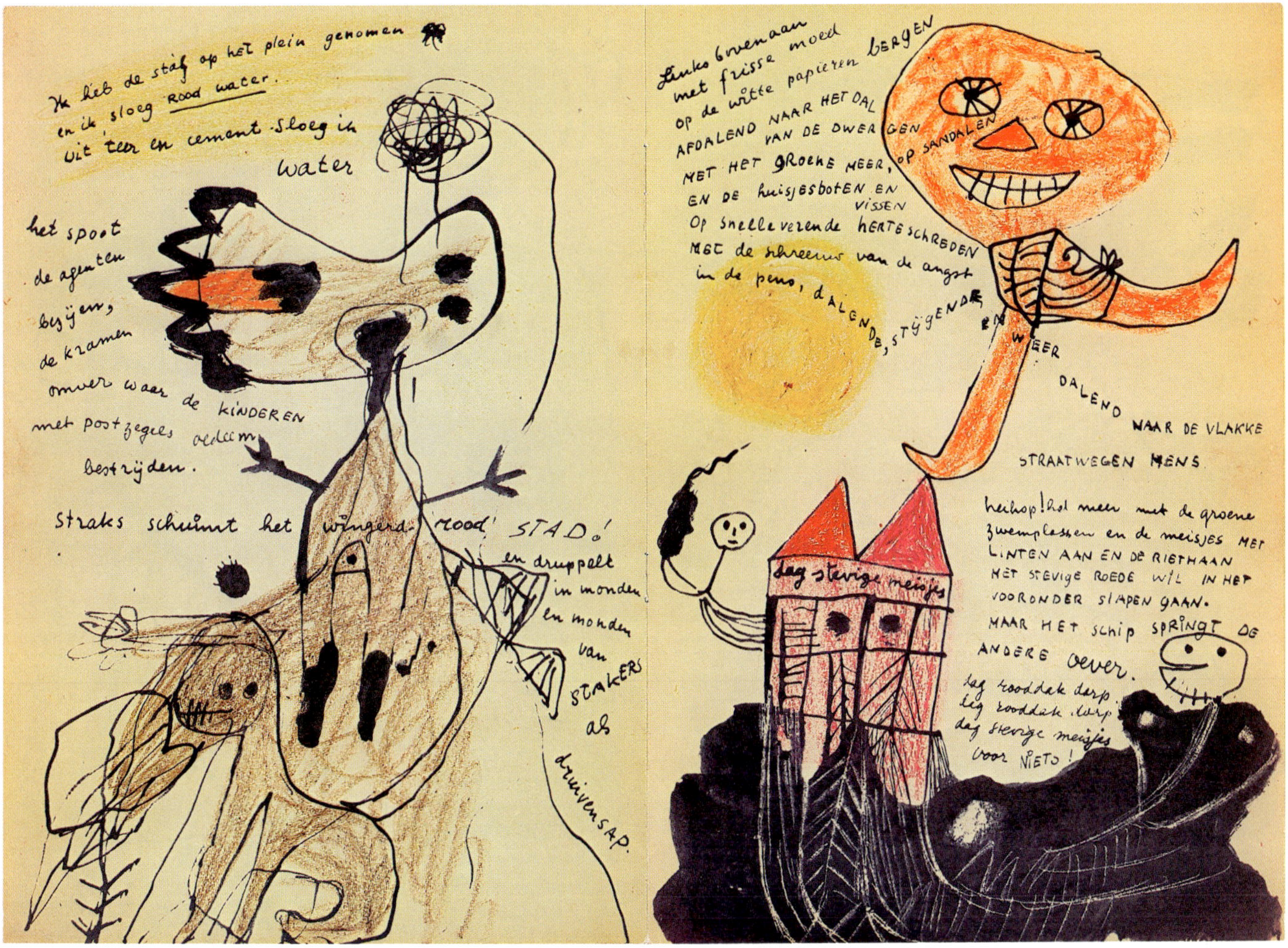
Ik heb de staf op het plein genomen
en ik sloeg rood water
uit teer en cement. Sloeg in
water
het spoot
de agenten
bijeen,
de kramen
omver waar de KINDEREN
met postzegels oedeem
bestrijden.
straks schuimt het wingerd-rood STAD!
en druppelt
in monden
en monden
van
STAKERS
als
druivensap.
Links bovenaan
met frisse moed
op de witte papieren BERGEN
AFDALEND NAAR HET DAL
VAN DE DWERGEN
MET HET GROENE MEER, OP SANDALEN
EN DE huisjesboten EN
VISSEN
Op snelleverende HERTESCHREDEN
MET de schreeuw van de angst
in de pens, DALENDE, STIJGENDE
EN WEER
DALEND NAAR DE VLAKKE
STRAATWEGEN MENS.
dag stevige meisjes
heihop! hol meer met de groene
zwemplassen en de meisjes MET
LINTEN AAN EN DE RIETHAAN
HET STEVIGE ROEDE WIL IN HET
VOORONDER SLAPEN GAAN.
MAAR HET SCHIP SPRINGT DE
ANDERE OEVER.
dag rooddak dorp!
dag rooddak dorp!
dag stevige meisjes
voor NIETO!

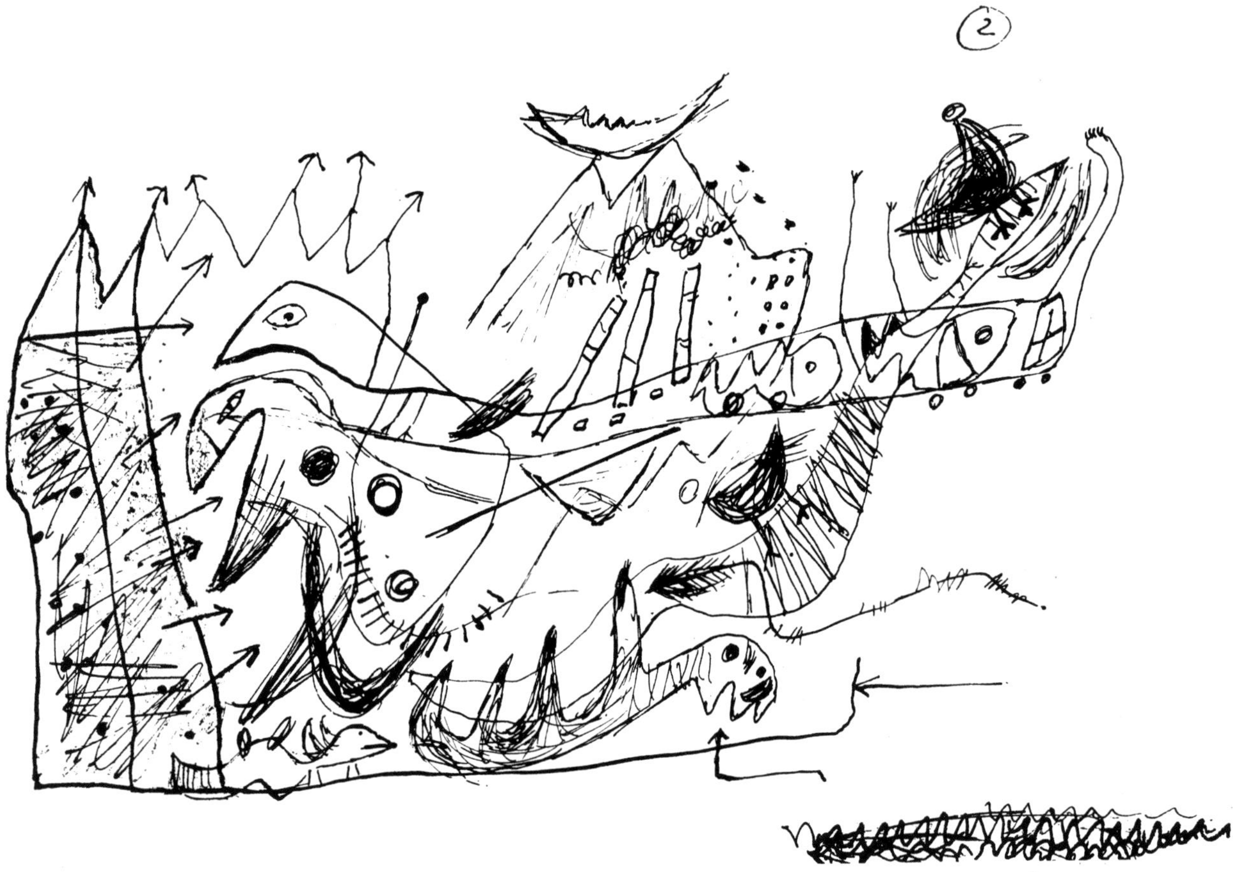

138 Christian Dotremont and Corneille
page from *Les jambages au cou*, 1966 (from 1949 maquette)
Downstrokes to the neck

Artists' Biographies

Peter Shield

The best source in English for further information on individual artists is Jean-Clarence Lambert's *Cobra* (see bibliography).

Pierre Alechinsky (Belgium, b. 1927)
Alechinsky studied book illustration and typography in Brussels (1944–48) and became a painter, exhibiting first in 1947. In March 1949, at *The Means and the End* exhibition in Brussels, he discovered Cobra and became involved in its organization, helping Christian Dotremont with the reviews and the co-ordination of exhibitions. His newly established studio co-operative – *Les Ateliers du Marais* – in a rundown Brussels building became the International Cobra Research Centre. A visit to Copenhagen in the winter of 1950 and the experience of both the cultural life and a retrospective of Carl-Henning Pedersen's work made a big impact on him. He organized the Cobra exhibition in Liège in 1951, which marked the end of Cobra. Immediately afterwards he obtained a grant to study graphic techniques in Paris at S.W. Hayter's Studio 17. Since then, he has participated in many collaborative enterprises, for example, with Karel Appel, Dotremont and Asger Jorn. He was given a retrospective exhibition in Paris in 1998 and is represented in major collections worldwide.

Else Alfelt (Denmark, 1910–74)
Together with her husband Carl-Henning Pedersen, Alfelt became a member of the Harvest Group (1942–49) and consequently of Cobra. Her type of crystalline Expressionism with its subject matter of mountains and natural phenomena, although spontaneous in execution, was somewhat removed from central Cobra preoccupations, but she took part in the 1949 Amsterdam exhibition and a couple of smaller Cobra shows, as well the 1949 Bregnerød Cobra congress. Whilst her subject matter remained the same throughout her life, her technique became looser, and she also made large mosaic murals.

Karel Appel (Holland, b. 1921)
Appel attended the Dutch Academy of Fine Arts (1940–43), and, in 1946, met Corneille, with whom he exhibited in the following year. The two then went to Paris where they saw recent works by Dubuffet and, in another exhibition, works by the mentally ill. On returning to Amsterdam, they encountered Constant and, in mid-1948, the three of them formed the Dutch Experimental Group, although Appel had already written a manifesto attacking Constant's theories. In 1949, his mural *Questioning children* for the canteen of Amsterdam Town Hall created such outrage that it was covered up for a decade. In late 1950, together with Corneille, he set up his studio by a tannery in Paris. He was a major participant in the large Cobra exhibitions in Amsterdam in 1949 and Liège in 1951 and several other Cobra manifestations. In 1954, he was awarded a UNESCO Prize at the Venice Biennale and also had his first American solo show. He is represented in most major public collections worldwide.

Jean-Michel Atlan (France, 1913–60)
Born in Algeria of Berber-Jewish stock, Atlan moved to Paris in 1930 to study philosophy and became engaged in student politics. He wrote experimental poetry and became a painter in 1941. His Resistance activity and Jewish origin resulted in arrest by the occupying Germans in 1942; he saved his life by simulating madness and was confined to the Saint-Anne psychiatric hospital. In 1944–47, he had several exhibitions in Paris and, after meeting Jorn in 1946, also exhibited in Copenhagen in 1948 and 1949. Atlan was active in the French section of the Surrealist Revolutionary Group and, when that collapsed, he supported the Cobra group, allowing his studio to become a rendezvous for like-minded artists. He developed a considerable artistic reputation in the decade before his death.

Ejler Bille (Denmark, b. 1910)
Bille was a founder member in 1934 of the Line, the Copenhagen group of 'abstract surrealists' that metamorphosed into the Harvest Group in the years 1938–45. He was one of the first to take up the mask motif after it was introduced to the group by Egill Jacobsen, and he developed an overall style where masks and animals emerge from coloured fields, which influenced Jorn, amongst others. His writings on the political significance of art were also influential and a couple of his articles were used in the *Cobra* publications. A retrospective selection of his works was included in the 1949 Amsterdam exhibition. Although highly regarded in Denmark, he has never made an international breakthrough.

Hugo Claus (Belgium, b. 1929)
A Flemish poet, playwright and novelist of considerable stature, Claus came into contact with members of the Cobra group in Brussels in 1949 and a self-illustrated poem appeared in *Cobra* 6 as well as a dramatic dialogue in *Cobra* 7. In late 1950, he co-operated with Karel Appel on an illustrated book, *The happy and unforeseen week* (cat. 134). His novel *The Sorrow of Belgium*, 1983 and several of his other works have been translated into English.

Constant (Constant Nieuwenhuis, Holland, b. 1920)

After a frustrating art education during the Second World War, Constant encountered Asger Jorn at a Joan Miró exhibition in Paris in 1946 and became aware of the free, expressive style developed by the Danes during the War. Jorn advised him to form a similar group and when, in the winter of 1947–48, he became acquainted with Karel Appel and Corneille, the possibility crystallized. The Dutch Experimental Group was formed in mid-1948, with a manifesto by Constant laying the foundation for the concept of 'experimental art' with no formal boundaries. He took part in all the major Cobra manifestations, issuing another powerful manifesto for the first Cobra exhibition in 1949 in Amsterdam. He moved to Paris in late 1950, but returned to Amsterdam shortly afterwards. After Cobra, he explored spatial problems with the architect Aldo van Eyck before turning to radical architecture with his *New Babylon*, 1959–74, a vast project for an ideal city. He was also associated with the Situationists and later the Provo groups in Amsterdam. He has since returned to painting and was a major participant in the 2002 *Documenta* exhibition in Kassel, Germany.

Corneille (Cornelis van Beverloo, Holland, b. 1922)

Born in Liège of Dutch parents, Corneille studied drawing at the State Academy in Amsterdam, where he became friends with Karel Appel. On a visit to Hungary in 1947 he came into contact with collections of German Expressionism and French Surrealism. After a trip to Paris together, he and Appel contacted Constant, and the three exhibited together in early 1948. A co-founder of both the Dutch Experimental Group and Cobra, Corneille was largely responsible for the organization of the 1949 Amsterdam exhibition and the editing of *Cobra* 4. In 1949, he made a series of experimental drawings with colour and text with Christian Dotremont. Together with Appel, he settled in Paris in late 1950. In the summer of 1951, he stayed and worked with Carl-Henning Pedersen in Denmark. He has made many study trips to Africa and South America. In 1956, he won the Guggenheim Prize and he represented Holland at the 1962 Venice *Biennale*. A prolific graphic artist, he is also an accomplished photographer.

Christian Dotremont (Belgium, 1922–79)

Born into a strict Roman Catholic family, the poet Christian Dotremont sought out the Belgian Surrealist movement during the Second World War, but became estranged from mainstream Surrealism when André Breton proclaimed a split with Communism in 1946. In 1947, he founded the Surrealist Revolutionary Group and held a definitive conference in Brussels, also attended by Asger Jorn. A second conference in Paris in November 1948, designed to clear up differences between French and Belgian adherents, failed, and Dotremont, together with Karel Appel, Constant, Corneille, Jorn and Joseph Noiret, formed a new group with the widest possible remit for experimentation outside formal boundaries in art and literature. Dotremont came up with the acronym 'Cobra' to suggest the nationalities of the founders. He became editor-in-chief of the *Cobra* magazine and took his duties very seriously. This led him into critical debate with Constant and Jorn about the nature of experimentation and its political uses. He participated in a number of collaborative books with Cobra artists and the *peinture-mots* series of oil paintings (1948–49) with Jorn. He was diagnosed with tuberculosis in mid-1951 whilst on a visit to Denmark, and admitted to the same sanatorium (and the same ward) as Jorn. After the collapse of Cobra, he vigorously promoted the idea of a continued Cobra spirit, making collaborative works with many artists and developing a kind of calligraphic painting he called the *logogramme*.

Jacques Doucet (France, 1924–94)

During the Second World War, Doucet encountered the avant-garde poet Max Jacob, who encouraged him to paint and study. He was invited to Budapest to exhibit in 1947 and there met Corneille, so making contact with the Dutch Experimental Group. He contributed a cover for the magazine *Reflex* 2. His work was included in both the 1949 Amsterdam and the 1951 Liège Cobra exhibitions. After Cobra, he exhibited regularly at Paris exhibitions such as *Le Salon de Mai* and *Le Salon d'Octobre*.

William Gear (Scotland, 1915–97)

After art education in Edinburgh, Gear won a travelling scholarship in 1937–38 with which he visited Italy and studied briefly with the French painter Fernand Léger in Paris. During his Second World War service (1940–47), he continued to paint while stationed in Italy and Germany. He moved to Paris in 1947 and came into contact with Constant and the circle around Jean-Michel Atlan's studio, and was invited to exhibit at the 1949 Amsterdam Cobra exhibition. He returned to Britain in 1950 and pursued parallel careers as a painter, gallery curator and later art education administrator. In 1951, his award of a Festival of Britain purchase prize provoked adverse press comment and questions in Parliament.

Stephen Gilbert (Scotland, b. 1910)

Gilbert studied painting at the Slade in London and spent the Second World War years in Dublin before settling in Paris in 1945. Asger Jorn saw his works at an open exhibition there and concluded that they had something in common. Gilbert was drawn into the Cobra group, attending the Bregnerød congress and taking part in the first Cobra exhibition in Amsterdam in 1949. He later became associated with Constant in formal experiments with painting and architecture and then turned to metal sculpture.

Henry Heerup (Denmark, 1907–93)

Although he studied at the Danish Academy, Heerup was mainly self-taught, both as a painter and sculptor. He took his inspiration from Romanesque imagery and folk art, especially from

Scandinavian sources. He preferred to exhibit with Danish groups as a guest but became a member of the Harvest Group (1941–48). Although he saw Cobra only as an opportunity to exhibit, his simple stone sculptures appealed to Constant and Corneille and he was invited to show with the group both in Amsterdam in 1949 and Liège in 1951. His witty assemblages of household articles have given him a special place in Danish art. He was also a Naive painter and graphic artist.

The Imaginist Group (Imaginisterna) (Sweden: C.O. Hultén (b. 1916), Anders Österlin (b. 1926), Max-Walter Svanberg (1912–94))

This loose Surrealist grouping existed in Malmö, Sweden, for approximately a decade from 1946. Asger Jorn encountered Hultén just after the Second World War and acquainted him with the work and ideas of the Harvest Group. When Christian Dotremont visited Denmark in late 1948, he crossed the Sound to enlist the Imaginist Group in Cobra. However, participation was only sporadic. Hultén and Österlin took part in the collaborative decoration at the Bregnerød congress in August 1949, and Hultén, Österlin and Svanberg made a collaborative lithograph with Appel, Constant and Corneille when they visited Sweden in late 1949. Österlin exhibited at both the Cobra exhibitions in Amsterdam in 1949 and Liège in 1951.

Egill Jacobsen (Denmark, 1910–98)

Largely self-taught as a painter, Jacobsen first visited Paris in 1935 and saw works by all of the leading modern artists there, including the mask-influenced portraits of Pablo Picasso. Back in Copenhagen the following winter, inspired by these and other influences (Oceanic art, Paul Klee, Danish folk art), he began to create pictures of great vitality based on the motif of the mask. In 1937, he became a member of the Line group at the same time as Asger Jorn and Carl-Henning Pedersen, and then a member of the Harvest Group (1938–42), before leaving for *Grønningen*, a more eclectic group. During the Second War War, he lived in the countryside outside Copenhagen and was a member of the Communist resistance. He wrote articles for the magazine *Helhesten* and signed the influential 1945 Harvest manifesto. His interest in Cobra was passive, and he took part in only one minor exhibition, but the influence of his earlier works on other Cobra artists was profound. He continued to develop variations on the mask motif for the rest of his life.

Asger Jorn (Denmark, 1914–73)

Jorn's family belonged to a strict Protestant sect and he did not come into contact with other ideas until his late teens. Trained as a high school teacher and active in Communist agitation, he decided to became a painter. After graduating, he bought a cheap motorcycle and, in 1936, drove to Paris to study with Wassily Kandinsky. As this was not possible, he enrolled in Fernand Léger's academy, where he spent a year. On his return to Copenhagen, he first joined the Line and then the Harvest Group (1942–48), becoming one of its leading theorists on experimentation and primitive expression. During the Second World War he was a major force behind the magazine *Helhesten* and took part in Resistance activities. As soon as the War was over, he began to travel all over Europe and soon had a network of friends in the art-world extending from Lapland to southern France. He met Constant in 1946, Christian Dotremont in 1947 and Karel Appel and Corneille in 1948 and, sharing a dissatisfaction with the debates around dogma in the Surrealist Revolutionary Group, to which they had all become attached, they became the founding members of Cobra. Jorn organized the first Cobra international congress in Bregnerød, but, because of his involvement with Constant's wife, stayed away from the events around the first Cobra exhibition (although his works were exhibited) and the second congress in Amsterdam in November 1949. He contributed several texts to the *Cobra* review, emphasizing both the primitive and the social aspects of experimental art. He moved to Paris in late 1950 but, in mid-1951, he was diagnosed with tuberculosis and malnutrition and returned to Denmark, taking no further part in Cobra. After his convalescence, he resumed his involvement with European art circles, joining or assisting in the foundation of several groups, the last of which being the Situationist International (1957–61). In his later years, besides painting at his usual hectic tempo, he launched a thirty-two volume project entitled *10,000 years of Scandinavian popular art*. Only one volume was published, but the associated survey of philosophy from the point of view of the artist came out in 1961–64 and 1980. He is one of the most important Scandinavian artists since Edvard Munch.

Gerrit Kouwenaar (Holland, b. 1923)

Kouwenaar was an important poet of the 50-ers group and the designation Kouwenaar School is sometimes used to express his influence on later Dutch writers. He is cavalier with the meaning of words, and, in one of his lines, he asserts, 'I cut the throat of a word'. He was associated with the Dutch Experimental Group in 1948–49 and made *Good morning cockerel*, 1949 (cat. 135), a small collaborative book, with Constant.

Lucebert (Lubertus van Swaanswijk, Holland, 1924–94)

In his youth, Lucebert assisted his house-painter father, and on the strength of a mural on a façade won a grant in 1940 for a term at the Amsterdam School of Decorative Art. For a time after, he squatted in houses as a tramp. In 1947, he was given his first commission to paint murals for a Franciscan monastery in return for food. He turned to poetry and became the most important poet of the 50-ers group, joining the Dutch Experimental Group in the winter of 1948–49, and playing a leading role at the opening of the 1949 Cobra exhibition in Amsterdam. One of his earliest poems was published in *Cobra* 4. From about 1950 onwards, gradually drawing and painting again became his major activity, although he never participated in exhibitions as an artist in the lifetime of Cobra.

Joseph Noiret (Belgium, b. 1927)

A poet and writer, Noiret became active in the Belgian Surrealist Revolutionary Group and then the Cobra group in 1948. He contributed several poems and articles to various Cobra publications. In Brussels in 1953, he co-founded the magazine *Phantomas* where most of his texts and poems were published. In 1962, he organized, with Christian Dotremont, the exhibition *Cobra and After (and Even Before) (Cobra et Après (et Même Avant))* in Brussels.

Erik Ortvad (Denmark, b. 1917)

Against the wishes of his parents, Ortvad became a self-taught painter associated with the artists around the Danish Line and Harvest Groups, who became known as the 'spontaneous abstract' painters. Initially a Surrealist, during the Second World War his painting developed in a more expressive direction with a distinctive flickering line and use of colour. He threw himself enthusiastically into work with the Cobra group, and, in 1948, he provided lodgings for the foreign visitors to Copenhagen and acted as their guide. After the demise of Cobra, he lost confidence in his painting and became a satirical cartoonist. He did this for a decade before settling in Sweden and returning to painting in the early 1960s.

Carl-Henning Pedersen (Denmark, b. 1913)

Born in straitened working-class circumstances, Pedersen was actively involved in several radical youth organizations. He attended the International Folk High School in Helsingør in 1933–34 and there met and married the painter Else Alfelt. He began to paint and draw, becoming a member of the Line (1937–39) and the Harvest Group (1942–50). He also collaborated on the production of the magazine *Helhesten*, contributing an influential article about medieval Danish church murals. His strong urge toward mythical representation struck a chord with Karel Appel, Constant and Corneille in Copenhagen in 1948, and a couple of years later with Pierre Alechinsky. He participated in both Cobra congresses (Bregnerød and Amsterdam, 1949) and both major Cobra exhibitions (Amsterdam, 1949 and Liège, 1951). After Cobra he travelled widely in Europe, Asia and Indonesia. His murals in the medieval cathedral of Ribe in Denmark in 1983 provoked a public debate because of his non-religious principles.

Anton Rooskens (Holland, 1906–76)

Originally a maker of both mechanical and electronic instruments, Rooskens was largely self-taught as a painter and was initially influenced by Constant Permeke and Belgian Expressionism. He met Karel Appel, Eugène Brands and Corneille in 1946, and this contact, combined with the experience of an exhibition of sculpture from New Guinea, inspired a new approach. He joined the Dutch Experimental Group in 1948 and became its treasurer, but left it after the Cobra exhibition in Amsterdam in 1949.

Raoul Ubac (Belgium, 1910–85)

Between 1928 and 1934, Ubac visited several European countries. In 1935, he made contact with the Surrealist group, contributing photographs to one of their magazines, *Le Minotaure*, and studied graphic art with S.W. Hayter in Paris. After breaking away from Surrealism, he became an artist in many media. In Savoy, France, in 1946, he discovered an unusual type of slate particularly suited to the creation of double-sided reliefs. Several of these were illustrated in *Cobra* and one was used as a basis for the cover of *Cobra* 7.

Simon Vinkenoog (Holland, b. 1928)

As a young man, Vinkenoog came into contact with all the experimental Dutch artists and poets. His only poetic contribution to Cobra was a collaboration with Corneille, but he was active in helping to publicize the group's work in the post-Cobra years, even though at one point he had criticized the Dutch Experimental Group as being a sheer repetition of Dada. He later became associated with the Beat poets and has also written about several Dutch artists.

Theo Wolvecamp (Holland, 1925–92)

Wolvecamp met Karel Appel, Constant and Corneille in 1947 when he moved to Amsterdam. He joined the Dutch Experimental Group when it was formed in 1948, exhibited at the first Cobra exhibition in Amsterdam the following year, but left the group after the notorious 'poetry evening' at the Stedelijk Museum. However, he exhibited with Cobra again at the Liège exhibition in 1951. Throughout his life, his work was characterized by a non-figurative free abstraction.

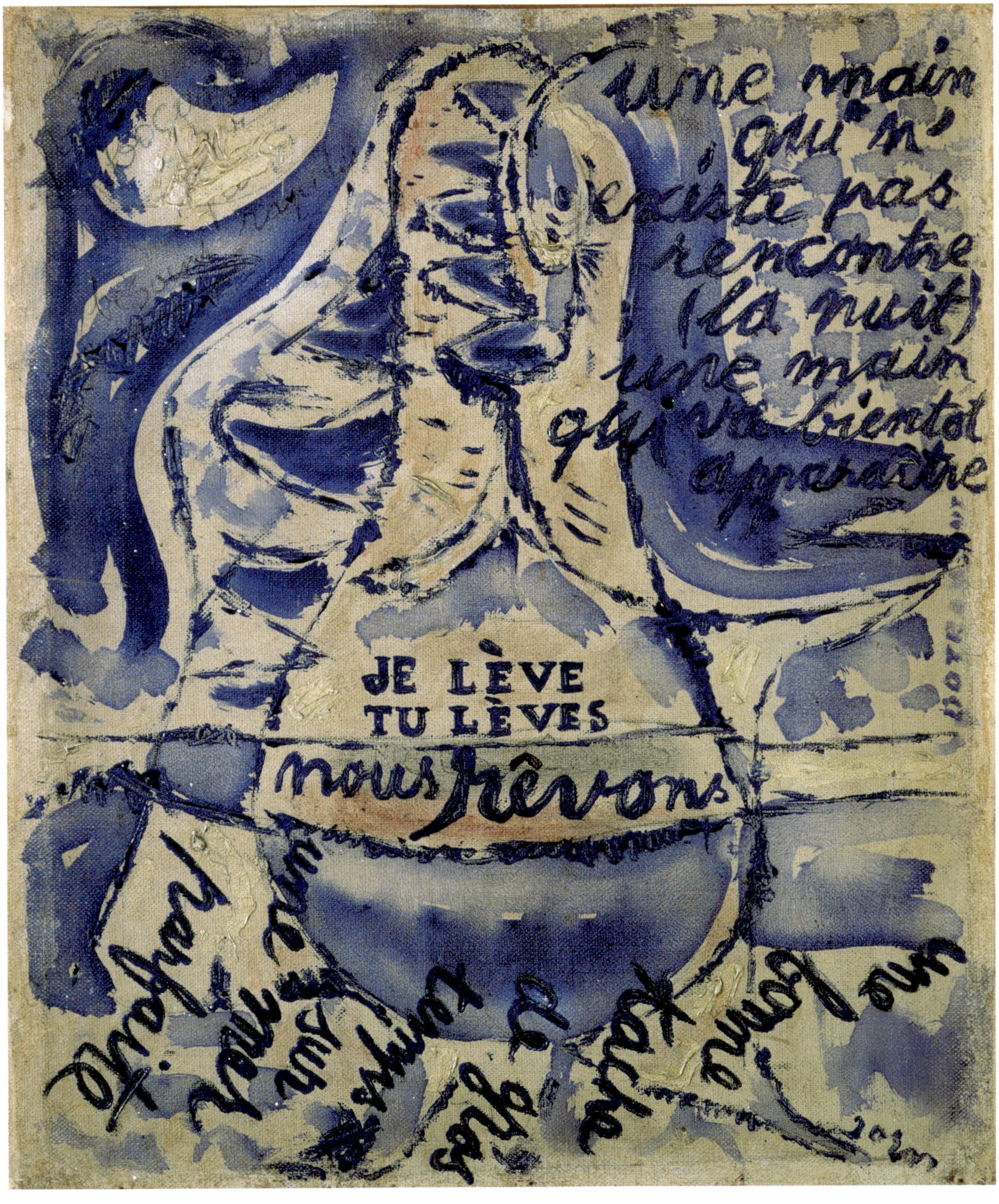

122 Christian Dotremont and Asger Jorn
Je lève, tu lèves, nous rêvons, 1948
I rise, you rise, we dream

Select Bibliography in English

Pierre Alechinsky, 'Souvenotes' in *Alechinsky. Paintings and Writings*, Pittsburgh, Museum of Art, Carnegie Institute, 1978, pp. 187–197.

Guy Atkins with the help of Troels Andersen, *Jorn in Scandinavia 1930–1953*, London, Lund Humphries, 1968.

Graham Birtwistle, *Living Art. Asger Jorn's comprehensive theory of art between Helhesten and Cobra (1946–1949)*, Utrecht, Reflex, 1986.

Graham Birtwistle, 'The Language of War Art. Constant and Picasso', in *Jong Holland* (Zwolle), vol. 7 no. 2, 1991, pp. 28–47.

Per Hovdenakk, *Danish Art 1930–50*, Copenhagen, Borgen, 1999.

Jean-Clarence Lambert, *Cobra*, New York, Abbeville Press, 1983.

Peter Shield, *Spontaneous Abstraction in Denmark and its aftermath in Cobra, 1931–1951*, unpublished doctoral thesis, The Open University, 1984.

Peter Shield, 'The Danish Ostriches', in *Jong Holland* ('s-Gravenhage), vol. 4, no. 5, 1988, pp. 21–33.

Peter Shield, 'Les Rencontres de Bregnerød. Cobra Myth and Cobra Reality', in *Jong Holland* (Rotterdam) no. 1, 1992, pp. 30–44.

Peter Shield, 'William Gear and Cobra', in *William Gear and Cobra*, Aberdeen Art Gallery, 1997.

Willemijn Stokvis, *Cobra: an international movement in art after the Second World War*, New York, Rizzoli, 1988.

Willemijn Stokvis, *Cobra 3 dimensions*, London, Lund Humphries, 1999.

Willemijn Stokvis, *The language of cobra*, Abcoude/Amstelveen, Uitgererij Uniepers/Cobra Museum for Modern Art, 2001.

Various authors, *Cobra 40 jaar later/Cobra 40 years after*, Amsterdam, Sdu uitgeverij, 1988 (Dutch and English texts).

Various authors, *COBRA 50 år/Cobra 50 years*, Ishøj, Arken Museum for Moderne Kunst, 1998 (Danish and English texts).

List of Works

All measurements are height by width. Page references are to illustrations in this book.

*** Denotes works not shown at all venues.**

1
Pierre Alechinsky
La Marche, 1948
The march
Paper collage; 30 x 29 cm
Collection Alechinsky, Bougival

2 (pp. 40–41)
Pierre Alechinsky
Les Métiers, 1948
The occupations
Nine aquatints and dry-points on paper; 31.5 x 24.5 cm
Collection Alechinsky, Bougival
© ADAGP, Paris and DACS, London 2003
Photo: André Morain, Paris

3 (p. 44)
Pierre Alechinsky
En plein air, 1949
In the open air
Ink and gouache on paper; 64 x 50 cm
Collection Alechinsky, Bougival
© ADAGP, Paris and DACS, London 2003
Photo: André Morain, Paris

4
Pierre Alechinsky
Gymnastique matinale, 1949
Morning gymnastics
Gouache on paper; 32.5 x 42 cm
Collection Alechinsky, Bougival

5
Pierre Alechinsky
Jardin bleu, 1949
Blue garden
Gouache on paper; 33 x 46 cm
Collection Alechinsky, Bougival

6
Pierre Alechinsky
Entrée de la grotte, 1950
Entrance to the grotto
Gouache on paper; 33 x 40 cm
Collection Alechinsky, Bougival

7 (p. 42)
Pierre Alechinsky
Épaves, 1950
Flotsam
Oil on canvas; 22 x 27 cm
Collection Alechinsky, Bougival
© ADAGP, Paris and DACS, London 2003
Photo: André Morain, Paris

8
Pierre Alechinsky
Serpent, 1950
Ink on paper; 41 x 43 cm
Collection Alechinsky, Bougival

9 (p. 42)
Pierre Alechinsky
Terre, 1950
Floor
Oil on canvas; 19 x 24 cm
Collection Alechinsky, Bougival
© ADAGP, Paris and DACS, London 2003
Photo: André Morain, Paris

10
Pierre Alechinsky
Totem, 1950
Gouache on paper; 65 x 18 cm
Collection Alechinsky, Bougival

11
Pierre Alechinsky
La Religieuse Portugaise, 1951
The Portugese nun
Seven ink drawings on paper; 68 x 81 cm
Collection Alechinsky, Bougival

12 (title page and pp. 20, 23, 28 and 35)
Pierre Alechinsky
Fifteen vignettes for *Le Petit Cobra* 4 and one for *Cobra* 8–9, 1951
Sixteen drawings, ink on paper; frame: 92 x 106 cm
Collection Alechinsky, Bougival
© ADAGP, Paris and DACS, London 2003
Photo: André Morain, Paris

13 (p. 43)
Pierre Alechinsky
Panoplie, 1951
Panoply
Oil on canvas; 21 x 27 cm
Collection Alechinsky, Bougival
© ADAGP, Paris and DACS, London 2003
Photo: André Morain, Paris

14 (p. 43)
Pierre Alechinsky
Promenade des épaves, 1951
Procession of flotsam
Oil on canvas; 21 x 27 cm
Collection Alechinsky, Bougival
© ADAGP, Paris and DACS, London 2003
Photo: André Morain, Paris

15
Else Alfelt
Universelt-grønt, 1943
Universal green
Oil on canvas; 102 x 102 cm
Carl-Henning Pedersen & Else Alfelts Museum, Herning, Denmark

16 (p. 45)
Else Alfelt
Regnbue-variation 1, 1948
Rainbow variation 1
Oil on plywood; 106 x 126 cm
Carl-Henning Pedersen & Else Alfelts Museum, Herning, Denmark
© Else Alfelt / Carl-Henning Pedersen and Else Alfelt Museum 2003

17*
Karel Appel
Droomdier, 1947
Dream animal
Mixed media on paper; 30 x 42 cm
TEK-1983-0022
Gemeentemuseum, The Hague

18*
Karel Appel
Composition of Heads, 1948
Felt-tipped pen on paper; 20.8 x 32.6 cm
TEK-1983X0200
Gemeentemuseum, The Hague

19*
Karel Appel
Face, 1948
Gouache and chalk on paper; 50 x 36.4 cm
TEK-1983X0171
Gemeentemuseum, The Hague

20*
Karel Appel
Ontwerp voor affiche, 1948
Design for poster
Pastel crayon on paper; 48 x 62 cm
TEK-1983-0033
Gemeentemuseum, The Hague

21*
Karel Appel
Untitled, 1948
Pastel crayon on paper; 29.8 x 24.5 cm
TEK-1983X0194
Gemeentemuseum, The Hague

22*
Karel Appel
Untitled, 1948
Felt-tipped pen on paper; 20.6 x 32.5 cm
TEK-1983X0202
Gemeentemuseum, The Hague

23*
Karel Appel
Untitled, 1948
Gouache on paper, glued; 51 x 34.7 cm
TEK-1983X0247
Gemeentemuseum, The Hague

24* (p. 46)
Karel Appel
Vragende kinderen, 1948
Questioning children
Chalk on paper; 20.4 x 30.5 cm
Gemeentemuseum, The Hague
© Karel Appel Foundation 2003

25 (back cover and p. 48)
Karel Appel
Vrijheidsschreeuw, 1948
Cry of freedom
Oil on canvas; 100 x 79 cm
Private Collection, London,
Courtesy Nancy Whyte Fine
Arts Inc.
© Karel Appel Foundation 2003
Photo: Mike Fear

26* (p. 29)
Karel Appel
Dieren, 1949
Animals
Oil on canvas; 171 x 240 cm
Stedelijk Museum, Amsterdam
© Karel Appel Foundation 2003

27*
Karel Appel
Figuren, 1949
Figures
Chalk and indian ink on paper;
40 x 47 cm
TEK-1983-0030
Gemeentemuseum, The Hague

28 (p. 49)
Karel Appel
Hiep, hiep, hoera!, 1949
Hip, hip, hooray!
Oil on canvas; 82 x 129 cm
Tate, London
© Karel Appel Foundation 2003
Photo © Tate, London 2003

29*
Karel Appel
Untitled, 1949
Felt-tipped pen on paper;
36 x 27 cm
TEK-1983X0283
Gemeentemuseum, The Hague

30*
Karel Appel
Untitled, 1949
Felt-tipped pen on paper;
36 x 27 cm
TEK-1983X0284
Gemeentemuseum, The Hague

31*
Karel Appel
Untitled, 1949
Chalk on paper; 49.5 x 32.5
TEK-1983X0333
Gemeentemuseum, The Hague

32* (p. 47)
Karel Appel
Vragende kinderen, 1949
Questioning children
Chalk on paper; 65 x 50 cm
TEK-1983X0296
Gemeentemuseum, The Hague
© Karel Appel Foundation 2003

33*
Karel Appel
Feestelijke stad no.2, 1950
Celebrating city no.2
Pen and ink on paper; 62 x 48 cm
TEK-1983-0036
Gemeentemuseum, The Hague

34 (p. 52)
Karel Appel
Glimlach, 1950
The smile
Welded iron sculpture;
48 x 44 x 23 cm
Collection Ellen and Jan
Nieuwenhuizen Segaar
© Karel Appel Foundation 2003

35 (p. 51)
Karel Appel
Petit Garçon, 1950
Young boy
Oil on canvas; 110 x 50 cm
Collection Ellen and Jan
Nieuwenhuizen Segaar
© Karel Appel Foundation 2003

36*
Karel Appel
Twee Hondjes, 1950
Two small dogs
Indian ink on paper; 45 x 54 cm
TEK-1983-0035
Gemeentemuseum, The Hague

37*
Karel Appel
Untitled, 1950
Pastel crayon on paper;
23.8 x 32.7 cm
TEK-1983X0345
Gemeentemuseum, The Hague

38*
Karel Appel
Untitled, 1950
Ink, gouache and black chalk
on paper; 35.5 x 27 cm
TEK-1983X0680
Gemeentemuseum, The Hague

39*
Karel Appel
Vogel, 1950
Bird
Gouache and chalk on paper;
43 x 55 cm
TEK-1983-0034
Gemeentemuseum, The Hague

40 (p. 50)
Karel Appel
The Look, 1950
Oil on canvas; 91 x 82 cm
ABN AMRO Collection
© Karel Appel Foundation 2003

41 (p. 12)
Karel Appel
African Mosquito, 1951
Oil on canvas; 80 x 104.5 cm
Private Collection
© Karel Appel Foundation 2003

42*
Karel Appel
Composition / Blowing Wind,
1951
Felt-tipped pen on paper;
35.7 x 27 cm
TEK-1983X0374
Gemeentemuseum, The Hague

43 (p. 53)
Karel Appel
Composition with animal figure,
1951
Oil on canvas; 67 x 142 cm
Karel and Rosemarie van
Stuijvenberg
© Karel Appel Foundation 2003

44*
Karel Appel
Paar, 1951
Couple
Oil on canvas; 81 x 100 cm
Stedelijk Museum, Amsterdam

45*
Karel Appel
Untitled, 1951
Pastel crayon on paper;
27.3 x 35.7 cm
TEK-1983X0378
Gemeentemuseum, The Hague

46*
Karel Appel
Untitled, 1951
Pastel crayon, pencil and ink
on paper; 30.5 x 24.8 cm
TEK-1983X0684
Gemeentemuseum, The Hague

47 (p. 21)
Ejler Bille
Untitled, 1942
Oil on canvas; 74.5 x 66.8 cm
Wørzner-Fonden / Vejle
Kunstmuseum
© DACS 2003

48
Ejler Bille
Lille Darum, 1944
Oil on canvas; 75.5 x 72 cm
Wørzner-Fonden / Vejle
Kunstmuseum

49*
Constant
J'ai visité les ours blancs, 1948
I have visited the polar bears
Oil on canvas; 144.3 x 109.6 cm
Nordjyllands Kunstmuseum,
Aalborg, Denmark

50 (p. 55)
Constant
Parelvisser, 1948
The pearl fisher
Oil on canvas; 100 x 54.5 cm
Karel and Rosemarie van
Stuijvenberg
© DACS 2003

51 (p. 54)
Constant
Satyr, 1948
Oil on canvas; 90 x 55 cm
The Asger Jorn Donation,
Silkeborg Kunstmuseum
© DACS 2003
Photo: Lars Bay

52 (front cover and p. 62)
Constant
Animaux, 1949
Animals
Oil on canvas; 84.5 x 69 cm
ABN AMRO Collection
© DACS 2003

53* (p. 57)
Constant
Après Nous la Liberté, 1949
After us liberty
Oil on canvas; 82 x 129 cm
Tate
© DACS 2003
Photo © Tate, London 2002

54 (p. 58)
Constant
Het laddertje, 1949
The little ladder
Oil on canvas; 90 x 75 cm
SCH-1978-0032
Gemeentemuseum, The Hague
© DACS 2003

55 (p. 59)
Constant
La femme terrible, 1949
The terrible woman
Oil on canvas on panel;
85 x 74 cm
SCH-1994X001
Gemeentemuseum, The Hague
© DACS 2003

56 (p. 56)
Constant
Untitled (Copenhagen) "KBHVN",
1949
Oil on canvas; 55 x 60 cm
Collection Ellen and Jan
Nieuwenhuizen Segaar
© DACS 2003

57
Constant
Vrouw met beest, 1949
Woman with beast
Gouache with black and coloured
pencil; 50 x 47 cm
Museum Boijmans Van Beuningen,
Rotterdam

58*
Constant
De oorlog, 1950
War
Oil on canvas; 101 x 70 cm
Stedelijk Museum, Amsterdam

59 (pp. 60–61)
Constant
8 x la guerre, 1951
8 x the war
Eight black-and-white lithographs;
each 31 x 48.7 cm
The British Museum, London
© DACS 2003

60
Constant
Moeder met kind, 1951
Mother with child
Pastel crayon, pencil on paper;
35.6 x 44.1 cm
TEK-1971-0136
Gemeentemuseum, The Hague

61* (p. 65)
Corneille
Het vrolijke rythme van de stad,
1949
The joyful rhythm of the city
Oil on canvas; 58.5 x 49 cm
Stedelijk Museum, Amsterdam
© ADAGP, Paris and DACS,
London 2003

62* (p. 63)
Corneille
Zomer, 1949
Summer
Oil on canvas; 100 x 100 cm
Stedelijk Museum, Amsterdam
© ADAGP, Paris and DACS,
London 2003

63 (p. 64)
Corneille
La ville, 1950
The town
Oil on canvas,two panels;
220 x 180 cm
Frans Hals Museum, Haarlem
© ADAGP, Paris and DACS,
London 2003

64 (p. 66)
Jacques Doucet
Hommage à Armstrong, 1949
Homage to Armstrong
Oil on canvas; 88.5 x 115.5 cm
Silkeborg Kunstmuseum, The Asger
Jorn Donation
© ADAGP, Paris and DACS,
London 2003
Photo: Lars Bay

65 (p. 67)
William Gear
Paysage au soleil couché, 1948
Landscape with setting sun
Oil on canvas; 45 x 54 cm
Private collection, Edinburgh
© the artist's estate 2003

66
William Gear
Untitled drawing, 1948
Ink on paper; 50 x 32 cm
Redfern Gallery, London

67
William Gear
Christmas Tree, 1950
Oil on canvas; 99 x 71.5 cm
The Arts Council Collection,
Hayward Gallery, London

68
Stephen Gilbert
Flower, 1944
Oil on canvas; 61 x 50.5 cm
Redfern Gallery, London

69 (p. 17)
Stephen Gilbert
Untitled (Butterfly), 1947
Oil on canvas; 30 x 39 cm
Collection Ellen and Jan
Nieuwenhuizen Segaar
© the artist 2003

70 (p. 69)
Henry Heerup
Nissemand, 1943
Sprite
Assemblage, iron, painted pine
and beech; 61 x 22 x 25 cm
Collection Ellen and Jan
Nieuwenhuizen Segaar
© DACS 2003

71 (p. 68)
Henry Heerup
Kvinde som tempel, 1949–50
Woman as temple
Granite; 46 x 26 x 13 cm
Collection Ellen and Jan
Nieuwenhuizen Segaar
© DACS 2003

72
Henry Heerup
Fugl, 1951
Bird
Granite; 38 x 42 x 53 cm
Collection Ellen and Jan
Nieuwenhuizen Segaar

73*
Egill Jacobsen
Eksotisk maske, 1939
Exotic mask
Oil on canvas; 100.1 x 75.7 cm
Nordjyllands Kunstmuseum,
Aalborg, Denmark

74* (p. 70)
Egill Jacobsen
Rødt Objekt II, 1940
Red object II
Oil on canvas; 131.4 x 91 cm
Nordjyllands Kunstmuseum,
Aalborg, Denmark
© DACS 2003

75*
Egill Jacobsen
Græshoppedans, 1941
Grasshopper dance
Oil on canvas; 91.3 x 116.1 cm
Nordjyllands Kunstmuseum,
Aalborg, Denmark

76 (p. 71)
Asger Jorn
Titania II, 1940–41
Oil on canvas; 120 x 115 cm
Louisiana Museum of Modern Art,
Humlebæk, Denmark
© fam. Jorn/DACS, 2003

77
Asger Jorn
La fleur du mal, 1946
The flower of evil
Pen, indian ink and crayon on
paper; 35 x 27.1 cm
The Asger Jorn Donation,
Silkeborg Kunstmuseum

78
Asger Jorn
Untitled, 1946
Pen, indian ink and crayon
on paper; 27.1 x 35 cm
The Asger Jorn Donation,
Silkeborg Kunstmuseum

79
Asger Jorn
Untitled, 1946
Pen, indian ink and crayon
on paper; 27.1 x 35 cm
The Asger Jorn Donation,
Silkeborg Kunstmuseum

80
Asger Jorn
Untitled, 1946
Pen, indian ink and crayon
on paper; 35 x 27.1 cm
The Asger Jorn Donation,
Silkeborg Kunstmuseum

81
Asger Jorn
Untitled, 1946
Pen, indian ink and crayon
on paper; 35 x 27.1 cm
The Asger Jorn Donation,
Silkeborg Kunstmuseum

82 (p. 73)
Asger Jorn
Drawing for *Ånden fra 48,* 1950
The Spirit of '48
Pen and indian ink on paper;
37.8 x 31.2 cm
The Asger Jorn Donation,
Silkeborg Kunstmuseum
© The Asger Jorn Donation,
Silkeborg Kunstmuseum 2003

83 (p. 74)
Asger Jorn
Dødsbranden, 1950
The burning city
Drawing for *Dødsbranden,* 1951
(cat. 90)
The burning city
Pen and indian ink on paper;
18.7 x 15.7 cm
The Asger Jorn Donation,
Silkeborg Kunstmuseum
© The Asger Jorn Donation,
Silkeborg Kunstmuseum 2003
Photo: Lars Bay

84 (p. 72)
Asger Jorn
Guldsvinet, 1950
The golden swine
Oil on canvas; 50 x 100 cm
The Asger Jorn Donation,
Silkeborg Kunstmuseum
© The Asger Jorn Donation,
Silkeborg Kunstmuseum 2003
Photo: Lars Bay

85 (p. 76)
Asger Jorn
La lune et les animaux, 1950
The moon and the animals
Oil on chipboard; 47 x 60.5 cm
Collection Alechinsky, Bougival
© fam. Jorn/DACS, 2003
Photo: André Morain, Paris

86 (p. 75)
Asger Jorn
Drawing for *Ørnens ret,* 1950
The eagle's share
Pen and indian ink on paper;
18.8 x 15.6 cm
The Asger Jorn Donation,
Silkeborg Kunstmuseum
© The Asger Jorn Donation,
Silkeborg Kunstmuseum 2003
Photo: Lars Bay

87 (p. 72)
Asger Jorn
Solsvinets kantate, 1950
The cantata of the sun swine
Drawing for *Guldsvinet,* 1950
The golden swine (cat. 84)
Pen (or matchstick) and indian ink
on paper; 20 x 25 cm
The Asger Jorn Donation,
Silkeborg Kunstmuseum
© The Asger Jorn Donation,
Silkeborg Kunstmuseum 2003
Photo: Lars Bay

88
Asger Jorn
Untitled, 1950
Pen and indian ink on paper;
31.2 x 32.9 cm
The Asger Jorn Donation,
Silkeborg Kunstmuseum

89
Asger Jorn
Untitled, 1950
Pen and indian ink; 29.7 x 37.5 cm
The Asger Jorn Donation,
Silkeborg Kunstmuseum

90*
Asger Jorn
Dødsbranden, 1951
The burning city
Oil on masonite; 87.4 x 121.7 cm
Nordjyllands Kunstmuseum,
Aalborg, Denmark

91 (p. 79)
Asger Jorn
Le droit de l'aigle II, 1951
The eagle's share II
Oil on masonite; 74.5 x 60 cm
The Asger Jorn Donation,
Silkeborg Kunstmuseum
© The Asger Jorn Donation,
Silkeborg Kunstmuseum 2003
Photo: Lars Bay

92 (p. 36)
Asger Jorn
(Return to) the Detested Town,
1951
Oil on panel; 160 x 128 cm
Collection Ellen and Jan
Nieuwenhuizen Segaar
© fam. Jorn/DACS, 2003

93 (p. 77)
Asger Jorn
Sentiment d'infériorité, 1951
Inferiority complex
Oil on canvas; 45 x 30 cm
ABN AMRO Collection
© fam. Jorn/DACS, 2003

94 (p. 78)
Asger Jorn
Sygelige fantomer, 1951
Morbid phantoms
Oil on plywood; 122 x 122 cm
Den Jyske Bank A/S
© fam. Jorn/DACS, 2003

95
Lucebert
Oordeel van Parjs, 1951
Judgement of Paris
Mixed media; 59.5 x 53.5 cm
Cobra Museum voor Moderne Kunst

96* (p. 82)
Lucebert
Zwevende Boer, 1951–52
Farmer floating in the air
Ink and watercolour on paper;
30.5 x 37 cm
Stedelijk Museum, Amsterdam
© Heirs Lucebert 2003

97*
Lucebert
De Dichter voedt de Poezie, 1952
The poet feeds the poetry
Ink and watercolour on paper;
42 x 56.5 cm
Stedelijk Museum, Amsterdam

98 (p. 80)
Lucebert
Gott mit uns I, 1952
God be with us I
Ink on paper; 41 x 27 cm
Cobra Museum voor Moderne Kunst
© Heirs Lucebert 2003

99
Lucebert
Gott mit uns II, 1952
God be with us II
Ink on paper; 41 x 27 cm
Cobra Museum voor Moderne Kunst

100
Lucebert
Gott mit uns III, 1952
God be with us III
Ink on paper; 41 x 27 cm
Cobra Museum voor Moderne Kunst

101
Lucebert
Gott mit uns IV, 1952
God be with us IV
Ink on paper; 41 x 27 cm
Cobra Museum voor Moderne Kunst

102* (p. 81)
Lucebert
Orpheus en de dieren, 1952
Orpheus and the animals
Gouache on paper; 42 x 56 cm
Stedelijk Museum, Amsterdam
© Heirs Lucebert 2003

103 (p. 80)
Lucebert
Partisans, 1952
Watercolour on paper; 34 x 21 cm
Cobra Museum voor Moderne Kunst
© Heirs Lucebert 2003

104*
Lucebert
Yoker the Smoker with Yardbird, 1952
Watercolour on paper; 33.5 x 21.5 cm
Stedelijk Museum, Amsterdam

105 (p. 83)
Erik Ortvad
Vegetation, 1948
Oil on canvas; 100 x 117 cm
Silkeborg Kunstmuseum
© DACS 2003
Photo: Lars Bay

106 (p. 85)
Carl-Henning Pedersen
Lyserød sol, 1942
Pink sun
Oil on canvas; 96 x 96 cm
Carl-Henning Pedersen & Else Alfelts Museum, Herning, Denmark
© Carl-Henning Pedersen / Carl-Henning Pedersen and Else Alfelt Museum 2003

107 (p. 84)
Carl-Henning Pedersen
Drømmen, 1947
The dream
Oil on canvas; 102 x 134 cm
Carl-Henning Pedersen & Else Alfelt Museum, Herning, Denmark
© Carl-Henning Pedersen / Carl-Henning Pedersen and Else Alfelt Museum 2003

108
Carl-Henning Pedersen
Fugl over by, 1948
Bird over town
from the series *Fantasifugle*, 1948–54
Birds of fantasy
Indian ink on Japanese paper; 31 x 41 cm
Louisiana Museum of Modern Art, Humlebæk, Denmark; Donation: Carl-Henning Pedersen

109 (p. 87)
Carl-Henning Pedersen
De fjærne bjerge, 1949
Distant mountains
from the series *Fantasifugle*, 1948–54
Birds of fantasy
Indian ink on Japanese paper; 41 x 31 cm
Louisiana Museum of Modern Art, Humlebæk, Denmark; Donation: Carl-Henning Pedersen
© Carl-Henning Pedersen / Carl-Henning Pedersen and Else Alfelt Museum 2003

110
Carl-Henning Pedersen
Krigeren, 1949
The warrior
from the series *Fantasifugle*, 1948–54
Birds of fantasy
Indian ink on Japanese paper; 41 x 31 cm
Louisiana Museum of Modern Art, Humlebæk, Denmark; Donation: Carl-Henning Pedersen

111
Carl-Henning Pedersen
Landskab med rød maske, 1949
Landscape with red mask
Oil on canvas; 102 x 134 cm
Carl-Henning Pedersen & Else Alfelts Museum, Herning, Denmark

112 (p. 86)
Carl-Henning Pedersen
Opretholderen, 1953
The upholder
from the series *Fantasifugle*, 1948–54
Birds of fantasy
Indian ink on Japanese paper; 41 x 31 cm
Louisiana Museum of Modern Art, Humlebæk, Denmark; Donation: Carl-Henning Pedersen
© Carl-Henning Pedersen / Carl-Henning Pedersen and Else Alfelt Museum 2003

113
Carl-Henning Pedersen
Sandhedens time, 1953
Hour of truth
from the series *Fantasifugle*, 1948–54
Birds of fantasy
Indian ink on Japanese paper; 41 x 31 cm
Louisiana Museum of Modern Art, Humlebæk, Denmark; Donation: Carl-Henning Pedersen

114
Carl-Henning Pedersen
Vinget hest, 1953
Winged horse
from the series *Fantasifugle*, 1948–54
Birds of fantasy
Indian ink on Japanese paper; 41 x 31 cm
Louisiana Museum of Modern Art, Humlebæk, Denmark; Donation: Carl-Henning Pedersen

115 (p. 88)
Anton Rooskens
Vliegende eg, 1951
Flying harrow
Oil on canvas; 100 x 130 cm
Museum Boijmans Van Beuningen, Rotterdam
© estate of the artist 2003

116
Raoul Ubac
Cover for *Cobra 7*, 1950
Incised slate; 30 x 20 cm
Collection Alechinsky, Bougival

117 (p. 89)
Theo Wolvecamp
Composition, 1949
Mixed media on paper; 54 x 44 cm
Collection Ellen and Jan Nieuwenhuizen Segaar
© estate of the artist 2003

118* (p. 90)
Theo Wolvecamp
Explosie, 1949
Explosion
Oil on canvas; 70 x 80 cm
Stedelijk Museum, Amsterdam
© estate of the artist 2003

Collaborative Works

119
Karel Appel; Constant; Corneille; C.O. Hultén; Anders Österlin; Max-Walter Svanberg
Some of these days, 1949
Lithograph on paper; 49 x 38 cm
Karel and Rosemarie van Stuijvenberg

120
Corneille; Simon Vinkenoog
Driehoogballade, 1950
Three stories high
Hand-coloured sheet folded in four, edition of 60; 28 x 22.5 cm (folded)
Karel and Rosemarie van Stuijvenberg

121
Christian Dotremont and Asger Jorn
Ici la chevelure des choses, 1948
Here is the hair-do of things
Oil on card; 17.5 x 21.5 cm
Collection Alechinsky, Bougival

122 (p. 101)
Christian Dotremont and Asger Jorn
Je lève, tu lèves, nous rêvons, 1948
I rise, you rise, we dream
Oil on canvas; 37.5 x 32.5 cm
Collection Alechinsky, Bougival
Dotremont: © DACS 2003.
Jorn: © fam. Jorn/DACS, 2003
Photo: André Morain, Paris

123
Christian Dotremont and Asger Jorn
Un visage suffit à nier le miroir, 1948
A face is enough to deny the mirror
Oil on canvas; 29.5 x 21.5 cm
The Asger Jorn Donation, Silkeborg Kunstmuseum

124
Christian Dotremont and Pierre Alechinsky
Ma raison n'est pas ma maison, 1950
My reason is not my mansion
Marker and gouache on paper; 34.5 x 50 cm
Collection Alechinsky, Bougival

Publications

125
Asger Jorn
Cover for *Abstrakt Kunst i Danmark* (Oslo/Gothenburg), 1947
Colour lithograph on coarse beige paper; 24.3 x 35.2 cm
The British Museum

126
Cobra 1: Bulletin for the Co-ordination of Artistic Investigations
Lithographed cover by Egill Jacobsen, Asger Jorn and Carl-Henning Pedersen, with inserted lithographs by Asger Jorn, Egill Jacobsen, Ejler Bille and Carl-Henning Pedersen
Copenhagen, March 1949
2 copies: The British Museum and Private Collection, The Netherlands

127
Cobra 2
Lithographed cover by Pol Bury
Brussels, March 1949
Private Collection, The Netherlands

128
Cobra 3
Lithographed cover by Pierre Alechinsky
Brussels, June 1949
Private Collection, The Netherlands

129 (p. 7)
Cobra 4: Organ of the International Front of Experimental Avant-garde Artists
Cover by Jørgen Roos
Amsterdam, November 1949
Private Collection, The Netherlands

130
Cobra 5
Hanover, September 1950
Private Collection, The Netherlands

131
Cobra 6
Lithographed cover by Léo van Roy
Brussels, April 1950
Private Collection, The Netherlands

132
Cobra 7: International Review of Experimental Art
Cover by Raoul Ubac
Brussels, Autumn 1950
Private Collection, The Netherlands

133
Cobra 10
Liège, October 1951
Private Collection, The Netherlands

134 (inside front cover and inside back cover)
Karel Appel and Hugo Claus
De Blijde en Onvoorziene Week
The happy and unforeseen week
Book, published Amsterdam, 1950
Collection Ellen and Jan Nieuwenhuizen Segaar
Appel: © Karel Appel Foundation 2003

135 (pp. 24 and 94–95)
Constant and Gerrit Kouwenaar
Goede Morgen Haan
Good morning cockerel
Book, published Amsterdam, 1949
Collection Ellen and Jan Nieuwenhuizen Segaar
© DACS 2003

136 (pp. 11 and 91)
Christian Dotremont and Asger Jorn
La chevelure des choses
The hair-do of things
Facsimile book of drawings, 1948–52, published Paris, 1961
Collection Peter Shield
Dotremont: © DACS 2003.
Jorn: © The Asger Jorn Donation, Silkeborg Kunstmuseum 2003

137 (pp. 39 and 93)
Les Artistes Libres
Artists' books, published Munksgaard, Copenhagen, 1950
15 booklets with lithographed covers; 17.5 x 13.5 cm
Cobra Museum voor Moderne Kunst
Alechinsky: © ADAGP, Paris and DACS, London 2003.
Alfelt: © Else Alfelt/Carl-Henning Pedersen and Else Alfelt Museum 2003.
Appel: © Karel Appel Foundation 2003.
Atlan: © ADAGP, Paris and DACS, London 2003. Bille: © DACS 2003.
Constant: © DACS 2003.
Corneille: © ADAGP, Paris and DACS, London 2003.
Doucet: © ADAGP, Paris and DACS, London 2003.
Ferlov: © DACS 2003.
Gilbert: © the artist 2003.
Gudnason: © estate of the artist/MYNDSTEF 2003.
Heerup: © DACS 2003.
Jacobsen: © DACS 2003.
Jorn: © fam. Jorn / DACS 2003.
Pedersen: © Carl-Henning Pedersen / Carl-Henning Pedersen and Else Alfelt Museum 2003

138 (p. 96)
Christian Dotremont and Corneille
Les jambages au cou
Downstrokes to the neck
Book (2nd edition), published Paris, 1966, from 1949 maquette
Collection Peter Shield
Dotremont: © DACS 2003.
Corneille: © ADAGP, Paris and DACS, London2003

139
Christian Dotremont and Jean-Michel Atlan
Les transformes
The transformations
Book, published Brussels 1950
2 copies: Collection Pierre Alechinsky, Bougival and Collection Peter Shield

140
Reflex 1: Organ of the Dutch Experimental Group
Cover by Corneille
Amsterdam, September–October 1948
Private Collection, The Netherlands

141
Reflex 2: Organ of the Dutch Experimental Group
Lithographed cover by Jacques Doucet
Amsterdam, February 1949
Private Collection, The Netherlands